Images of the Passion
The Sacramental Mode in Film

Images of the Passion
The Sacramental Mode in Film

Peter Fraser

PRAEGER

Westport, Connecticut

Published in the United States and Canada by
Praeger Publishers, 88 Post Road West, Westport, CT 06881
An imprint of Greenwood Publishing Group, Inc

English-language edition, except the United States and Canada,
published by Flicks Books, England

First published in 1998

Library of Congress Cataloging in Publication Data

Fraser, Peter, 1957–
    Images of the passion : the sacramental mode in film / Peter
Fraser.
        p.   cm.
    Filmography: p.
    Includes bibliographical references and index.
    ISBN 0-275-96464-7 (alk. paper). -- ISBN 0-275-96465-5 (pbk. :
alk. paper)
    1. Motion pictures--Religious aspects--Christianity.   2. Religion
in motion pictures.   3. Religious films.   I. Title.
PN1995.9.R4F73   1998
791.43'6823--dc21   98-19469

Library of Congress Catalog Card Number: 98-19469

ISBN: 0-275-96464-7
        0-275-96465-5 (pbk.)

Printed in Great Britain

Contents

Acknowledgements

This book would not have happened without the patient support and wise advice of Virginia Wright Wexman of the University of Illinois at Chicago (UIC). Linda Williams, now at the University of California, Irvine, also added shape to the original themes for the study. John Huntington, Lawrence Poston and Clark Hulse, all of UIC, added ideas and encouragement along the way.

I am unable adequately to express my gratitude to my dear friend, Arthur Livingston, who helped me through several of the more difficult films around which this work is based, and whose conversations provided much stimulation. I am likewise grateful for the insights and support of my wife, Martha.

Thanks also to Diane Koser of the Wisconsin Lutheran College in Milwaukee, who typed the majority of the manuscript into her computer through all its drafts. Similar thanks to Starla Siegmann of the Marvin Schwan Library at Wisconsin Lutheran College for help in locating research materials, and to the staff of the Golda Meir Library at the University of Wisconsin-Milwaukee.

Introduction

> But when you pray, go into your room and shut the door and
> pray to your Father who is in secret; and your Father who sees
> in secret will reward you. (Matthew 6: 6)

Sacramentalism in film

In the climactic sequence of Rouben Mamoulian's film, *We Live Again*
(1934), the young Russian nobleman, Nekhludov (Fredric March),
overcome with guilt at having debauched and then deserted a young
peasant girl named Katusha (Anna Sten), enters his private room and
closes the door. At this moment, the previously straightforward narrative
flow of the film comes to an abrupt halt. What occurs is a montage of
cinematic gestures, a prolonged search into Nekhludov's soul. March
slowly walks across the room to a piano; he sits and begins to play a
doleful hymn. The shot dissolves into the interior of a church during
Mass, and then back to Nekhludov whose head is lifted with emotion
as he plays. He rises from the piano and moves towards a mantle, upon
which the camera reveals an icon. The soundtrack continues the hymn
which Nekhludov played, which increases in volume and fullness the
nearer the man draws to the icon. With a gesture of despair, Nekhludov
bows before this altar and asks God's forgiveness so that he might "live
again".

This shift in narrative technique, a shift towards formalism that
intends to describe an underlying concurrent narrative track – the
spiritual – sets this film apart from the conventional Hollywood drama.
The unique spiritual montage of Nekhludov's conversion in *We Live
Again*, which occurs within a frozen or static moment of the surface
narrative, permits a complete reshuffling of character behaviour and
narrative pattern from this moment onwards. The spiritual realm has
broken through the physical, and will now redeem it. Nekhludov leaves
the room a changed man, merciful, sacrificial and heroic, and we as
spectators are offered participation in this conversion through the same
potent grace by virtue of our identification with Nekhludov and
embrace of the film's dramatic conclusion. *We Live Again* represents

a distinct filmic mode which offers a unique form of entertainment and experience for an audience. In its enfleshment of a divine presence and subsequent liturgical offer of that presence through identification and assent, the mode approaches a sacramental experience.

Religious films of this type are many and diverse, for they operate in a performative context that is open to both religious and quasi-religious content. The essence of the mode is the incarnational gesture at the film's centre, in which a primary narrative is disrupted and made "holy". The introduction of the holy presence then typically transforms the narrative of the film into the most recognisable of all Christian narrative patterns: the Passion. The specifics of the spiritual dimension in these sacramental films are secondary to their function within the causal realm of the narratives. The Christian foundation of *We Live Again* can be ambiguous without greatly disturbing the experience offered by the film.

In fact, Mamoulian's film very loosely adapted its source material, Leo Tolstoy's Christian novel, *Resurrection*. The incarnational moment in the film is merely the beginning of repentance for Tolstoy's Nekhludov. The character in the novel will not fully recognise his need for God until he has joined himself to the peasant girl, Katusha, after she is imprisoned for prostitution, and suffered degradation with her. Tolstoy's Nekhludov converts at the very end of the action (it occurs only two-thirds of the way through the film) in a non-emotional, highly rational recognition of life's overall futility. He decides to seek an answer to his broken spirit through the Gospels (as Tolstoy himself did):

> We were sent here by some one's will and for some purpose. And we have made up our minds that we live only for our own enjoyment, and of course things go ill with us, as they do with labourers when they do not fulfil their master's orders. The Master's will is expressed in these laws. As soon as men fulfil these laws, the kingdom of heaven will be established on earth, and men will reach the greatest good they can attain.
>
> "'*Seek ye first his kingdom and his righteousness; and all these things shall be added unto you.*' But we seek for *these things*, and have evidently failed to obtain them.
>
> "And so here it is – the business of my life. Scarcely have I finished one task, and another has commenced."
>
> A perfectly new life dawned that night for Nehlúdof; not because he had entered into new conditions of life, but because everything he did after that night had a new and quite different meaning for him.
>
> How this new period of his life will end, time alone will prove.[1]

Mamoulian's film places Nekhludov's conversion much closer to his initial encounter with the ruin of the peasant girl, and it recontextualizes the conversion into an emotionally charged moment of time. This throws into question the impetus for the man's repentance. Is it a sense of sin and helplessness, or is it "the woman"? Here Hollywood convention seems to have had its way by bringing faith into the arena of the analogous sphere of sentimental romance. Tolstoy has been secularized; yet, the mystification of romantic love in the standard Hollywood drama acts as a spiritual principle of its own.

However the gesture is read – whether it is the pull of the Holy Spirit or of "romantic love" – Nekhludov is still reborn, and the literal film narrative is transformed into a redemptive performance. Since the moment of divine intrusion cannot be rendered literally in film (just as it cannot in the linguistic characters of Tolstoy's written pages), it must be told or evoked metaphorically. This moment may be cued either by character gesture (for example, facial or body gesture in Bresson, Dreyer or De Sica) or by cinematic gesture (juxtaposed stills of nature in Ford, Godard or Murnau; non-diegetic musical cues and artificial effects in the Hollywood epics; lighting effects in Lang, Dreyer or Borzage; narrative rhythm and symbolic compositions in Tarkovskij; and so on). In all cases, there is some mixture of the two gestures, with individual directors playing off standard conventions and their own style. In addition, there are degrees of subtlety, dependent to some extent on how much needs to be expressed to convey the alteration in narrative.

Religious films of this type have a decidedly evangelistic tenor, as the audience is invited to participate in the Passion celebration that begins once the divine and the human merge in the film narrative. Audience identification and assent function as metaphoric acts of faith.

These films mingle strategies found in two disparate genres, the musical and the horror film. They take from the musical the method by which lyrical and fanciful forces invade a narrative. From the horror film they take the idea of an audience experiencing a purgative identification in a sacrificial ritual. In these sacramental films, the lyrical, musical intrusion is a heavenly chorus, and the purgation is a means towards the elevation of feeling.

To understand the framework of this unique religious style in many films, one must consider the long-standing liturgical tradition in Western culture, since the narrative pattern of the sacramental film echoes the narrative pattern of common Christian liturgies. However, before tracing the similarity between these films and Christian liturgy, it may be helpful to recollect the impulse behind liturgical celebrations.

Characteristic of many of the messianic predictions written in the two centuries before the birth of Christ was the insistence that certain of the great Jewish prophets, particularly Elijah and Jeremiah, would again walk the earth in the great days when the Messiah would come to restore Jerusalem. The rabbis read Old Testament Scriptures as political and legal promises for themselves and their heirs. The Messiah would return the prosperity to the Jewish nation, and the power of God would permanently reside with man, as it had only temporarily in the past.

After the coming of Christ, the Church rejected the literal Jewish hermeneutical method as untenable.[2] Instead, the Church Fathers interpreted the Old Testament as a book entirely about Jesus, although their attempts to do so led at times to extremely symbolic and esoteric readings of the individual texts. As theological controversies pressed the Church in the second and third centuries, it became apparent that an authoritative hermeneutical method had to be established if there was to be consistency in the voice of the Church as it went out through the nations.

The codified hermeneutic came from Augustine in his treatises on Christian doctrine. Augustine, following the general consensus of the Fathers, argued that all Scripture pointed to Christ and could be understood only in the light of the Gospel; however, he also argued that such an understanding required a careful examination of the layers of meaning in the written texts. Divine signification led to Christ, and this signification came from both divine words and divinely placed signifying things, types, that needed to be classified and subordinated to a larger conception of the Word made flesh, the ultimate signifier.[3]

Augustine's hermeneutic firmly established orthodox Christian understanding of Christ's importance, both as the incarnate God within history and as the centre of God's many layers of communication with the believer. Without an embrace of Christ as The Word, there could be no saving knowledge of and approach to God. Largely for this reason, the Incarnation, Christ as The Word becoming flesh, is the centrepiece of all orthodox Christian theologies.

Thus, vital to the life of the believer in every age has been access to a means by which the incarnate Christ can be approached in individual and collective experiences. The evolution of the liturgy of the Mass inevitably led to a progressive subordination of all its elements – songs, readings, homily – to the Eucharistic celebration of the presence of Christ with its myriad physical rituals involving concrete objects, such as icons, relics and the various trappings of pageantry. Private religious exercises likewise evolved in the direction of increased communion with Christ through mystical experiences.

It is this yearning for a personal relationship with God in the physical realm that most closely relates to the present discussion of religious films. The popular exercises for spiritual communion that developed throughout Christendom, particularly after the Reformation, can be seen as precursors of the type of sacramental technique that is apparent in films such as *We Live Again*. The exercises were based on an incarnational principle which would lead to an identification with God entering the affairs of men. Consider, for example, one section of Ignatius's *Spiritual Exercises* (1548), which was widely used as a devotional manual for the Jesuit order:

> 106. First Point. This will be to see the different persons: First, those on the face of the earth, in such great diversity in dress and in manner of acting. Some are white, some black; some at peace, and some at war; some weeping, some laughing; some well, some sick; some coming into the world, and some dying; etc. ...
> 107. Second Point. This will be to listen to what the persons on the face of the earth say, that is, how they speak to one another, swear and blaspheme, etc. ...
> 108. This will be to consider what the persons on the face of the earth do, for example, wound, kill, and go down to hell. ...
> 109. Colloquy. ... I will think over what I ought to say to the Three Divine Persons, or to the eternal Word incarnate, or to His Mother, our Lady. According to the light that I have received, I will beg for grace to follow and intimate more closely our Lord, who has just become man for me.[4]

The key difference between this method of conceptualizing the entrance of God to the world and embracing it and the methods of certain films is one of means. French theorist André Bazin exalted the apparatus of cinema as the ideal means for re-creating life through art. Ignatius was content with the art of pure imagination through the means of contemplation of religious experience and Christian doctrine. Cinema projects the contemplation forward to the screen and then draws the individual to it.

Sacramental mechanics in film

The sacramental film allows for the appropriation of spiritual presence sought by the devotional writers, but in a public experience. Thus, it brings together the ritualistic aspects of Christian liturgy with the more private concerns of popular piety. The sacramental film can well be analyzed according to the principles of mystical contemplation: composing the space, applying the intellect, understanding, will, affections, and so on. The medium of film, like the devotional exercise, is displayed in fixed time periods, on a rotational basis, and with a regular sequence of participatory steps.[5] The structures of the individual films follow certain generic and stylistic patterns as they address particular audiences with set conventional understandings, and they find presentation publicly, following liturgical methods. These films uniquely synthesize the diverse practices of the Christian devotional and liturgical traditions, and it will not be surprising if the passage of time finds them becoming more prominent in popular practices of Christian piety.

To illustrate how certain sacramental techniques in film can enhance the expression of popular piety, it is useful to look beyond the better known religious vehicles (i.e. Hollywood epics or films by recognised Christian filmmakers) to the more esoteric and religiously tendentious group of films produced exclusively for evangelical purposes by companies such as Moody Films International, Ken Anderson Productions or Billy Graham Association Films. Since 1960, these companies have produced an increasing number of narrative films geared for limited private showings in churches or private sectarian schools. Most of these films operate on an extremely low budget, and only a handful – *The Cross and the Switchblade* (1970), *The Hiding Place* (1974) and *Jesus of Nazareth* (1977) – have been marketed for theatre showings. *The Cross and the Switchblade* provides a clear example of how these narrative films are designed.

The Cross and the Switchblade is ostensibly the spiritual biography of David Wilkerson, a rural minister who began an outreach programme to gangs and drug addicts in New York City in the late 1960s, which blossomed into a nationwide halfway house network known as Teen Challenge. The film loosely adapts a book-length study of Wilkerson's ministry, also entitled *The Cross and the Switchblade.*[6]

Whereas the focus of the book is the expansiveness of Wilkerson's programme, the film narrows its attention to one incident in Wilkerson's ministry that gave him an early sign of his potential success. This is the conversion of one of the warlords of a New York gang, Nicky Cruz. The narrower focus – a necessary measure in all film adaptations – has a specific function in this film beyond making the work more filmable; as with Mamoulian's adaptation of the Tolstoy novel in *We Live Again*, the film of *The Cross and the Switchblade* shifts the narrative point of view from an objective factual account of the Wilkerson ministry to a direct address that will culminate in a sermon by Wilkerson within the narrative. As the change in Nicky Cruz's life is foreshadowed and then pressed home in the climactic setting of Wilkerson's sermon, so the spectator is carried through the narrative on a persuasive emotional line that is designed to encourage spiritual introspection.

With Pat Boone in the lead as David Wilkerson and Erik Estrada playing Cruz, the film is structured in a "Hound of Heaven" motif that has Wilkerson pursuing Cruz through back alleys and tenements, and telling him over and over again that God loves him. Cruz largely resists, but a developing pattern of facial close-ups suggests that his defences are steadily falling. In the climactic scene, Wilkerson gathers two rival gangs into a theatre for a youth rally and, after quieting them, begins the sermon that wins over Cruz and several of the others.

The pattern of close-ups that has developed to this point becomes intensified as rapid cuts scan the facial reactions of Cruz and various listeners. Wilkerson's sermon reaches a crescendo of emotion as he tells the gatherers: "Open up your heart and let all that bitterness run out, and let Jesus Christ come in". As he says this, the frame freezes. Boone's voice is echoed through a synthesizer and the background is lit with an artificial blue that has a streak of light extended across it diagonally; then a bell begins to ring softly. This frozen image with its artificial gestures holds for a full ten seconds. When the narrative resumes, the soundtrack carries a chorus which sings, "God loves you, God loves Nicky Cruz". Cruz is revealed in close-up with tears of conviction in his eyes. From this moment onwards, the narrative follows new principles. Cruz's conversion triggers a complete reshuffling of character-allegiance, as the "message" has altered heart motivations. Nicky Cruz now loves Wilkerson, the gangs find a peaceful compromise, and Wilkerson is recognised as a hero.

The stylistic devices of *The Cross and the Switchblade* are obvious and clumsily done in key sequences, but they differ only in technique and quality from many Hollywood religious films and several other varieties of religious filmmaking. In fact, some of Hollywood's more overwrought productions, such as De Mille's *The Ten Commandments* (1956), have moments of incarnation conveyed in even more startling and artificial fashion (the sudden transformation of Charlton Heston's appearance as Moses after the episode of the burning bush, for example). The devices, however employed, serve to symbolise spiritual intrusion.[7] The evocative shift of narrative style towards formalism signals the transformation of the stable text "religiously" that characterises what might be called "the sacramental style".

The sacramental film characteristically narrows its focus to a symbolic conversion of one individual.[8] The conversion is synecdochic, since the complete text is also typically redeemed. The conversion marks the incarnational centre of the text, and it is conveyed through some cinematic metonym in which space and time converge symbolically – the freeze-frame; ten-second delay; stylised background; and non-diegetic bell and chorus in *The Cross and the Switchblade*. As a formalistic device, the incarnation, which is most manifest within Cruz during the sermon, takes on a sacramental dimension as the spectator has been drawn to identify with Cruz as the centre of dramatic tension. In *We Live Again*, space and time are isolated in an apostrophe when Nekhludov enters his chamber to repent. As the chamber dissolves into the church and then returns again, screen space is declared openly as a spiritual field. Similarly, time is halted in the sequence, or it is translated from the narrative's causal realm to the internal realm of Nekhludov's soul, where it becomes a signifier for spiritual communion. In both cases, the artifice that signals incarnation becomes the signified itself, with its source behind the narrative – God, daemon, and so on.

The symbolic functions of space and time within the incarnational moment of the sacramental film make the complete performance of the work a type of liturgical ceremony. As such films often follow a stable ideological base, and urge moral and spiritual enlightenment through the embrace of a form of divine presence, they operate ritualistically. Variation within sacramental films may be seen as liturgical preference. In addition, it may well be argued that these liturgical preferences have immediate relationships with the religious tendencies of the artistic and social presences behind the works. In the United States, where popular evangelistic styles, born in 19th-century revivalism, move through a hierarchy of emotional appeals – songs, testimonies, readings – towards the potent sermon, it can be expected that sacramental films will follow a similar emotional incline towards a more direct and didactic incarnational gesture. This is clearly the case in *The Cross and the Switchblade*, as the film literally stops to present Wilkerson's sermon to the spectators, as well as to the gang members – "Open up your heart". It is true also of Mamoulian's film, although to a lesser degree, due to the director's own European heritage and, of course, the influence of Tolstoy. A contrary example might be Dreyer's *Ordet* (*The Word*, 1955), in which the highly integrated liturgy of European Lutheranism, with its dual emphasis on Word and Sacrament, forms a liturgical balance in the narrative between the preaching of the mad son, Johannes, and the raising of Inger from the dead: liturgy of the Word gives way to Eucharistic celebration.

The Passion

If the Incarnation is the pivotal impulse in the formal mechanics of many religious films, the Passion is the pattern for the narratives of these films, as well as many other "inspirational" films. The suffering and death of the Saviour, Jesus Christ, completes the redemptive act begun with the Incarnation. The Passion is sublime. God enters history and takes the form of man in order to suffer and die. Believers and non-believers together puzzle over this paradox. Films that have even the faintest hint of Christianity in them tend to make some allusion to the suffering of Christ.

Typically, this allusion is focused in the plight of the central character, and that character can have presences as diverse as Sylvester Stallone in the *Rocky* series (1976-1990), Gary Cooper in *Meet John Doe* (1941) or Jennifer Jones in *The Song of Bernadette* (1943). What these characters undergo is a form of holy pilgrimage towards suffering that redeems them and the communities that they represent. Therefore, in *Rocky* (1976), the pummelling that Rocky Balboa receives from Apollo Creed is necessary to give him validity as a worthwhile individual in his own eyes and in those of his girlfriend, Adrian; it also vicariously regenerates the many down-and-out Philadelphians who stake their hopes on this nobody's title chance. In *The Song of Bernadette*, Bernadette's perseverance in the face of scepticism and criticism validates her "divine call", and carries along the many broken men and women who stream to Lourdes in the hope of a divine touch.

Characters who undergo a Passion experience in a film narrative will first take on a representational role as bearers of the desires of a community. This, of course, is fundamental to Christian doctrine, since Christ "bore the sins of many" and died to reconcile God and humanity. Often this represented community will be explicitly described within the film narrative, as in the three films mentioned above. In other cases, the film audience will be immediately drawn in as the redemptive community by virtue of an especially strong identification created with the main characters. *Chariots of Fire* (1981) or Dreyer's *La Passion de Jeanne d'Arc* (*The Passion of Joan of Arc*, 1928) might serve well as examples of this pattern, where the audience enters the psyche of the redemptive figure in the process of his or her pilgrimage through the means of lingering close-ups, internal monologues, and doubling with antithetical figures. In the climax of *Chariots of Fire*, Eric Liddell's victorious run in the 400-metres race is cross-cut with reaction-shots of the crowd in the Olympic stadium, completing the narrative thematically, but also inviting the viewer to join in the celebration of Liddell's victory. This gesture finds reinforcement in a flashback interior monologue reminding the viewer that Liddell's power to see the race to the end comes from "within". In Dreyer's *The Passion of Joan of Arc*, the audience is forced into a deep sympathy with Joan through the director's relentless facial close-ups of actress Maria Falconetti against washed-out backgrounds.

The redemptive figure in many films will typically undergo a lonely purgative ritual in the course of the narrative. This ritual includes either physical, emotional or spiritual suffering, and it concludes as the character resigns to the forces compelling this trek and accepts whatever consequences the narrative movements decree. Gary Cooper as Frederick Henry in Frank Borzage's *A Farewell to Arms* (1932) deserts the Army and marches across Europe to rejoin his beloved (pregnant and dying) Catherine. Borzage makes numerous references to the cross in a lengthy montage of Henry's difficult, lonely journey. Father Laforgue in *Black Robe* (1991) finds all his companions leaving him as he continues up river to the Indian mission where he will administer communion to a small, sickly band. En route, his closest friend betrays him, he is tempted sexually and psychologically, tortured and consistently misunderstood. In the Borzage film, Henry resigns himself to Catherine's death, lifting her from the bed to an open window and, metaphorically, to the hands of God. In *Black Robe*, Father Laforgue accepts the miserable circumstances at the Huron mission and the certain failure of the whole enterprise; yet, he will love and serve the Indians as long as he is called.

Passion narratives in films are remarkably common, in part because the full concept of heroism in the Western tradition hearkens back to medieval descriptions of saviour-warriors. The patterns have been passed unmistakably from *Beowulf, La Morte d'Arthur* and *Sir Gawain and the Green Knight*, through Shakespeare and Spenser to Tennyson and even Dickens. The historical and literary heritage of such a long tradition is hard to shake. Thus, in seemingly secular vehicles as removed from the traditional Christian material as *The Karate Kid* (1984), *The Terminator* (1984), *Batman* (1989) and *Unforgiven* (1992) we find echoes of the same heroic motifs grounded in the primary Christian model of redemption.

Sacramentalism and the Passion

The aim of this book is to describe a few of the best films which portray Christ's Passion in a sacramental format. In doing so, the mechanics of sacramental films will be fully illustrated and, ostensibly, shown for what they are, the details of a unique film genre which has received little attention.

By choosing films which have a strong Passion motif, the purest and most obvious narrative thread in these films will also be shown to be the most powerful. There is something unusually compelling in each of the films which fall under careful scrutiny in the following chapters. Scholars have typically praised films such as *The Word* or *Journal d'un curé de campagne* (*Diary of a Country Priest*, 1950) on the basis of their artistic virtuosity, but the moving experiences which these films provide are not grounded simply in their aesthetic merit. They are moving because they take the viewer through a liturgical pilgrimage into an experience that can only be called sublime. Whether or not the viewer is a believer, the experience of these films cannot easily be dismissed.

It has been aptly said by more than one critic that *Diary of a Country Priest*, to continue with this example, offers the clearest portrayal of holiness to be found on film. But what is the nature of this holiness? It is the face of Christ that emerges from the face of the young French priest dying of cancer. Holiness, after all, is simply the presence of God, and the presence of God in the flesh in Christianity is Christ himself. When Bresson's film is embraced – that is, when viewers allow the film to guide them as Bresson intends – viewers are brought into a sacramental experience with the living God. An incarnational presence of Christ is metaphorically offered up, through the imaginary yet physical, iconic world of film. The little priest is Christ enfleshed, his life is an agonising journey to a cross, and his death is salvation for the viewer who receives it as such.

Diary of a Country Priest serves well as the defining film of this special genre, but each of the films chosen for study operates towards a similar end. What makes the group of films discussed particularly interesting is their international flavour and stylistic variety. Unlike other film genres, the sacramental style seems to have emerged not from a movement in art or a particularly popular set of films, but from something outside the world of art: traditional Christian liturgy. With this source, one would expect what one finds – an uncanny similarity in formal method and narrative pattern in a geographically and historically disparate group of works.

In these films one also expects and finds some strong Christian impulse behind the making of the film. With Dreyer, Bresson, Tarkovskij or Borzage, the impulse is clearly the director's own faith. But the impulse need not be so abiding. Pasolini was moved to make *The Gospel According to St Matthew* upon reading the Gospels, but his epistemology remained more Marxist than Christian. Martin Scorsese considered the priesthood early in life, but gave it up. His scriptwriter for *Raging Bull*, Paul Schrader, was raised a strict Calvinist, but he gave that up. Nevertheless, *Raging Bull* in an idiosyncratic way moves in a sacramental direction that becomes rather evangelistic in the film's closing moments. In some cases, the stories behind the creation of these unique films are as intriguing as the works themselves.

One last comment that deserves attention before beginning a closer examination of these sacramental images of Christ's Passion concerns the remarkable ability of the Christian faith to integrate with changes in culture and art. Throughout the history of the Church there have been movements against new artistic media, from the theatre to verse, the novel and new forms of music, and now to film. Yet, ironically, the Christian faith has powerfully impacted every sphere of art in the West. At the same time that the Church, particularly in the United States in the 20th century, cautions filmmakers about the potential dangers of film as a corrosive influence on society, films emerge, such as those chosen here, which will be recognised as masterpieces of Christian art for at least the next 100 years. Despite the shortsightedness of the messengers of the faith, there is an abiding power in the Christian religion which finds a way to express itself regardless of time, place or voice.

Notes

[1]   Leo Tolstoy, *Resurrection*, translated by Louise Maude (London: Oxford University Press, 1931): 513-514. Emphases in original.

[2]   For an excellent comprehensive discussion of the evolution of Biblical hermeneutics in the early Church, see Jaroslav Pelikan, *The Emergence of the Catholic Tradition (100-600)*, volume 1 of *The Christian Tradition: A History of the Development of Doctrine* (Chicago; London: University of Chicago Press, 1971): especially 1-108.

[3]   Saint Augustine, *The Writings of St. Augustine*, volume 4 (Washington, DC: Catholic University of America Press, 1966).

[4]   Ignatius Loyola, *The Spiritual Exercises of Saint Ignatius of Loyola*, translated by Louis J Puhl (Chicago: Loyola University Press, 1951): 50-51.

[5]   See Louis L Martz, *The Poetry of Meditation: A Study in English Religious Literature of the Seventeenth Century* (New Haven: Yale University Press, 1954).

[6]   David Wilkerson, with John and Elizabeth Sherrill, *The Cross and the Switchblade* (Chicago: Moody Press, 1972).

[7]   Michael Bird discusses the broader conception of hierophany as metaphor for cinema, and the religious base for such a conception, in "Film as Hierophany", in John R May and Michael Bird (eds), *Religion in Film* (Knoxville, TN: The University of Tennessee Press, 1982): 3-22.

[8]   In this aspect, the revivalistic Protestant root of the mode is quite evident.

1 · *Diary of a Country Priest* (*Journal d'un curé de campagne*, 1950)

Robert Bresson's *Journal d'un curé de campagne* (*Diary of a Country Priest*, 1950) plays masterfully at themes of solitude, austerity and grace. Bresson enables the viewer to contemplate, with his heroic priest, the conflict between God and Satan as experienced in the quiet and rather dull lives of the members of a small French country parish in Ambricourt. The turning of a door handle, a glance through a window, downcast eyes, the pouring of wine, the carrying of a lantern – such gestures are packed with private significance for the players in the film, just as they are in the common experiences of most of the film's viewers. In these lie Bresson's appeal and the brilliance of this work.

One leaves a Bresson film – whether it is *Diary of a Country Priest*, *Mouchette* (1967) or *Pickpocket* (1959) – with the sense that souls have been won or lost, that the profound suffering and groaning of all humanity has been briefly revealed. Bresson's films are full of action by virtue of their stillness, a stillness which allows viewer identification and sympathy on a profound level. Bresson's unhurried, deliberate camera and his symphonic editing lead the viewer to moments of self-revelation that produce a much greater impact than that derived from the typical frenetic commercial film, even the commercial religious film. In his own words, Bresson reveals that "the flattest and dullest parts [have] in the end the most life".[1]

The slow pace of *Diary of a Country Priest* allows the viewer to step into the film and walk through its images in a rather sacramental way. Bresson particularly allows his camera to linger on shots of the priest looking at the varying facets of his parish, and these shots allow the viewer to share that same look and curiosity. The priest looks at his subjects and, through them, at their participation in the spiritual war in which they unwittingly find themselves. We are given time to do the same. Consequently, there is a haunting quality in *Diary of a Country Priest*, which many viewers and critics have identified as a mood of sanctity or holiness.

Bresson typically uses sparse settings in his films as attempts at developing subjectivity. Several minutes of *Un Condamné à mort s'est échappé* (*A Man Escaped*, 1956), for example, are shot in nearly complete darkness, to allow the viewer full empathy with a French convict breaking from prison under the cloak of night. One of the key scenes in *Diary of a Country Priest* is similarly shot in such thick darkness that the image of the priest walking along a hillside is barely discernible; when he falls in a faint, he is virtually swallowed up by that darkness. Similarly, the priest's final moments are only briefly shown to the viewer. Instead, they are recounted through a letter read by a companion priest over a plain image of a cross against a pure, white screen.

Bresson used non-actors for *Diary of a Country Priest* and for other films. Claude Laydu was chosen for his combined youthfulness and solemnity to play the young priest from Ambricourt. Bresson was thus free to mould the character portrayal as he desired, rather than having to contend with the actor's own interpretations. The consequence of this idiosyncrasy and of those mentioned above is a remarkable unity of purpose and vision in the Bressonian world.

The story for *Diary of a Country Priest* was taken with great care from Georges Bernanos's 1936 novel of the same title. It is the story of a young country priest's Christ-like submission to his own suffering and insignificance. The priest, dying of stomach cancer and imprisoned in an unbelieving parish, slowly gives himself over to what he himself calls "the holy agony". The priest arrives at his first parish at Ambricourt, and experiences trouble and resistance at every point in his parish ministry. He is misunderstood and shy to speak directly about issues. Children in a communion class mock him. When he steps into the affairs of a local Count who is in an adulterous relationship with a castle governess, he is opposed and urged to leave his work. In addition, the young priest must also weather the internal physical and spiritual struggle of his developing illness. The priest endures his sufferings and continues his ministry, sharing his inner burden only with God as he writes his thoughts in a diary. He dies a painful and lonely death. Yet, before his life is over, his ministry begins to bear fruit, as his example of holiness affects all in the parish, even those who opposed him. His final words are "All is grace".

Bernanos and Bresson share a profound Catholic vision. Two of Bresson's films derive from novels by Bernanos, and others seem to share the same devotion and precise description of private experiences. The great Bernanos themes are the satanic hold of decay and despair on the modern world; the corruption and redemption of childhood; and the relationship between suffering and salvation. These same themes might be described in Bresson's films, although whereas Bernanos often worked out his plots in religious settings, Bresson typically did not. The priest of Ambricourt stands in contrast to Bresson's usual collection of heroes – pickpocket, prisoner, peasant girl, student, labourer, knight, and so on.

Bresson adapted the novel by condensing the action around the significant events of the plot, and by trimming the narrative around the most telling passages of the priest's diary. Bresson thus adjusted the priest's struggle to allow for a more visual and visceral display onscreen. The viewer can find all of Bernanos in the film, but the discovery must come by projection outwards from Bresson's images.[2] Perhaps this tightening of the Bernanos novel is most apparent in the description in the film of Mademoiselle Chantal, whose peculiar depravity explained in detail in the novel is conveyed in the film through her tempting and elusive glances, and the darkness in which she is often enshrouded.

Bernanos used the priest's diary in his novel in the same way that Samuel Richardson used letters to advance his plots, in order to allow for the development of a single character's voice. With his use of the diary, Bresson creates a counterpoint between the priest's understanding of his life and our discovery of it. Bresson thus underlines the dominant theme in the novel: the priest's growing sense of inconsequence and frailty vs. his developing humanity and saintliness.

In the novel, the diary kept by the young priest chronicles his inner struggles of soul that accompany his ministry and physical sufferings. In terms of the film, however, the diary serves the much larger function of introducing subsequent images and of providing an interpretive frame for them. An analysis of this function reveals Bresson's thematic arrangement of religious ideas and symbols throughout the film.

The film begins with a close-up of the diary opened by a hand, presumably that of the priest, and a blotched fragment of paper is moved aside to reveal the first entry. In voice-over, the priest recites: "I do not think I would be doing any harm if I write down, day by day, the humble, indeed insignificant, secrets of a life which in any case contains no mystery".

The diary gives way to the image of a road sign for the town of Ambricourt, where the priest has arrived. This image dissolves into a close-up of the priest wiping sweat from his brow. His eyes are fixed in no definite direction. This close-up is replaced by a shot of a fence which surrounds an estate, and another cut presents a medium shot of a couple, the Count and his governess, embracing. They both look towards the camera, and pull from the embrace as they see the priest. The following shot reveals the priest in full figure beside the bicycle which he had apparently ridden to the spot. His glance is curiously directed towards the scene behind the fence. The next cut shows the couple walking off in the distance in a less familiar attitude. The camera returns to the priest who watches as he takes a package from the back of the bicycle; apparently, the package contains his few belongings. He walks towards a building, the vicarage, advances to the door and opens it. The door opens to complete darkness, and the camera looks into this darkness with the priest. The final cut of the sequence looks up at the priest as the voice-over recites, "My parish, my first parish".

The diary entry that introduces the sequence evokes the paradox that controls the entire film: the priest's insignificance and his surrender to it have allowed for the work of the Holy Spirit to become fully manifest in his life – "the wind bloweth where it listeth".[3] This idea will be confirmed throughout the film, as he is counselled by the curé of Torcy, an older and more rigorous companion priest, to be mindful of the little things, for they will keep him peaceful; moreover, he will convey to Chantal, the Count's suicidal daughter, that she will one day give in to the mystery of life, and, having done so and received life, give it to others who will pass it on. The way of life is through self-denial, surrender to the little things, and then self-surrender in love to others. Because of the humility of the young priest, he has achieved the level of greatness that the film compels us to follow.

The little things matter a great deal, therefore, and we are prepared early in the film to think through the images that Bresson's camera reveals to us.[4] The Ambricourt sign, the mopping of the brow, the stolen embrace of the couple, the bicycle, the dark doorway – each captures an essential theme of the complete procession of the film. The sign tells of the remoteness of the place, and also of that of the priest's inner odyssey and his loneliness of soul. The mopped brow comments on the priest's hard journey to the vicarage and on his failing health. He has sacrificed and suffered to come to this parish, and his sufferings shall continue. (The mopped brow has greater significance as the film progresses: it is later wiped by Séraphita, then by Dufréty, the lapsed priest who cares for the priest before he dies, and then by Dufréty's woman; it suggests also the wiping of Christ's face during his Passion.) The stolen embrace of the Count and the governess tells of the dark secrecy of their relationship and the foreign nature of human social relations to the priest throughout his life – later, with the children, with Chantal, and with Dufréty. But their guilty response reveals the reverse side of this – i.e. that is, the priest's ability to look through exteriors into people's souls. The bicycle suggests the priest's transience, both in his concern to reach others (he will continually be going to meet someone) and in his passage towards death and a resurrection. The dark doorway suggests the coldness of attitude shown him in the village, and his look into his own death – which is the underlying purpose of the diary.

These are isolated synecdochic images that assist the narrative. Two more central visual motifs, developed further by the sequence, reveal the larger thematic structure. The first of these is a set of images that revolve around the looks of both the priest and the couple – the curious look of the priest, and the couple's offended return look. These looks define the priest's relationship to the community and the world from the very start. He is an outsider, guilty by character and presence. Despite his numerous attempts to penetrate the world that surrounds him, he remains an enemy to it.

This leads to the secondary motif, that of the gate and the door. The priest is separated from the couple by a fence. Several times through the film, he will pass through the castle gate to achieve the world on the other side, and each time Bresson will grant special attention to the priest's movement through the gate. At first, it seems that the world of the castle is thus imprisoned, and, in a spiritual sense, it is. However, the true prisoner of the film is the priest: imprisoned by his poor health, his simplicity, his poverty and, ultimately, his participation in Christ's Passion.

The opening images of the film thus set a clear liturgical structure. The priest represents the holy soul, Christ, moving towards God within the world but remaining separate from the world. As he moves forward, he moves towards his own death: the symbol of the mopped brow, and, even more, the vault-like darkness of the vicarage. His rite of passage, which was that of Christ and is that of the Church, will be lonely and painful, for it carries through a hostile, fallen world where God's immediate presence cannot be felt. There is no comfort for the priest beyond his knowledge of the lack of significance of his own life compared to the mystery of Christ's, as he implies in his diary entry and acts out in laying prostrate before his bed when unable to pray.[5]

Another illustration of the mechanisms of the film which reveals the same relationship between the diary and the visual motifs that follow can be traced in one of the more visually gripping segments of the film, in which the priest's cancer begins to worsen and he collapses on a hillside while visiting members of the parish. Torcy has encouraged him to pray to the Virgin for peace, after the priest has been blamed for triggering the Countess's death by confronting her for not resigning herself to God's will in the death of her young son. The priest narrates that the words affected him deeply, and in the subsequent sequence we follow him on his visitations.

The sequence begins with the priest in a chair in a home, where an old woman is serving him tea. The camera fixes on the priest's painful, downward gaze. It appears that he is being helped by the woman, but when he gets up to leave and is led outside by the woman and a companion, we realise that he has come to visit and bless her. The two women watch from the top of a porch as the priest wearily leaves and proceeds down a dark street. The camera cuts to a close-up of his note pad on which he crosses out a name. The priest narrates that he was feeling especially ill and should have returned home, but chose to make one final visit. This last visit would be to the home of Séraphita, the girl who had openly mocked him.

As the priest journeys over the hillside, the camera approaches him from a distance below and to the left. As already mentioned, the scene has little light, the light coming from behind the hill and casting an eerie glow over the hillside. The priest is silhouetted beside a lifeless tree, and, because of the placement of the camera and the slant of the hill, the priest's weariness makes the entire hillside seem close to toppling.

The priest stumbles forward, the camera exploring his tortured face. Suddenly he falls and tries to move but cannot. Again, the camera explores his face, as the voice-over records that he did not know how long he lay in the mud. He slowly rises and begins to stagger forward again, but this time his head is lifted up and his eyes closed as if in prayer. He narrates that he was afraid he would see the Virgin should he open his eyes. The screen goes blank for a moment. The priest narrates that he opened his eyes to see the face he expected: "It, too, was a child's face, but without any splendour". The darkness is replaced by a ground-level shot of dirty and awkward feet moving towards the prostrate man. The camera ascends to reveal Séraphita, who carries water and a cloth to wipe his wounds. She cleans him and then explains that she knows he is not drunk, and that she will punish any children who should say so. She leads him back to the road and then returns, lamp in hand, towards her home.

The obvious feature of this sequence is its resemblance to Christ's journey to the cross. Women minister to the priest, who is actually ministering to them. The road is uphill, the tree recalling the cross, and the priest can barely make it. He falls and is helped to the journey's end. The priest bleeds and sweats profusely; his face is wiped by a woman. However, more than through these symbols of the priest as Christ, the sequence is understandable within the larger context of his reflections on the Virgin recalled in the opening narration.

The sequence begins with older women giving the priest tea, and ends with the girl giving him water. When Séraphita helps him on the road, he imagines it is the Virgin, and when he finally sees her, he sees a virgin, but with no splendour. Her words to him reveal the operation of grace in her heart, and it is significant that she carries a lantern as she departs from him on the road, the lantern which here and throughout the film suggests the light of the Gospel.

The narrative of the film at this point is not only telling of the saint's life, it also speaks of the complete work of the Church. Woman, who fell first in the garden, is captured by grace and made the mother of God, and, as His mother, the only human heart fully capable of feeling the pain of the divine suffering that alone could redeem humanity. Furthermore, as woman, Séraphita is the Church that carries the light of truth on through generations of children, processions of life and death.

In recording his meditations and memories, the priest has produced a kind of lesser Scripture. We understand the fuller relationships that he can see only in part. His limitations become a stamp of divine authorship, for they preserve the integrity of the sacrifice which is his life. These writings also proclaim the glory of what we see, which he cannot see. The scene is night, but the sense is full of brightness, the lamp that lights the way and the lamp of the priest's brilliant soul.

Such symbols of holy glory can be followed throughout the film. The priest is bereft of comfort, fearing the loss of God's love, and, as he looks out of a window at carefree passers-by, he hears the crowing of a cock, the symbol of Peter's denial of Christ. A subsequent scene introduces Séraphita who initially betrays his trust. In several instances, as the priest agonises in his room, the background is marked by a cross, either the crucifix over his bed or the shadow of window bars. When he confronts Chantal about her lack of love for her parents, she backs into a confessional booth where only her face is lit in a frame of black darkness. Out of the darkness her face seems devilish, as are her attitudes, but, as the priest reads her heart and asks for the suicide letter she has written, she steps from the booth into the light. Later, the priest will assume that her conversion is inevitable.

Bresson's film, despite his often-expressed position that filmmaking should strip artifice to reveal essential realities, teems with visual, auditory and stylistic symbols. In his attempt to reach the soul of people and events, Bresson depends upon synecdochic and metonymic reductions that link images and sequences. Diary of a Country Priest is typical of what characterises his complete style. The image may be the bowed head of the priest or the bowed figure of Michel the pickpocket; the feet of Séraphita or the feet of Joan of Arc; the open door and window of Une femme douce (A Gentle Creature, 1969), or the vacated hillside of Mouchette – in each case, the symbol is packed.

These packed images allow Bresson to approach the souls of his characters, and make them people and not types, as Ayfre argues in her telling analysis of Bresson's style.[6] By suppressing the realistic tendency towards an over-abundance of narrative detail, Bresson is able to make individual details more communicative.[7] Objects interpret people and events which in turn reinvest the objects. The world is simplified idealistically, both to emphasise the unique individuality of all things, and to relate all things in terms of their shared life and communion.

This idealism produces both a biting naturalism and a divine allegory. The naturalism follows from Bresson's care in documenting his images and in allowing them to linger in the mind to suggest relationships with other images. He begs us to see things with all their multidimensionality, and yet stops just short of removing the mystery from the material presented to us. The allegory grows out of the arrangements of Bresson's images, which force certain theological interpretations: for example, the crowing of the cock or the presence of the crosses. These symbols come to the film with conventional interpretations which cannot be sterilised and made mere existential details. Nor would Bresson want them to be: the film has a large pattern to it that is as idealistic as Bresson's concern to capture essences in objects.

The pattern for *Diary of a Country Priest* is the Mass. The vocation of the main character allows for such an equation superficially in terms of narrative development: the priest becomes what he performs – that is, the sacrificial saviour. But the liturgical structure is more pronounced than this. The performance of the entire filmic text is liturgical, not just the movement of the characters. The design of the film compels viewer identification with universal religious types and with Christian redemptive history.

The priest whom we follow poses as Everyman, fallen and subject to death, yet potentially beautiful of soul, and the one son of Adam whose sacrifice allows for the eternal life of his followers: Christ. The souls to whom he ministers are ultimately lost, in need of redemption, and incomplete – the Count, Countess, Chantal, Séraphita, Dufréty. In the procession of the film, we watch the priest take on the weight of these guilty souls until his own death. In that death, these sins find atonement in the grace that covers all. In the cases of Séraphita, Chantal, the Countess and Dufréty, the motions of grace have already become evident by the end of the film.

What informs us of these situations is typically firstly the camera, then the narrative. The camera studies Séraphita's feet and face as she cares for the priest when he collapses, and then studies her again as she leaves the priest with the lantern that he had previously carried. With Chantal, the camera lingers on certain expressions and gestures, unseen by the priest, that indicate her internal rebelliousness and the later softening of it. In the case of the Countess, the camera flashes from the pendant of the woman's son to the fire in the fireplace to indicate the weight of the priest's ministry to her, a camera gesture foreshadowed by earlier lingering shots of the priest's pained expressions that suggest the spiritual importance of the ensuing interchange between the two. With Dufréty, the introduction of his letter to Torcy into the voice-over narration previously held by the priest places him in a position of succession to the vacant ministry. In all these cases and many more throughout the film, the significance of events, which we have been urged from the start to witness as mystery, is defined and interpreted as Christian redemptive mystery by the camera.

The final image of the film, the cross imposed on a pure white screen, is the resolution of all the relationships developed by Bresson in the film. All the represented humanity resides under the shadow of Bresson's cross, either giving in fully to it, as does the young priest, or running from it. This image is the consummate symbol, the synecdoche not only for the whole film, but also for relationships in the reality beyond the film.

This is the prototypical pattern for the sacramental film that follows Western liturgical conventions. The silence of God must lead to the proclamation of the Gospel, which is to say that the consummate realistic representation leads to the consummate theological symbol – the liturgical rehearsal of redemptive history. These films make no attempt to justify or resolve the existential tensions they pose in their factual representations, for they follow an inherent liturgical compulsion which is based on the same tension. They are paradoxical rehearsals of the human dilemma of the necessity for faith and hope in a bleak world. Rather than reason, they seek to develop praise.

Notes

[1]   Cited in Phillip Lopate, "Films as Spiritual Life", *Film Comment* 27: 6 (November-December 1991): 26.

[2]   André Bazin provides a useful discussion of the relationships between the novel and film in "Le Journal d'un Curé de Campagne", in Ian Cameron (ed), *The Films of Robert Bresson* (New York: Praeger Publishers, 1969): 51-66.

[3]   The text from the third chapter of John's Gospel was to have been the title (and is the subtitle) of *A Man Escaped*. It was and remains a favourite Bresson meditation.

[4]   Bresson's cinematographic tendencies are best defined in his own short notebook, Robert Bresson, *Notes on Cinematography*, translated by Jonathan Griffin (New York: Urizen Books, 1977).

[5]   In analyzing the texts of Bresson, one is forced to read symbols and stylistic cues across the films in a manner somewhat different from the techniques that would typically be employed in a standard narrative film. David Bordwell explains and justifies this necessity by identifying Bresson's narrative style with what he calls "parametric narration", a type of narration in which a film's stylistic system creates patterns that operate distinctly from the demands of plot. The parametric film tends to operate primarily as an aesthetic performance. As such, it relates closely to the type of liturgical film that I am defining here, insofar as both subordinate story to the phenomenological experience of viewing the film in a given stylistic mode. See David Bordwell, *Narration in the Fiction Film* (Madison: University of Wisconsin Press, 1985): 274-310.

[6]   Amédée Ayfre, "The Universe of Robert Bresson", in Cameron (ed): 8-18. Dudley Andrew summarises Bresson's concentration on the priest as follows: "Bresson...pared down the novel by cutting off its public half. He bored straight to the center of the curé, where he was temperamentally at home, and from there he refused to budge". (Dudley Andrew, *Film in the Aura of Art* [Princeton: Princeton University Press, 1984]: 124.) See also Susan Sontag, "Spiritual style in the films of Robert Bresson", in *Against interpretation and other essays* (London: Eyre & Spottiswoode, 1967): 177-195; Marjorie Greene, "Robert Bresson", *Film Quarterly* 13: 3 (1960): 4-10.

[7]   Lindley Hanlon ties this to the tradition of narrative traced in European literature from the Old Testament by Erich Auerbach in his *Mimesis: The Representation of Reality in Western Literature*, translated by Willard R Trask (Princeton: Princeton University Press, 1953). Although Hanlon does not treat Bresson's *Diary of a Country Priest*, she provides an excellent framework for tracing the multiplicity of interrelationships within the Bresson text. See Lindley Hanlon, *Fragments: Bresson's Film Style* (London: Associated University Presses, 1986): 19-23ff.

The Christian doctrine of immanence states that God is everywhere present in the fullness of His being. For Christians, this concept is acutely mysterious because Christ is God in the limitations of human flesh. The only way to reconcile God's immanence with Christ's Incarnation is by appeal to the mystery of God's own being. Religious artists must bow here.

Apart from the image of Christ himself and symbolic renderings of the Trinity, the liturgical tradition of the West, and of the United States in particular, has no mechanism for the representation of immanent divinity within space and time, largely because of the theological complexity surrounding the doctrine of the Incarnation in relation to the doctrine of immanence. The God in the flesh has ascended into heaven. In general, Western liturgics avoid attempts at literal divine representation because of the fear of pantheism or idolatry. Many Protestant churches, in particular, remain strongly iconoclastic. The mystery of God's nature would seem to be violated if representations were attempted, for the rendering would depict either the omnipresent God or the physical form of Christ, not both together.

Nevertheless, two types of representations are frequently used in the West to hint at a conception of Christian immanence. The first is the image of the saint with a halo – a literal halo, as in Catholicism, or an implied one, usually elevated verbal descriptions accompanying ordinary images, in Protestantism. The halo casts a certain aura around the physical representation of the saint, and so suggests metaphorically her or his divine attributes. The second representation that carries hints of immanence is the depiction of a mythical world which surrounds or enfolds the image of the saint. One often finds this representational style, the lion at rest with the lamb, in stained glass windows or book illustrations, often in children's books or in illustrations accompanying parables in Bibles. Each of these types of representation touches on one side of the divine mystery. The halo approaches the notion of God incarnate within human beings. The mythical style portrays a world dominated by the providence and presence of God. Both styles, especially when joined, are highly symbolic, and therefore pose no immediate threat to orthodox teachings.

The medium of film, however, offers the potential to bring to these symbolic approaches a verisimilitude which can lead to theological complication. A case in point would be Martin Scorsese's *The Last Temptation of Christ* (1989), which attempts to demythologize typical representations of Christ. By adding human elements to the typical Hollywood mythological approach, Scorsese seems to be threatening orthodox doctrines regarding the person of Christ. What he has attempted is a literal representation of Christ as both man and God, with perhaps a heavy hand towards the former. That attempt, by its very nature, violated the mystery of the doctrine for many people.

The problem is partly cultural. The liturgical tradition that is built upon the doctrine of God's immanence, and which in turn has generated an acceptable iconography of immanence, is that of Eastern Orthodoxy, and this faith is little understood in the Protestant and Catholic West outside the Greek and Slavic communities. It finds little place in current theological or philosophical discussions of any kind, because it has remained a static tradition since almost the 9th century. The Orthodox aesthetic strikes the Western eye as ornate and somehow primitive, almost pagan with its gilded edges and heavily symbolic images. It is common for those who first approach Orthodox film art – for example, the films of Sergo (Sergej) Paradžanov or Andrej Tarkovskij – to feel somehow put off by the esoteric nature of their works.

Yet, a thread of Orthodox, iconic filmmaking has infiltrated the United States from abroad, most evident in the works of Paradžanov and Tarkovskij which have begun to circulate freely. It also can be recognised in the later work of Carl-Theodor Dreyer, perhaps because of the affinity between Lutheran theology and that of Orthodoxy.[1] Unquestionably the largest entrance has been through Gothic horror films,[2] which derive in part from German Expressionism and its combined Manichaeism and theatricality. There is a form of negative immanence in Expressionist-influenced works, from Gothic horror to the films of Werner Herzog and the Hollywood genre of film noir.[3]

Films built upon conceptions of immanence have a representative style characterised by a rich atmosphere. Something surrounds the characters and the action, which has a compulsory power over the whole. This something is not merely a claustrophobic tension, as in Welles's films, nor the metaphoric expiration of intense living, as in those by Sternberg; it is not a mere symbol, but a living moral presence imposed upon the materials of the narrative. Typically, this presence conflicts with the will of a group of individuals and, finally, with a single individual. The heart of the conflict becomes the inability or refusal of characters to acknowledge or "see" this presence and recognise its own will in regard to their own. Within the narrative, the presence will finally take a single physical shape (will undergo an incarnation), often a miraculous shape, or will finally be identified in a single shape, and there will be some climactic struggle between the wilful and usually heroic human, and the incarnate "thing".

This motif can indeed be most clearly followed in the dark conflicts of horror films, but it can also find positive treatment within the mode of the sacramental film. As sacramental films typically posture the viewer in an attitude of liturgical worship, those which follow concepts of immanence follow tendencies related to Orthodox devotional practices. In particular, they imitate the Orthodox liturgical posturing that enhances spiritual detachment and the concentration of focus. The object of devotion becomes climactically the God-man in his passion.

Morning and evening prayers and devotional instructions in the Orthodox faith are collected in the *Canonicon*, the book of rules and patterns for worship. A sample instruction touches on both the attitude and content of prayer:

> 'When you awake, before you begin the day, stand with reverence before the all-seeing God. Make the sign of the Cross and say: In the name of the Father, and of the Son, and of the Holy Spirit. Amen. Having invoked the Holy Trinity, keep silence for a little, so that your thoughts and feelings may be freed from worldly cares. Then recite the following prayers...'[4]

The detachment from the world which these instructions promote is triggered by mental concentration and physical positioning. This positioning is quite important, as it relates to the iconicity of Orthodox art. The soul cannot be separated from the body in worship, for the mystery of the Church is that Christ "dwells and abides in the faithful".[5] This indwelling is appropriated by faith, but this faith is not ethereal; it is the attitude of the complete person. Thus, the worshipper stands, makes the sign of the cross, and voices prayer. These actions turn the worshipper physically and spiritually from the world and towards God.

The positioning that detaches the believer from this life initiates a concentrated focus on God. The goal of prayer is to "realise the presence of God". In a similar fashion, the liturgical sacrament of the Eucharist is "a true *re-presentation*" of Christ.[6] Thus, divinity, which is everywhere present, is to be received through the senses and enjoyed in prayer, particularly through the sacramental elements. Spiritual detachment and concentration trigger the experience.

An Orthodox liturgical aesthetic is one that turns the participant from the ordinariness of a fallen world to perceive a wholly different divine presence. Beyond the Eucharistic celebration, this turning is most often prompted by concentration on an icon. The icon is a physical representation that reveals divinity when contemplated. Icons usually incorporate human representations, because Christ dwells most explicitly in humanity. However, the icon is not necessarily an artefact, for Christ himself was a living icon as he walked upon the earth.[7]

This conception of immanence can be traced in a small number of films once the stylistic and narrative elements associated with the theology are exposed and examined. Such films are often labelled as "difficult" because of their aesthetic biases, but I hope to illustrate a different and more precise source of their complexity: the liturgical representation of God's immanence played out in a Passion narrative. Perhaps the best example of a film which pointedly follows such a pattern is *Ordet* (*The Word*) by the Danish director, Carl-Theodor Dreyer.

Dreyer's *The Word* enfleshed

Dreyer's film version of *The Word* restates a popular Scandinavian play of the same title by Kaj Munk. Both play and film recount the story of the reconciliation of men and women of different faiths that occurs as the result of a miracle which many witness. The miracle is the resurrecting of a woman, Inger, who has died in childbirth, by her brother-in-law, Johannes, thought by his family to be mad as a result of too much religious study. The differing faiths are manifest both within Inger's family, the Borgens, and between the Borgen family and a rival family, the Petersens. The father, Morten Borgen, represents an old, traditional variety of Lutheranism that allows but doubts the potentiality of miracles. His eldest son, Mikkel, Inger's husband, is sceptical of his father's faith because the family has suffered so much through the years – Borgen's wife has died and Johannes is considered mad. The third son, Anders, has fallen in love with Anne, the daughter of Peter Petersen, a tailor who is a leader of a pietistic Lutheran sect. Anders has sought out Inger's help in the situation, since Inger sees through the divisions between Borgen and Peter, and shows sympathy even to Johannes. Inger's sudden death breaks down the hostility that has alienated the different characters – Peter consents to Anne's marrying out of her faith to Anders, and the family is gathered in a context of mutual sympathy. Her resurrection then propels this reconciliation to a new level of spirituality.

As an aid to reveal the liturgical mechanisms of *The Word*, it is useful to interact momentarily with David Bordwell's structural analysis of Dreyer's film.[8] Bordwell's reading aligns well with a sacramental reading, as he singles out Inger's resurrection as the narrative moment that generates the film's peculiar style:

> The miracle is *represented on film* as a return to cinematic intelligibility, to a space and time responsive to narrative demands, to stylistic figures immediately meaningful. In Inger's resurrection, verisimilitude is violated in the name of narrative order, and the sense of order is justified by the return of conventional filmic comprehension.[9]

The basis for Bordwell's argument is the sudden shift from the long takes with sweeping, unbiased camera movement that characterise the main portion of the film to the concluding sequence which relies on conventional editing techniques. In order to prepare the film viewer for the "unbelievable ending" of this cinematic version of the Munk play, Dreyer frustrates the viewer's ability to contain the narrative until the miraculous sequence; thus, the miracle is a relief in terms of its accessibility, and therefore it is at least visually welcome, if not believable.

Bordwell builds his analysis upon the premise that the figure of Johannes and his concluding miracle trouble narrative logic, largely because of their explicit supernaturalism. They suggest that Dreyer is "'a religious director' and has found in *Ordet* the perfect narrative".[10] Bordwell's contention is that Dreyer was primarily an independent artist who created films that challenged dominant cinematic practices with highly experimental styles, and whose narratives can be best considered as attempts to explore the interactions of these styles against conventional narratives. Thus, *The Word* is not a religious film by a religious director *per se*, but a perfect vehicle for the kind of narrative integrations that mark the filmmaker's signature. Its religiosity is a subordinate issue to its formal structures.

Bordwell supports his hypothesis with meticulous shot analyses. He argues that the unusually long shots of *The Word*, each lasting approximately 65 seconds across the film, underline the passing of time within the drama, and the shot is consequently a durational block, rather than the conventional spatial block. This creates a feeling of rhythm within the narrative that captures the theatrical quality of the film. He argues that the film's abstract camera movement, often presenting a circular three-dimensionality within given rooms (the Borgens's parlour or Peter's shop) and following characters from one place to another, presents a contrast between the live environment and the flat, distanced women and men, another stylistic curiosity. Moreover, Bordwell argues that the film evidences a sparseness of cinematographic varieties – few camera positions, straightforward lighting, and so on – that highlights the particular variances that occur within the narrative pattern. All the patterns set up through the narrative of *The Word* are broken in the miraculous conclusion:

> Once the space [of the death room] has been laid out, in a manner characteristic of Dreyer's circular *mise-en-scène*, it is quickly made subordinate to the cause-effect progression of the narrative. The characters announce the scene's agenda: 'The Vicar will soon be here.' 'And so, Inger, we shall put the lid over you.' 'Let the Parson say a prayer.' 'Any news of Johannes?' The narrative problems are about to be resolved, and at just this point the final sequence rapidly returns to the conventions of the classical norm. *Ordet* rediscovers the match-on-action cut, shot/reverse-shot, the eyeline match, analytical editing, and the close-up.[11]

This shift in style returns the viewer to a cinematic legibility and stability. For Bordwell, it subordinates the narrative matter to the narrative form; that is, the fact that the family is brought back together and that life is now restored to normalcy is signalled by the sequence's conventionality. The only problem which Bordwell finds in the structural unities of this final sequence in relation to the whole film is the presence of Johannes, who remains alive and miraculously gifted even at the narrative conclusion. Bordwell points out, however, that Johannes absents himself from the concluding frame by exiting left, thus spatially eliminating his troubling presence. Bordwell concludes:

> He becomes the only character whose final position in the room remains unknown to us. This tiny gesture poses as slight a problem as one can imagine. Yet even in a scene as massively unified as *Ordet*'s miracle, space refuses to lie completely under the sway of narrative structure.[12]

Bordwell's rigid formalism provides a certain relief from some of the more subjective treatments that the film has been given through the years,[13] but it needs to be countered precisely on his concluding point of the troubling presence of Johannes. By dismissing Johannes, Bordwell has dismissed the religious core of the film's narrative and stylistic structure, and, in doing so, he has overlooked the nature of the text as a vehicle for religious experience. One would suppose that any reading of the film which sidesteps its liturgical experience must end in the kind of denial that characterises Bordwell's concluding remarks.

Johannes is the primary subject of the camera's gaze throughout the narrative. The question posed at the opening of the film is: Where is Johannes? Anders and Inger both gaze out of windows to search for him at daybreak in the opening sequence. The family forms a search party, and, when they finally find him on a hill, the camera observes him mysteriously from below and at a distance, as he begins to proclaim himself as Christ. This same motif recurs towards the film's conclusion. Johannes leaves the Borgen house through a window after Inger's death, and the family forms a party to search for him. This time he will not be found, but a series of wipes connecting the different aspects of the search, the only wipes of the film, underlines the significance of Johannes's absence: even the camera searches for him. In this context, his sudden appearance in the death room at the conclusion, his miraculous words, and his final absence from the screen cannot merely be passed over.

Similarly, the camera follows Johannes each time he is present in a scene. His presence stops not only the actions of the characters, as when he proclaims that the man with the scythe has come for Inger, but also, consistently, the camera. All his actions – even the more trivial, as when he moves a candle to a window – are conveyed as significant by the camera's attention. The viewer shares this attention. These actions are never fully explained on the narrative level, except as "madness", and they continue to trouble the viewer until Johannes's final appearance. If madness, why are they foregrounded? Why is the search for him given such significance?

The answer is that, regardless of how Dreyer's style interacts with conventional norms, *The Word* centres on the religious presence of this one character. Paul Schrader underlines this same feature in his illustration of how Dreyer manifests a transcendental style based on conceptions of disparity. However, Schrader considers Johannes an allegorical presence, rather than what the film literally suggests: the manifest physical reincarnation of Christ.[14] *The Word*'s narrative structure does not contain and secularize Johannes; rather, it poses him as a religious mystery. The function of the film's concluding sequence is primarily to answer the mystery. The miracle itself, not the stylistic mechanics of the film, restores family unity. As for narrative unity in the restoration of conventional techniques, I think it can be much better argued in reverse: the conclusion poses a set of artificial formal devices designed to underline the incarnational occurrence in the resurrection of Inger. The abstraction of lighting behind the coffin and the sparseness of furnishings in the room, coupled with the more rapid editing style and almost sentimental reaction-shot of Maren watching Inger rise, signal the extraordinary occurrence that now answers all the metaphysical questions raised in the narrative. These are, of course, the metonymic cues that mark the sacramental film.

The mystery of Johannes is answered by Inger's resurrection. Johannes has been mad, but his madness is a form of radical holiness. Dreyer changed the source of Johannes's madness from an aborted love affair in Munk's play, to over-intensity in theological studies. In Dreyer's film, Johannes has become absorbed, temporarily, *in his pursuit of God*. This is a crucial understanding because it is a form of the same crisis that overwhelms Morten Borgen throughout the narrative, and Mikkel at the end. The "shock", as the doctor puts it, that restores Johannes to normalcy at the end – his altered dress, relieved voice inflection, and restoration within the Borgen family – has been the death of Inger. He collapses in her sickroom and then later leaves the house. What Inger's death has accomplished is Johannes's recollection of his own previous humanity – his collapse paralleling Inger's death. It has not altered his apprehension of the family's faith nor his belief in the power of faith, as the final sequence shows. It has simply brought his communion with God's presence back to a human form. In a sense, both Johannes and Inger are resurrected, and the physical manifestation of God that marks the sacramental conclusion is shared by both.

It is impossible to dismiss the supernatural message of the film's conclusion, as Bordwell has done, once the function of the character of Johannes is carefully considered within the film's thematic context. To do so is to overlook that aspect of the film that is most noteworthy: its representation of the immanent presence of Christ.

All the disruptions and theatricalizations of Dreyer's style in *The Word*, which Bordwell skilfully uncovers, charge the film's *mise en scène* with a mysterious atmosphere, a holy aura. The long takes that suggest shot duration also suggest a presence overlooking – considering or contemplating – the action. The viewer is forced to concentrate on the flattened narrative plane in a posture of anticipated discovery. Similarly, the circuitous camera movement, following one character and then gradually shifting to another, anticipating entrances and pondering disappearances, suggests a presence overseeing the action, and thus links the camera's point of view to divine perception. Dreyer's style, which supplants classical narrative continuity editing by replacing it with a more theatrical representational technique, acts as a catalyst to the *contemplation* of meanings and relationships within a much less active visual plane. The sparseness of the images in the film encourages a deeper *penetration* into the specific images given.

In terms of the narrative elements that I have previously linked to the immanent style – the question of "seeing"; the climactic confrontation between the "God in the flesh" and a small group of resistors; and the final revelation of divine presence – these can all be observed in *The Word*. Johannes is again the key figure, since he is literally the manifest presence of God, up until the last sequence when his work of power reveals that the presence of God is potentially available to all who believe, from the little child to the sceptical doctor or the now-converted Mikkel. The resurrection and highly stylised final framing of Mikkel and Inger reinforce the meaning; in fact, the bright, diffused lighting of the frames that end the film suggests the type of holy aura that is a classical stylistic metonym for transcendence.

The posture of concentration upon a physical mystery and subsequent detachment from the world is enacted visually many times throughout the film. Midway through the narrative, the vicar calls upon the Borgen household. The scene begins with a cut to Johannes standing alone in the sitting room. The vicar enters and engages Johannes who tells him: "I am a bricklayer but people want to build their own homes...Most wander homeless". The camera follows Johannes as he speaks, and leaves the vicar in the back of the field. "People believe in the dead Christ, but not the risen", Johannes pronounces, "thus speaks my Church". The camera follows Johannes as he leaves the room after this statement, and excludes the vicar entirely from the frame in doing so. Finally, the camera pans from the door and reintroduces the vicar who concludes, "How awful".

This exchange between the vicar and Johannes is synecdochic for the whole film. The camera follows Johannes and forces our attention on him; thus, the vicar enters a plane of vision which Johannes dominates. Johannes tells the vicar that he is the Christ and that he alone can create and sustain lives. The vicar expresses his doubt in the supernatural. The camera resists his presence, framing him at a distance and only briefly, and follows Johannes. The return to the vicar is almost an afterthought. His expression of Johannes's "awful" condition is questioned, and, with the mounting evidence presented through the course of the film, seen as rather trite and insignificant. The double-edged sense of the word "awful" even adds a touch of irony. The viewer is drawn to Johannes and cued to penetrate his mystery; the scepticism of the world is left in the background and finally dismissed altogether.

The point I am arguing here is that Bordwell's formalist analysis of Dreyer's style denies that style a meaningful connection with particular images and with the overall thematic arrangement of the film. Bordwell is correct in arguing against the notion that Dreyer is a religious director with a religious style, although the director certainly was well versed in

Biblical subjects.[15] *The Word* is, however, contrary to Bordwell's text-bound conclusion, an explicitly religious film, and Dreyer does tailor his style to offer the film material in a specifically religious manner. The sacramental mechanics are clearly manifest in the concluding sequence, in the sudden transformation of stylistic gestures and overall *mise en scène* that accompanies the resurrection. In addition, the quality of immanence that characterises the visual structure – the dialectic between Johannes's visual presence and the denial of his divinity, together with the aura of spiritual concentration and detachment from the world – is likewise marked.

Munk's play provided Dreyer with the thematic motif of "the Word made flesh". Dreyer would well know the context of this idea:

> In the beginning was the Word, and the Word was with God, and the Word was God...He was in the world, and the world was made through him, and the world knew him not...And the Word was made flesh, and dwelt among us. And we saw his glory – glory as of the only-begotten of the Father – full of grace and truth. (John 1: 1, 10, 14)

This passage is at the heart of any doctrine of immanence – God enfleshed, omnipresent creator and yet man, visible as such to a few, but rejected by the world at large. Dreyer presents this concept thematically in the overall narrative structure of *The Word*, and he draws attention to the doctrine through his style.

Notes

[1]   Both Lutheran and Orthodox theologies emphasise the state of grace in which the Church now resides after the atonement. Consequently, both faiths have liturgical structures which encourage a concentration on the process of sanctification by which believers are lifted to God. See Robert E Webber, *Common Roots: A Call to Evangelical Maturity* (Grand Rapids, MI: Zondervan Publishing House, 1978): 41-116. Luther felt sufficient affinity to the Orthodox faith to cite it against Johann Mayer von Eck in his anti-papal debates; the Catholic Church, of course, had dismissed the Eastern Church over their "heretical" understanding of the Trinity after the 9th century. Philip Melanchthon later translated Luther's Augsburg Confession (1530) into Greek for the sake of the patriarch of Constantinople, and Luther's discussion of justification by faith found its way into Orthodox theologies after the 16th century. See Roland H Bainton, *Here I Stand: A Life of Martin Luther* (Nashville; New York: Abingdon Press, 1950): 88-89.

[2]   An incarnate evil presence in a Manichean universe became a standard generic expression within horror film, particularly after Polański's *Rosemary's Baby* (1968).

[3]   Foster Hirsch frequently personifies the *noir* universe in *The Dark Side of the Screen: Film Noir* (San Diego; New York: A S Barnes & Company; London: The Tantivy Press, 1981). Consider, for example: "The city in *film noir* is never merely neutral, never simply a shapeless background. In both studio and location thrillers, it participates in the action, 'comments' on the characters, supplies mood and tension." (79).

[4]   Cited in Georges Florovsky, "Orthodox", in Pehr Edwall, Eric Hayman and William D Maxwell (eds), *Ways of Worship: The Report of a Theological Commission of Faith and Order* (New York: Harper & Brothers, 1951): 55.

[5]   Ibid: 60.

[6]   Ibid: 56, 59. Emphasis in original.

[7]   In the 8th century, John of Damascus definitively described an icon as "a likeness, an illustration, and a representation of something, showing forth in itself that which is imaged" (cited in Jaroslav Pelikan, *The Spirit of Eastern Christendom [600-1700]*, volume 2 of *The Christian Tradition: A History of the Development of Doctrine* [Chicago; London: The University of Chicago Press, 1974]: 119). Christ's physical presence as the image of the invisible God became a focus of debate during the iconoclastic controversy of the 9th century. The Eastern Church saw the Incarnation as the fulfilment of God's presence with His people which was lacking in the Old Testament. Therefore, Old Testament prohibitions against depicting God no longer completely applied, as God had depicted Himself in the New Testament. Worship of Christ was worship of God. Similarly, worship of holy images was worship of the presences behind them. See Pelikan: 83-138.

[8]   David Bordwell, *The Films of Carl-Theodor Dreyer* (Berkeley; Los Angeles; London: University of California Press, 1981).

[9]   Ibid: 170. Emphasis in original.

[10]   Ibid: 147.

[11]   Ibid: 167.

[12]   Ibid: 170.

[13]   For example, see Robin Wood's attack on Dreyer's dogmatic approach to filmmaking in "Robin Wood on Carl Dreyer", *Film Comment* 10: 2 (March-April 1974): 10-17. See also Tom Milne, *The Cinema of Carl Dreyer* (New York: A S Barnes & Co; London: A Zwemmer; 1971).

[14]   Schrader (*Transcendental Style in Film: Ozu, Bresson, Dreyer* [Berkeley: University of California Press, 1972]: 135) writes: "John [i.e. Johannes] is not the central character of *Ordet*. He is used as an allegorical figure,

representing what the other characters must come to believe." This is a curious argument, since Johannes is a literal presence in the film. However, it suits Schrader's larger concept that *Ordet* is a "self-conscious" attempt at transcendental style by Dreyer. The transcendental style defined by Schrader takes its model from Zen Buddhism, which is naturalistic. In such a frame, miracles must be allegorical.

[15] For some of Dreyer's more candid observations on historic Christianity, see his comments in Donald Skoller (ed), *Dreyer in Double Reflection* (New York: E P Dutton & Co, 1973): 55ff.

Andrej Tarkovskij's conception of filmmaking is conveyed through the metaphor he chose as the title of his film memoirs, *Sculpting in Time*. His film moments fit together thematically, rather than chronologically or even teleologically: he cuts separate shapes out of time and pieces them into a whole as an artist would create a collage. Tarkovskij's film narratives serve the overall unity of a complete artistic conception; they do not create that conception. Ivor Montagu calls Tarkovskij "a *realist poet in images*...he digs deep beneath the surface structure of his narrative to load his treatment with overtones and undertones, hints, symbols".[1]

Tarkovskij's masterpiece, *Andrej Rublëv*, ostensibly tells the story of the aesthetic evolution of Russia's greatest icon painter, a monk who lived in the late 14th and early 15th centuries. However, unlike similar reverential artist biographies, such as *Rembrandt* (1936), *Lust for Life* (1956) and *The Agony and the Ecstasy* (1965), Tarkovskij finds little interest in the standard historical matters that usually fill these films, such as the artist's early history, relation to large political movements, and private relationships. What is to be known of these matters must be taken to the film, not gathered from it. The matter of this life history is the depiction of the anguish and joy of the soul that produced Rublëv's great icons and frescos.[2] In this anguish and joy of soul, Tarkovskij details a unique conception of Christ's Passion as played out in the life of a great artist.

Tarkovskij's internal portrait also strays from the customary norms of psychological drama. Very little immediate attention is given to the personal struggle within Rublëv as such; rather, the viewer is made to experience Rublëv's conflicts, and so experience the story from a perspective parallel to that of the artist. The more immediate subject-matter of the film is the barbarous history which unfolded around Rublëv's life. In the climactic sequences of the film, such as the casting of a great bell or the ransacking of the town of Vladimir, Rublëv is little more than a spectator himself. The film's final images dismiss him altogether in favour of his art and the spiritual beauties of that art, metaphorically conveyed by a graceful shot of horses standing in a rainswept field.

Tarkovskij's aesthetic in *Andrej Rublëv* seems to be modelled on the aesthetic style of Rublëv and other iconographers, and this makes the film both remarkable and difficult. There is no muttering of "Rosebud" or use of stasis shots to resolve questions which the narrative has raised. The large conception of the film emerges only when the complete portrait is considered from a distance. Moreover, the emergent meanings are both theologically suggestive and mysterious. Tarkovskij's style has been appropriately compared to the iconostasis in an Orthodox church, the collection of icons that form a screen between the nave and church sanctuary.[3] The viewer must contemplate and penetrate the internal thematic complexities of the icon screen to have full access to the altar.

Tarkovskij builds the film narrative towards the images of Rublëv's art that fill the screen in the final moments, even more than in the film's climax, when Andrej will break a long vow of silence and return to painting. The film concludes when the screen suddenly fills with brilliant blues, golds and reds, as the camera in close-up observes the charred edges of Rublëv's great fresco in the cathedral at Vladimir. The images are startling because they are the first introduction of colour, and because they seem so rough and abstract in close-up. Over the images is the sound of a choir singing a joyous chant, beautifully scored by Vyacheslav Ovchinnikov. The camera scans the indefinite forms and locates small, recognisable and beautiful details: a donkey, the faces of disciples, a hand, a church. Slowly, the camera circles back to reveal more and more of the detail and beauty of Rublëv's surviving icons. The last images are of the famous icon of the Holy Trinity, climaxing in the image of Christ's face. This icon is perhaps the most famous of all Russian paintings, and the icon which would inspire an Orthodox Church Council to proclaim Rublëv's style as the true Russian iconographic style "to be followed in all perpetuity".[4]

The camera gesture of this artistic reverie can be taken as a symbol of how Rublëv's life is presented: small, abstract and striking details that reveal elegance and beauty only when seen as a whole and from a distance, from a transcendent position. The pastoral images of horses, and the rain that falls over the final shots, signify the spiritual character of the complete artistic conception and the soul which created it.

The film itself might well be considered as a collection of icons, a kind of cinematic fresco. The structure of the narrative suggests this: a compilation of ten separate episodes, all related thematically to the personal and artistic development that occurred throughout Rublëv's life. The episodes contain their own structural unities, while building upon one another to preface the final resolution – the extant Rublëv icons themselves. This structure might be seen as analogous to certain medieval narrative structures, which are vertical, reflecting upward on larger spiritual truths for their organisational purpose. Erich Auerbach has related this episodic structure to the Old Testament narratives:

> [C]ertain parts brought into high relief, others left obscure, abruptness, suggestive influence of the unexpressed, 'background' quality, multiplicity of meanings and the need for interpretation, universal-historical claims, development of the concept of the historically becoming, and preoccupation with the problematic.[5]

The episodic structure of *Andrej Rublëv* enables Tarkovskij to explore Rublëv's life as a kind of romantic and religious pilgrimage. It also partially dissolves Rublëv's individuality into a larger religious type.

The prologue of the film begins with a man crossing a river in a boat, and then climbing a church tower in order to launch a primitive air balloon. The man takes off in the balloon and soars over the meandering waterways of the Russian countryside. The flyer marvels at the beauty of the land and the diminution of its occupants. However, the balloon begins to lose altitude, and the man and craft crash horribly on the bank of a river. A shot of the wreckage completes the sequence.

This prologue introduces a pair of oppositions that will be restated in each subsequent episode. The former is natural beauty vs. human barbarity and mortality. As the flyer prepares to launch the balloon, Tarkovskij shows in the background a chaotic assembly of monks and peasants who shout their opposition to the experiment, and apparently prepare to burn the flyer as a witch. These women and men shrink to insignificance as the balloon ascends, and they are replaced onscreen by the grandness of the flyer's aerial vision. The beauties of flight are then replaced again with the calamitous crash. In the final shot, the serenity of the shore where the crash occurs is paradoxically united with the horrible image of the rustling balloon.

The second opposition is spiritual optimism vs. pessimism. The flyer obviously represents the first as he rushes to achieve humanity's ancient dream of flight. His vision is fulfilled, and we find joy with him as he soars across land and water. The clamourers form the primary opposition to the flyers, as their shouting and gesticulating contrast with the grace of flight. But the balloon itself, made of pieces of skin and cloth, forms another pessimistic image. We know that it will not fly long. Similarly, the flyer lacks grandeur as he babbles, laughs and gasps during the flight. These oppositions are likewise united in the

37

paradoxical final image. The balloon is destroyed on the shore, but the breeze causes it to rustle, and there is some hint of human movement underneath. The vision has both succeeded and failed.

These pairs – natural beauty/human ugliness, and spiritual optimism/ pessimism – can be traced most explicitly in the several dialogues in the film between Andrej and Theophanes the Greek, the other important iconographer of the period. In each discussion, Andrej emphasises God's love, and the need for unity in Russia and compassion in art. Theophanes argues for a more realistic portrayal of man's depravity and the ensuing judgment to come. (In one early discussion between Theophanes and Andrej's assistant, Kirill, men are being tortured on a rack outside Theophanes's quarters.) This polarization of attitudes marks Andrej's inner struggle with the horrors he experiences outside the monastery. He cannot paint a fresco of the Last Judgment which the Duke has commissioned, because it is too harsh and cruel; he spends his time painting the Duke's playful daughter. However, the paradoxical result of his artistic gentleness will be the blinding of several artisans who take a commission with the Duke's brother out of impatience with the project's delay – an officer of the Duke blinds them in consequence of the Duke's jealousy. Similarly, Andrej vows silence after the ghastly Tartar pillage of the town and cathedral of Vladimir, during which he is forced to kill a man who intends to rape a holy fool under his care. This silence, however, renders him impotent to restrain the fool later when she is enticed into riding off with a Tartar chieftain. The dichotomies of beauty/ugliness and spiritual optimism/pessimism will torture Rublëv's spirit throughout the narrative, since they are irreconcilable in his human experience. They simultaneously become the paradoxical conflicts that enable Andrej to produce an art which exudes sensuality while transcending physicality.

Rublëv's spirit reflects a New Testament emphasis on God's love, while the projected world of the film seems to align more directly with Old Testament barbarism. Tarkovskij remarked:

> Unlike Theophanes the Greek, who propounded the idea of Judgement Day, who found in Man only the embodiment of sin and vice, and in God a vengeful, punitive being, Rublev placed Man first. In Man he sought God, he regarded him as the house in which God lived.[6]

In one perhaps visionary conversation between Rublëv and Theophanes, Rublëv first imagines (or at least the viewer sees) ants climbing up Theophanes's legs. As they discuss the potential for a true

Russian art – Rublëv seeing a virtue in the mass suffering of the Russian people – Rublëv's words are projected over a vision of a crucifixion. The mourners are Russian peasant women; the Christ figure bears some resemblance to Rublëv; and the setting is a snowy Russian countryside. The realisation of Rublëv's inner vision, and the realisation of Gospel hope, can thus only be approached through faith in glimmers of vision, in dreams, and in art. These thematic elements first offered by the prologue form the backdrop for the nine episodes of Rublëv's life which follow. They also detach the viewer from standard theological methods of understanding film, and set the rule for the religious concentration on Rublëv's passion that Tarkovskij encourages.

The first episode, set in the year 1400, presents Rublëv with fellow monks, Kirill and Danilov, taking shelter from a heavy rain in a hut where a jester performs bawdy songs for a group of peasants. The appearance of the three monks quiets the crowd, although the jester continues to offer lewd comments. After a time, soldiers appear at the door and drag the jester off, slamming his head into a tree in the process. The suggestion is that he is an escaped serf and that someone has reported him. (The jester will later falsely accuse Rublëv of this.) After the arrest, two men fight in the mud outside the hut.

Beyond the dichotomies set out in the prologue, new motifs emerge in this segment. The radical separation of Andrej from the world is plain in the almost hostile silence that descends upon the hut after the monks arrive. This silence is related to the brutal silencing of the jester when the soldiers arrive. In addition, contrasting visual perspectives are introduced in parallel shots, first of a group of peasant women peeping through a window at the festivities in the hut, and then of Andrej looking out of the window from inside at horses and men slogging through the mud. Similarly, the camera pans slowly around the room while the jester performs, catching the myriad raucous expressions of the peasants, and a similar pan catches the sudden solemnity that the monks bring. After the monks leave the hut, the camera beautifully frames a group of horses lingering under trees in a mist. The effect of these contrary images is to foreground perspective as it bears upon an evaluation of people and things. The peasants are alternately crude and respectful, exploitive and exploited. The hut is a sanctuary from the rain, but not all are offered the sanctuary – the women looking in. The horses and all of nature are caught in chaotic struggle, and then allowed to rest pastorally in a refreshing mist. We are offered a penetrating glimpse of the world's depravity, while alongside there are images of a world still bearing the divine stamp and ruled by the divine presence.

The next episode begins in 1405 in the quarters of Theophanes the Greek, in a church where the artist has a commission. Kirill comes to Theophanes on behalf of Andrej, whom Theophanes would like to employ as an assistant. Kirill offers his help instead, but Theophanes sends a messenger to the monastery requesting Andrej. Andrej asks Danilov to accompany him, and, after an argument motivated by Danilov's jealousy, Danilov agrees. Kirill then rejects the monks in a jealous rage and leaves the monastery; on the way, he brutally kills his dog with a staff.

The new theme introduced in this segment is the artist's place among his peers. Andrej's "gift", as Kirill will later call it, has separated him even beyond the separation of his monastic calling. Alternately, Theophanes, Kirill and Danilov reject Andrej, and yet each will return to Andrej before the film ends. The rejection becomes a rejection of God, as evidenced in Kirill's brutality and the intimate and moving reconciliation of Andrej and Danilov. It places Andrej in the position of the crucified Christ, the image that will close the next sequence (set a year later, in 1406), the imagined or visionary discussion between Andrej and Theophanes that has already been discussed.

The subsequent episode takes place in 1408, and concerns the encounter between Andrej and his companions and a group of pagan revellers. The painters see an orgiastic festival in the distant forest near a river. Andrej wanders off and encounters two of the male revellers. He rebukes them and they respond by tying him to a post. A naked girl comes to Andrej and attempts to seduce him. He asks to be untied, and, after she complies, he leaves. He returns, with several facial scratches, to his companions who assume the worst and look at him with disappointment. The monks then leave to cross the river in a small boat. As they do so, authorities chase two of the revellers into the water. One of them, the girl who tempted Andrej, swims away, passing the monks' small boat. Andrej makes no sign of acknowledgement and offers no help.

This segment, following the visionary sequence of the Russian crucifixion, enhances the theme of Andrej's separation from the world. He is obviously tempted by the young girl's beauty; yet, he rejects her twice. His companions, however, doubt his purity, and their glances condemn him unjustly. Several compositions in the sequence emphasise Andrej's isolation, especially as he is framed viewing the pagan festivities and this one woman from a distance.

A further suggestion of this episode is the impotency of Rublëv within his environment. His piety renders him unable to help the girl when she is evidently in distress – we have seen how officials treat law-breakers, both in the prologue and in the capture of the jester. The frustration that comes from his sense of propriety will take shape after the artisans are blinded and after the Tartar purge. In the first instance, he throws paint against a cathedral wall and smears it, while, in the second, he takes his vow of silence. Both actions are negations, of art and love, and their reversal at the end of the film will provide emotional impetus for the explosion of colour and vitality in the icons that fill the last frames.

Finally, the episode displays Andrej's rejection of natural beauty and passion. One possible fulfilment for the artist's longing after beauty in the midst of the chaos and ugliness of the time would be a classical contemplation of nature. One could read Andrej's temptation as an allegory of such longing. He must reject the appeals of nature in favour of the glories of heaven. Nature is a type of heavenly perfection, but not the thing in itself. Tarkovskij plays out this motif more completely in his film, *Nostalghia* (*Nostalgia*, 1983).[7] The beauties of sight and sound, past and present, became the channel through which faith and hope pass on the way to final rest and fulfilment.

All these themes interweave and build the tension within the painter that is evident in the subsequent episodes. The brutality of the Duke, his brother and the Tartars, and the barbarous warfare that rolls over the landscape in the following sequences metaphorically convey the turmoil within Rublëv caused by the paradox of his own existence. When a horse crashes through a rail of a stairway and falls some fifteen feet to the ground, when Danilov is savagely tortured by Tartars, and when the holy fool is given foul meat to enjoy, the entire world seems to be given over to despair. Andrej is driven to reject art and speech. Yet, Tarkovskij relentlessly offers hope on top of the horror: snow falls on the nave of the church after Andrej's vow of silence.

The long concluding episode underscores this hope. It is eleven years since the vow. The Duke commissions that a bell be built for his church. Soldiers search for a bell-maker named Nikolai, but they find a boy at Nikolai's home who tells them that everyone in the family has been killed by the plague. The boy, Boriska, claims that he has been given the bell-maker's secret to the proper cast, and the soldiers reluctantly take him along. The project is begun under the boy's authority and proceeds with a myriad of problems: the boy cannot find the proper clay for the cast; there is need for most of the Duke's silver; the workers question the boy's knowledge; it rains. Rublëv watches the entire scene from a distance and several times the boy rebukes him for his silent presence. Finally, the work is completed and the bell is hoisted into the tower. It rings clear and true. The boy leaves the joyous scene and collapses in tears. Andrej goes to him and comforts him, and, in doing so, he breaks his vow of silence, saying, "You have created such joy and you cry". The boy confesses that he never was given the secret of the bell. The two embrace and the camera leaves them to pan across the people leaving the area around the church. The screen then gives way to the brilliance of Rublëv's icons, which then dissolve into the image of horses on the field in the rain.

This final sequence of the epic functions allegorically: Boriska is a double for Rublëv. Surrounded by death, opposed both by his peers and by hostile civil authorities, threatened by problems of nature, carefully guarding his own inner doubts – the boy perseveres and produces a masterpiece. The boy's compulsion to continue in the work of the bell despite potential failure mirrors and rebukes Rublëv's rejection of life and art. The secular attitude taken by the boy, who seems driven only by some internal necessity to live out his dream and who exhibits great cruelty in moments, further rebukes Rublëv, whose calling implies a greater measure of faith than the struggling artist has shown.

What the sequence of the bell affirms is the power of faith within the context of the world. Tarkovskij shows here that faith must always act positively: negation is despair. As the Orthodox Christian faith so clearly proclaims, the Church embodies Christ in the world. Christian art must find a base in the material world and display the love of God there. To reject action is to reject not only faith, but also love, and "God is love".

The significance of this allegory for Rublëv's life and art is marked by the film's grand conclusion displaying Rublëv's art. This triumph is foreshadowed several times through the film by the sound of bells ringing in the background. The auditory cue occurs most apparently during the opening credits; it also occurs in the key scenes when Danilov and Andrej make peace after their quarrel, and when Kirill returns to the monastery to seek absolution. The bell represents the work of the Church. It involves the long, hard and dirty labour of many workers. Visually, it looks crude and heavy, but, hoisted into its proper place and rung, its sudden beauty draws many to it.

A visual image that seems for Tarkovskij to parallel the auditory sound of the bell is that of the horses. There are many beautiful compositions involving horses in the film, particularly the concluding shot. For Tarkovskij, the horse embodies perfect innocence and peacefulness. In chaotic scenes, such as the rainstorm that opens the action, and the rape of Vladimir, Tarkovskij juxtaposes a scene of great ugliness and cruelty with a shot of horses grazing or walking sedately. It could be said that these horses testify to the often hidden but always manifest presence of God in the world. They represent the still-present grace of the original creation, and this grace becomes the spring of Rublëv's and Tarkovskij's art.

The iconographic qualities of the narrative of *Andrej Rublëv* can be discovered primarily in the thematic arrangement of the material. Each segment in the film functions as a shot in a large montage. Tarkovskij gives the viewer essences in glimpses, and so evokes the final understanding of the artist's genius subjectively. There is no definitive statement regarding the relationship between Rublëv and his icons; instead, the viewer is left to contemplate the ambiguous intermeshing of both, and thus sense or feel the nature of both.

The film also operates as an icon through its highly symbolic individual images. An icon captures in time and space the interplay between divinity and humanity. It produces a stillness that inspires a feeling of devotion. Such images dominate the film's *mise en scène*:

> Tarkovsky's vital allegiance, actually, is...to Brueghel and Dürer. This means: every living corner of the canvas is animated. The distant individual incidents of a given scene seem to have the autonomy of such incidents in life, produced out of their own internal logic and necessity. Scenes, for example, surrounding the casting of the bell: the horseman in the far distance mounting the little hill, the dog pausing in the snow to scratch itself, the group of peasants huddled round the brazier: and beyond the peasants, the walls of the city itself.[8]

Tarkovskij's iconography is much more richly naturalistic than usual devotional images are, partly due to the increased verisimilitude allowed through the medium of film. Its function is the same, however. Many images present visual paradoxes that mimic the struggles of Rublëv's art and the overarching struggles of fallen humanity straining towards some greater good. There is an elegance and a corruption to each composition, and the viewer feels both sublimely moved and grossly repelled.

Typical of all sacramental films, *Andrej Rublëv* builds towards a final moment of convergence between heaven and earth. This moment would be the embrace between Boriska, the young bell-maker, and Andrej. It is stylistically signalled by the appearance of Rublëv's colour icons on the screen. The image of the two embracing has an interesting similarity to the ending of Dreyer's *Ordet* (*The Word*, 1955). Both display double miracles – the conversion of Mikkel and quickening of Inger matching the conversion of Andrej (from despair) and the success of the bell-maker. Andrej and Boriska, like Mikkel and Inger, will go forward together to bear testimony to the miracle and what it signifies.

In addition, as in Dreyer's film, the miraculous ending resonates back through the film and recontextualizes all previous images. God was everywhere present. All Tarkovskij's elemental images – water, fire, earth and air, the images he uses so effectively in all his films[9] – take on new connotations. Following classical iconographic references, water and fire purify, earth is humanity's domain, and the air is God's. These new connotations add another level of contemplation to the already complex compositions. With this, God's presence in every thing and person makes the interpretive potential of the film endless. It is hardly surprising that viewers of *Andrej Rublëv* find highly complex religious associations in the most ghastly of images. Like the Song of Solomon, the potential of Tarkovskij's film as a religious text is in large part due to its sensuality. Like an icon, and like the Passion, it is meant to be contemplated, not contained.

Notes

[1]   Ivor Montagu, "Man and Experience: Tarkovsky's World", *Sight and Sound* 42: 2 (spring 1973): 92. Emphasis in original.

[2]   The loose historical structure of the film, coupled with its aesthetic bias, caused considerable problems with Soviet censors, who nearly succeeded in blocking distribution of the film altogether. See Jeanne Vronskaya, *Young Soviet Film Makers* (New York: George Allen and Unwin, 1972): 33.

[3]   Vincent Canby makes this same observation in his review, "*Andrei Rublev* From Russia is Shown", *The New York Times* 10 October 1973: 43, 1.

[4]   Cited in Mark Le Fanu, *The Cinema of Andrei Tarkovsky* (London: British Film Institute, 1987): 36.

[5]   Erich Auerbach, *Mimesis: The Representation of Reality in Western Literature*, translated by Willard R Trask (Princeton: Princeton University Press, 1953): 23.

[6]   Quoted in Vronskaya: 34.

[7]   See Peter Green, "The Nostalgia of the Stalker", *Sight and Sound* 54: 1 (winter 1984-85): 50-54. I am thinking particularly of the remarkable concluding image of *Nostalgia*. See also Peter Green, "Apocalypse & Sacrifice", *Sight and Sound* 56: 2 (spring 1987): 111-118.

[8]   Le Fanu: 46-47.

[9]   See Peter Green (1984/85): 53-54.

Christian liturgy celebrates the relationship between God and His people. That relationship has been consummated in the Incarnation of Jesus Christ. It has been developed in Christ's sacrificial ministry and death, and then applied to believers through Christ's Resurrection, which guarantees the Christian's victory over the grave. Christ's birth, death and resurrection are the focal points in any Christian liturgical ceremony.

The liturgical tradition in the Church has been generated by the tension between these facts of the faith and the believer's hope in his own participation in the coming kingdom of God. Liturgical celebrations typically emphasise one of two aspects of this tension. The first is the (apparent) absence and silence of God, as the Church awaits Christ's return. The Church, as eschatological community, fills the void of God's physical absence by reciting prayers and praise responses that rehearse His previous activity as described in the text of Scripture. Worship is partly an exercise of faith and hope. The second aspect is the incarnate presence of God in Word and sacrament, in which the Church celebrates the Incarnation and Resurrection as pattern for life now. The congregation participates with more immediacy through physical symbols and rituals in the means of grace by which this miraculous newness of life is appropriated. Worship is here partly an exercise in contemplation.

These are both tendencies, not rules, which usually manifest themselves, one way or another, in various liturgical traditions. The Western Church, as a whole body, structures liturgy in the Mass or worship service around the text of Scripture in preparation for Christ's return towards the enhancement of faith and hope, while the Eastern Church longs for saintliness, an appropriation of the divine life, through a tradition of greater contemplation by the use of icons and symbolic physical rituals. Within each tradition, the same tendencies towards eschatological faith in the God of the text or contemplation of God's immanent presence mark differences among the various branches of Christianity. For example, within the Protestant community of the West, the Lutheran tradition is far more contemplative than the Baptistic or

Calvinistic tradition. Likewise, post-Vatican II Roman Catholicism has evolved from a more contemplative towards a more Protestant textual orientation.

Since the sacramental experience for Christians, regardless of the strength of an individual's devotion, is most accessible through the experience of the Church as worshipping community, it is no surprise that films which build upon a sacramental model would tend to follow the same tendencies as traditional liturgies. Films such as Dreyer's *Ordet* (*The Word*, 1955) or Tarkovskij's *Andrej Rublëv* (1966) lean in the direction of the liturgy of contemplation, the celebration of divine immanence. The film to be considered in this chapter, Roberto Rossellini's *Roma, città aperta* (*Rome, Open City*), celebrates the Church's awaiting Christ's return and enduring his absence.

In his praise of Italian neo-realist film, André Bazin defined the unit of cinematic meaning in these films as the "fact".[1] It is the ambiguous mechanical presentation of uninterpreted reality in the films of Rossellini, De Sica or Fellini that makes their films "realistic" in a new way. In his analysis of the effective realism of *Ladri di biciclette* (*Bicycle Thieves*, 1948), Bazin writes: "The events are not necessarily signs of something, of a truth of which we are to be convinced, they all carry their own weight, their complete uniqueness, that ambiguity that characterizes any fact".[2] The power of *Bicycle Thieves* resides not in the artifice of the medium, nor in the significance of the film's thesis, but in the beauty of the phenomenon of the relationship between the protagonist father and son, caught here and there in poignant gestures by the camera.

These facts block easy interpretation by leaving the ambiguity of things as they are. The author of the work places his creatures in the same predicament that he experiences, alone in the world without the aid of convention or artifice to resolve definitively the many problems of existence. As individuals of the world, their lives commune with others in the larger ambiguities of a world controlled by divine mystery. People, places and things in these realistic vehicles have life beyond representation; they are not mere characters, types and symbols.

This view of filmic realism has been challenged by postmodern criticism, which labels it naïve in the light of the constructedness even of human perception.[3] Film can produce no "facts" of existence – at least, none that we can certainly identify – since all phenomena filters through unstable human perceptions. Even the most seemingly factual and objective film can be deconstructed to reveal its identity as a product of imaginative perception, reconstructed memory, or illusion. The semblance of reality, in fact, that we label as "realistic" merely defines a conventional and familiar border of perception. Peter Brunette summarises some of the criticism of neo-realism:

> We perceive something as realistic, in short, when it corresponds to a set of conventionalized expectations (largely derived from previous film or novelistic practice) about what people in movies do, not when it corresponds to actual empirical experience. All of this provides the comforting envelope of believability of the conventional film that enables us to be inserted into the complex dual process of what we loosely call audience identification. We are not actually meant to take what we see as *reality*, of course, or we would try to jump into the screen...But when we experience, with excitement, a film as *more* realistic than usual – that is, more like 'real life' than previous films we have seen – I would argue it is because it is pushing against the currently accepted boundaries of the realistic, closer toward the dangerous unpredictability of the (represented) *real*.[4]

To argue in this manner against the phenomenology of Bazin is thus to argue against Bazin's previously discussed idealist metaphysics. There can be no "truly" realistic film because there can be no identifiable, absolute fact of existence, only conventions based on perceptions regarding motion and our subsequent illusion of reality.

It is not my intention to critique Bazin here, but rather to underline the presuppositions that govern his phenomenology. Bazin clearly presupposes that there are absolute things and occurrences which have built within them the potential for human identification and interpretation, and which exist with or without interpretation.[5] Amédée Ayfre, following Bazin's metaphysical logic, goes so far as to suggest that the formal vehicles of art, by which the real is expressed, and the interpretation of art may be inherent in the nature of events: "But the all-inclusive nature of the event takes in both the spatio-temporal reality and a relation to human consciousness which is part of its essence and is its 'meaning' or 'sense'".[6] Ayfre ties this philosophy to its root in a Christian theology of immanence, which teaches that the hand of God is manifest in the divine image within human beings, the excellencies of creation, and the proverbial course of history:

> Where everything is susceptible of a natural explanation there is still room for a transcendent reality within the natural development of determinations, and indeed this is one of the characteristics of that transcendence itself...For if the psychology

in the proper sense is infinitely less elaborate, grace is no more hidden and the ambiguities are not fundamentally greater; it is in any case in the very nature of grace to be hidden and ambiguous precisely because it is the human face to the transcendent Mystery of God.[7]

In short, reality is created and controlled with all its ambiguities built in, and through these ambiguities of perception and consciousness we still can and must recognise its objective origin, the substance of order, God. This philosophy is most easily understood as a synthesis between a strong philosophical idealism and an equally strong realism: the face of God emerges through the facts of existence when seen as they are, for God creates and uphold all things.

Bazin's aesthetic principles, as Ayfre develops them, can be traced to a traditional Christian hermeneutic that goes as far back as the Church Fathers when they condemned the theatre not only for its immorality, but also for its idolatry – that is, as St Paul argues (I Corinthians 8: 1-6), a worshipping of things that do not exist apart from God who created them.[8] Atheistic art is, by this definition, unrealistic, while theistic art traces the mystery of all existence. As late as the Reformation, when mystery plays had fully evolved towards more fictional dramatic, less canonical lines, the Church tended to approve or condemn them according to criteria of realism grounded in the assumption of the world as created and providentially upheld by God.[9] If the truth of God's presence was evident in the performance, the performance was realistic.

The summation of the philosophy in this Christian context is that the progress of history plays out the saving work of God through Christ. When people colour and interpret reality according to their individualised, "unredeemed" sense, apart from grace, they bring to it the effects of their own depraved nature; they humanise the grace of God and invariably profane what is manifestly holy. The analogy for the artist would be the model of the Scripture writers: "Holy men of God wrote as they were carried along by the Holy Spirit" (II Peter 1: 21). The canonical writers were not considered mechanical secretaries; rather, by the Spirit of God they saw the work of God and were able to tell of it without error.[10] Realistic fiction is accordingly inspired, although to a lesser degree.

A working principle of such an aesthetic when applied to historical subjects by a Christian artist, or by one working within a cultural or textual Christian frame, is that *the manifest absence of God in the facts of reality reveals the presence of God when seen in the totality of human existence*. This principle defines the mechanisms of the greater number of sacramental films that have been made. It is a principle that has been an integral part of the Church's art and practice of liturgy for centuries. That Bazin and his followers applied this aesthetic principally to Italian neo-realist films follows from the inherent Catholicism in the neo-realist movement. Beyond social realism, there is a strong theological realism in the films of Rossellini, De Sica, Fellini, Pasolini and others in the school. It is easily traced in these filmmakers because of their cultural heritage and aesthetic starting-points, but the thread also leads through a variety of different schools, directors and films, from sentimental Hollywood vehicles such as Capra's *Meet John Doe* (1941), to films of other established genres such as John Ford's allegorical western, *Three Godfathers* (1948), to more recent religious films such as Alain Cavalier's *Thérèse* (1986) on the life of the "Little Flower".[11]

To illustrate how this hermeneutic of Christian realism is manifest in the type of sacramental filmmaking which regards the absence of God, the following discussion is devoted to *Rome, Open City*, which, despite its initial reputation for unadulterated naturalism, is overtly constructed according to religious themes. The other film which could serve as an illustration here is by the French Catholic director, Robert Bresson, who was heavily influenced by the neo-realists and the French New Wave, but who has defined his own idiosyncratic style of realistic filmmaking. The film, *Journal d'un curé de campagne* (*Diary of a Country Priest*, 1950), treated in the opening chapter of this book, is in some ways radically different from the Rossellini film in its source material and dramatic execution, but shares a remarkably similar philosophy of presenting God's entrance into the world of the film.

Rome, Open City is primarily the account of Rome's struggle under German occupation during the Second World War. Rossellini claimed to have completed the script for the film in a week, and the claim is validated by the overtness of its themes. While the suffering of the film's protagonists suggests the existentialist mood that God is not watching, the film's thematic motifs suggest redemption and rebirth.

The great paradox of the film is, of course, its reputation as an accurate historical portrait of wartime Italy.[12] *Rome, Open City* is hardly "historical" in the strict objective sense; rather, it is heavily polemical, even parabolic or allegorical. Its historical aura grows out of its documentary style and production history, as the film was spliced together from whatever fragments of film stock Rossellini and his associates could find and use. In fact, the narrative patterns strongly resemble what Peter Brooks expresses as the patterns for melodramatic fiction:

Melodramatic dilemmas and choices are constructed on the either/or in its extreme form as the all-or-nothing. Polarization is both horizontal and vertical: characters represent extremes, and they undergo extremes, passing from heights to depths, or the reverse, almost instantaneously. The middle ground and the middle condition are excluded.[13]

The crucial difference which separates *Rome, Open City* from typical melodrama is the narrative resolution. Virtue is not fully "liberated" or "freed from what blocked the realization of its desire",[14] except on a transcendent level. The Christian symbolism of the climax suggests that justice will occur in a future age or day of judgment. Thus, like Borzage, Rossellini employs the terms of melodrama to underline the narrative clash between good and evil, innocence and corruption, which he places in a larger Christian epistemology. The Manichaeism of typical melodramatic plots becomes recontextualized in *Rome, Open City* to fit the more orthodox theme of the Church struggling to maintain faith in a fallen world, and awaiting a final liberation in Christ's return.

Rome, Open City begins with a grainy image of German soldiers marching in Rome in lock step. Then, in an apartment building, they pursue Manfredi, a leader of the Italian Resistance, who manages to escape over rooftops with help from some of the local tenants. When the commander of the local Nazi war office, a brutal man named Bergman, hears of the escape, he is determined to increase the effort against the leader. Thus, the pattern of the film's plot is immediately established in simple terms. The Nazis, who are evil, are in pursuit of the good Italian liberator, who is aligned with the common family- and Church-oriented Italians (this by virtue of the setting in which Manfredi is pursued).

The Resistance against the Nazis is widespread, although weak. Manfredi is aided in his work by a printer, Francesco, who helps produce literature for the Resistance, and a priest, Don Pietro, who acts as a go-between for Manfredi and the leaders of the liberation junto. Francesco is engaged to be married immediately to a widow named Pina, who is already pregnant with his child. Pina's son, a young boy named Marcello, has joined the Resistance with some local boys. On the day of Pina's wedding, Nazi agents come to the apartment to search for Manfredi. They find Francesco and take him into a truck; when Pina runs after her lover, she is gunned down in the street. Francesco is later rescued by members of the Resistance.

Manfredi and Francesco go to Manfredi's lover, an actress named Marina, to find shelter for a while. Marina is broken-hearted by

Manfredi's coldness to her; she lacks the depth and maturity to interest him further. As a consequence, she has been vulnerable to the seductions of a lesbian Nazi named Ingrid, who is an associate of Bergman. Francesco and Manfredi leave her, and Manfredi joins Don Pietro to discuss the work of the Resistance, but Marina informs and the two men are arrested together with an Austrian deserter seeking the priest's help. Francesco is able to escape the Nazis' attention and rejoins Marcello, whom he treats as a son now that the boy's mother is dead.

Bergman interrogates Manfredi and Don Pietro, but neither is willing to discuss the work of the junto; Manfredi is therefore brutally tortured and Don Pietro is forced to watch. The Austrian deserter hangs himself. Bergman is confident that the tortures will break Manfredi, but he is contradicted by Hermann, an officer who is drinking with other Nazi officers in a room adjacent to Bergman's office and the torture room. Hermann insists that the cruelty and pride of the Nazis will destroy them, but Bergman is convinced that Italians are weak and Germans alone strong. Hermann is proved correct in part when Manfredi dies at the hands of his torturers without talking.

Don Pietro is able to bless Manfredi just prior to his death, and the priest is so moved that he pronounces a curse on the Nazis, that they will be trampled to death like vermin. The introduction of music, rare in the film to this point, and the look of exaltation on Don Pietro's face bring the drama to a climax at this moment. However, Don Pietro catches himself and falls on his knees, asking forgiveness for his lack of love. The next day, Don Pietro is led into the military yard and shot by a firing squad. The soldiers originally fail to kill him, so an officer must finish the job. Watching and whistling their support from behind a wire fence are the children of the neighbourhood, who played with Don Pietro at the parish and had tried to resist the Nazis on their own by bombing Nazi vehicles. The children walk back to the city after the priest's martyrdom.

The film's concluding sequences make the Christian thematics unmistakable. Both Manfredi and Don Pietro die in Christ-like fashion. Manfredi plays out the physical courage of Christ as he bears up silently under torture to protect his fellow nationalists, at one point with arms extended as on a cross. Don Pietro plays out the integrity and mildness of Christ. He speaks to Bergman with restraint and devotion, and prays for Manfredi during his tortures. When, after Manfredi's death, he bursts out in his curse of the Nazis (a divine curse spoken, as it were, by a prophet shy of his own calling), and falls to his knees before them to ask forgiveness for his own lack of love, he performs a gesture reminiscent of Christ's dying pardon of his murderers. Most significantly, immediately after Don Pietro's execution, the children, who have watched the execution through the fence whistling their support and love for the priest, head back for Rome with heads bowed in mourning, but arm-in-arm with a new constitution as a brotherhood of disciples.[15] The ending bears remarkable similarity to the end of Roland Joffé's *The Mission* (1986), where the children of the ravaged Jesuit mission of San Carlos escape the slaughter at the hands of the Portuguese to become a new community defined by their position as the heirs of the martyrdom that established the mission in the first place.

Once this structure of redemptive death emerges out of the apparent realism of *Rome, Open City*, the tragic silences of the film begin to speak. Earlier in the film, Pina asks Don Pietro, "Doesn't Christ see us?", and this question takes on great force when Pina is unexpectedly arbitrarily shot down by the Fascist soldiers looking for Manfredi. The camera pulls away from her body, as does the truck of soldiers, in apparent unconcern. The answer to Pina's question comes when the soldiers, asked to fire into Don Pietro's back, somehow miss, and the Nazi officer must kill the priest. The unconcern was a mere posture. The soldiers' joint act of conscience (assuming that they consciously misfire) acknowledges that Christ does see. Don Pietro, the martyr with his head bowed and body turned, sees into their souls as clearly as he might their faces. The subsequent murder of the priest by the officer implies the awkwardness of denial and guilt, and Pilate's handwashing.

Rome, Open City is less manifestly Christian by its subject than by its method. The cinematic symbols we see and hear, protagonists and antagonists in their various postures moving across the screen, give way to the types and attitudes identified with the Christian way of redemption. The narrative structure likewise is transformed into a much larger transcendent pattern. The forward motion of the film progresses towards a consummate moment, the incarnation where the equations are completed – here the whistled song of the children and the misfire of the soldiers – which seems to signal the grace of God and power of the Holy Spirit, grace and power revealed in the climax but then cast in retrospect over the entire performance. The question suggested is: Were not Pina, Manfredi and Don Pietro all brought together in this time and place from the very beginning for just this noble and holy purpose?

Once the voice of God is heard at the end, all other facts find interpretation, and the complete filmic procession becomes a rehearsal of redemptive history. The audience takes the familiar position of worshippers vicariously enacting a liturgical celebration. Through the metaphor, we respond with the shared hope that our own silences and redemptive longings are played out in the narrative of Rossellini's film.

The point here is not that *Rome, Open City* is intentionally created for the sole purpose of playing out a liturgical model; such an assumption would hardly fit the political climate that drove Rossellini to the material. The sacramental model of the film is more a part of the cultural heritage of Italy that Rossellini tapped for his material. Rossellini was a believing Catholic, but his earlier films are more socially oriented than the overtly religious films he would later direct for television – *Atti degli Apostoli* (*Acts of the Apostles*, 1968), *Agostino di Ippona* (*Augustine of Hippo*, 1972), *Blaise Pascal* (1975) and *Il Messia* (*The Messiah*, 1978). The film's sacramentalism is less intentional than built into the cultural and historical context of the film materials. After all, one can find inherently religious material even in films by directors who openly deny the faith, such as Luis Buñuel, because what is harder to deny than dogma is a cultural epistemology.

However, it is useful to carry this thematic reading of *Rome, Open City* further along liturgical lines to illustrate how deep the roots of the Christian tradition can go in sacramental films. Just as Christian theology and liturgical practices have drifted towards different emphases, so the conception of the relationship between a worshipper and God has evolved in its definition.

In the East, the Incarnation traditionally has been viewed as a step in man's assumption into the divine presence. Christ redeemed the human flesh he wore, and the Holy Spirit draws humanity towards godliness. In the West, the Incarnation has been viewed in terms of the divine humiliation. Christ became flesh to save humanity, and the Holy Spirit strengthens and preserves the saints throughout their lives. These paradoxical ideas stress aspects of the mystery of the Incarnation. Worship in the West – and this is our positioning in a discussion of neo-realism – builds upon humanity's duty as creatures made in the image of God, as opposed to the Eastern emphasis on the effects of God's holiness on creation. Traditionally, three strands to this human situation are woven into liturgies. The first is humanity's obligation to love and serve God; the second is the militant duty of the Church upon earth; the third is the call of God's people to live as a community.[16] These three grow out of the fundamental doctrine of the Church that God made His people in His image, and so requires their devotion. They are manifest in both the liturgical structure and the contents of prayers, hymns and responses in a most fundamental way in the Mass and in Protestant services. For example, a typical prayer in a Good Friday Mass reads:

Let us pray, dearly beloved, for the holy Church of God: that our God and Lord would be pleased to give it peace, *maintain it in unity and preserve it over the earth; subjecting to it the princes and potentates of the world:* and grant us, that live in peace and tranquillity, *grace to glorify God* the Father almighty.[17]

It might seem strained to suggest that *Rome, Open City* develops such a devotional theme, given the film's harsh anti-Fascist focus; yet, it would be equally strained to imagine the film locked in time as nothing more than a reaction to a particular historical circumstance. The climatic narrative line of *Rome, Open City* builds upon transcendent relationships. Pina wants a church wedding because she believes in God. The priest Don Pietro aids the Resistance for the love of humanity. Manfredi gives over his body, rather than betray friends. Even the children find their identity as patriots defending their city and on the high plane of spiritual fellowship when Don Pietro is killed. But beyond these more obvious relationships, the film carries an aura of hope. How else can we interpret the mixture of comedy and grimness that characterises the early segments? The slapstick moment of the priest clubbing an old man with a frying pan would be out of place when juxtaposed with Pina's useless killing, were it not for the overarching devotion of the film. Only in a context of faith defined as love for God and hope in His larger promises can the brutality and irony of the film's resolutions be connected with the kind of warmth and levity felt earlier. It is the lack of faith, the sterility and calculation of the Nazis, that makes them so terrible, and that lack of faith is what also defines them as grotesque caricatures, specimens of inhumanity.

The martyrdoms of Manfredi and Don Pietro furthermore play out the striving for glory that is a central motif in the film. This glory is distinct from the Nazi pride most evident in Bergman's angry denunciation of Hermann for insinuating that the hatred bred by Fascism would destroy the Germans. Heavenly glory, the consummate affirmation of the dignity of the human soul, moves the Resistance leaders and common people. Such glory must be purchased with death, ultimately Christ's death, but also that of all those who want to taste it in the chaos of the times. Francesco and Pina's longing for better times; Manfredi's broader path of Communism for the sake of dignity; the priest's compromises as both political activist and Christian pacifist – all these build the tension which propels the film towards the resolutions of sacrificial death which alone brings to mankind the redemptive glory which all desire. This glory is the final hope for the lovers of God.

A second liturgical tendency manifest in the film is the constitution of the persecuted Italian resistors as a militant congregation set apart to fight an impossible battle against the world for the sake of something unreachable. The Italian people are represented, especially early in the film, as an active, working people. On the other hand, the Nazi Bergman gathers his knowledge of the Resistance movement from his chair by examining photos. The whole tone of the headquarters exudes sluggardliness and decay, especially when juxtaposed with the energy of the apartments (particularly in the hallway) and shops of the people. The heroic community is far more militant within the course of the film than are the persecutors. Furthermore, the conclusion of the film has children moving towards Rome, still striving together for their own paradoxical rest.

A third liturgical aspect, closely related to the aspect of militancy, is that of society. Christian worship performs the fellowship that sets the people of God apart. Traditionally, the keynote of that fellowship is communion (although, in Protestant worship, an intellectual fellowship based upon mutual assent to the preached Word can highlight worship). Rossellini begins his film in midstream of the life of the people to develop the feeling of community that binds them. They eat, work, sleep and suffer together. They drink of a common cup, so to speak, with even a Catholic priest and a Communist leader partaking together. As with the issue of militancy, the Italian community is juxtaposed with that of the Nazis in the aspect of fertility. Pina, already pregnant before marriage, is counterpointed with Ingrid, the lesbian who displaces Manfredi as Marina's lover. The faithfulness of the believing Italians finds God's ample blessing, and guarantees the continuation of the community, as the film's conclusion suggests. Human pride, evidenced by the Nazis, leads to corrupted relationships and attitudes that guarantee extinction.

Beyond these liturgical structures operating within the film, there is a host of individual symbols that increase in significance in the given context. Already mentioned are the priest's prayer of forgiveness after cursing the Nazis, Manfredi's Christ-like posture, and the children's whistled hymn. Further mention could be made of the silence of Manfredi under torture, like Christ's silence, and the conversation between Don Pietro and Bergman, which resembles the scene of Christ before Pilate and Herod. In addition, the children march back towards Rome with St Peter's in the background in the final images. All these and other small symbols that refer to Christian iconography colour the larger religious structures of the film, and make its mode of appeal to the audience unmistakable. They are like the ringing of bells or the swinging of a censer during a procession.

[1] André Bazin, *What Is Cinema?*, volume II, essays selected and translated by Hugh Gray (Berkeley; Los Angeles; London: University of California Press, 1971): 47-48.

[2] Ibid: 52.

[3] See Colin MacCabe, "Theory and Film: Principles of Realism and Pleasure", in Philip Rosen (ed), *Narrative, Apparatus, Ideology: A Film Theory Reader* (New York: Columbia University Press, 1986): 179-197. Of course, the extreme of this criticism leaves no hope for traditional notions of realism. See Michel Foucault, "'What is an author?' (extract)", in John Caughie (ed), *Theories of Authorship: A Reader* (London; Boston; Henley: Routledge & Kegan Paul, 1981): 282-291.

[4] Peter Brunette, *Roberto Rossellini* (New York; Oxford: Oxford University Press, 1987): 58. Emphases in original.

[5] See Dudley Andrew's discussion of the influences of Henri Bergson and Roger Leenhardt on Bazin's intellectual formation in *André Bazin* (New York: Oxford University Press, 1978): 19-37.

[6] Amédée Ayfre, "Neo-Realism and Phenomenology", in Jim Hillier (ed), *Cahiers du Cinéma. Volume 1. The 1950s: Neo-Realism, Hollywood, New Wave* (Cambridge, MA: Harvard University Press, 1985): 187.

[7] Ibid: 190.

[8] The Calvinistic Westminster Confession of Faith of 1646 puts it most strongly by limiting any human good only to those who are considered regenerate: "Works done by unregenerate men, although for the matter of them they may be things which God commands, and of good use both to themselves and others; yet because they proceed not from a heart purified by faith, nor are done in a right manner, according to the Word, nor to a right end, the glory of God; they are therefore sinful, and can not please God, or make a man meet to receive grace from God. And yet their neglect of them is more sinful and displeasing unto God." As extreme as this position may seem, the attitude carried typifies that of the larger branches of the Church. See John H Leith (ed), *Creeds of the Churches: A Reader in Christian Doctrine from the Bible to the Present*, third edition (Atlanta: John Knox Press, 1982): 211.

[9] An interesting discussion of Martin Luther's evolving definition of the relativity of the arts to Christians is found in Thomas I Bacon, *Martin Luther and the Drama* (Amsterdam: Editions Rodopi, 1976).

[10] An exhaustive discussion of the traditional doctrine can be found in Benjamin Breckinridge Warfield, *The Inspiration and Authority of the Bible*, edited by Samuel G Craig (London: Marshall, Morgan & Scott, 1951).

[11] See the review by Arthur Livingston, "Theresa", *The Living Church* 194: 16 (1987): 12. Livingston relates the film to a Bressonian stylistic system.

[12] Brunette (especially 368-369) offers some explanation of the interrelationships between the script of the film, the historical subjects, and popular reception.

[13] Peter Brooks, *The Melodramatic Imagination: Balzac, Henry James, Melodrama, and the Mode of Excess* (New Haven; London: Yale University Press, 1976): 36.

[14] Ibid: 32.

[15] See Ben Lawton, "Italian Neorealism: A Mirror Construction of Reality", *Film Criticism* 3: 2 (winter 1979): 8-23.

[16] An extended discussion of these and other liturgical themes occurs in Geoffrey Wainwright, *Doxology: The Praise of God in Worship, Doctrine and Life* (New York: Oxford University Press, 1980). See also Cheslyn Jones, Geoffrey Wainwright and Edward Yarnold, SJ (eds), *The Study of Liturgy* (New York: Oxford University Press, 1978), and Josef A Jungmann, SJ, *The Early Liturgy To the Time of Gregory the Great*, translated by Francis A Brunner (South Bend, IN: University of Notre Dame Press, 1959).

[17] Emphases added. Such attitudes can be most easily identified in the architecture and arrangement of churches and shrines and the physical movement of standard liturgies.

Bruce Beresford's film, *Black Robe*, tells a story that bears strong similarities to Bresson's *Journal d'un curé de campagne* (*Diary of a Country Priest*, 1950). An extremely zealous young French Jesuit finds himself in a hostile mission field, in which his own perseverance in faith and physical courage are strongly tested. Although seemingly defeated in his evangelical mission, his piety presents a powerful witness to the cross of Christ, and succeeds in some measure in winning the hearts of those around him. Both films present images of holiness in action, and both conclude with images of Christ's cross. Both also skilfully adapt successful novels.

While sharing some of the same redemption motifs with Bresson's film, *Black Robe* arranges these motifs in a markedly different context. Whereas Bresson's austere, nameless priest follows the way of the Cross in the obscurity of a rural French village, Beresford's Father Laforgue acts in the grander epic of Jesuit missionary enterprises in North America in the 17th century. Although the underlying picture of Christ's Passion is much the same in both films, the largeness and more overt historical and cultural positioning of *Black Robe* make it more accessible to the average viewer.

The novel on which *Black Robe* is based and the film's screenplay were both written by the Northern Irish-born author, Brian Moore (now resident in Canada), who came to the material through Francis Parkman's chronicle of early settlements in North America. In particular, it was a single passage from Parkman about the canonised French Jesuit, Noel Chabanel, which provided Moore and then Beresford with a central theme for *Black Robe*:

> Noel Chabanel came later to the mission for he did not reach the Huron country until 1643. He detested the Indian life – the smoke, the vermin, the filthy food, the impossibility of privacy. He could not study by the smoky lodge fires, among the noisy crowd of men and squaws, with their dogs and their restless, screeching children. He had a natural inaptitude to learning the language, and labored at it for five years with scarcely a sign of

progress. The Devil whispered a suggestion in his ear: Let him procure his release from these barren and revolting toils and return to France where congenial and useful employments awaited him. Chabanel refused to listen: and when the temptation still beset him he bound himself by a solemn vow to remain in Canada to the day of his death.[1]

In a profound way, *Black Robe* lauds the commitment of men such as Chabanel, clearly the model for Laforgue, who model Christ's own willingness to die for the salvation of others. However, Moore's story does not in any sense idealise the journey of faith. Near the end of both the novel and the screenplay, Laforgue seriously questions the entire purpose of his missionary work, and a conspicuous absence from the story until the concluding images is evidence of the presence of God; in this, *Black Robe* again parallels Bresson's film and also Tarkovskij's *Andrej Rublëv*.

An expensive Canadian and Australian co-production, Beresford's film won six César awards and much praise in Canada, but sold poorly in the United States, perhaps partly due to its grim depiction of American Indians, which strongly contrasts with the images in Kevin Costner's highly successful *Dances with Wolves* (1990), released at approximately the same time. Moore's and Beresford's Indians are not idealised, but depicted with insight and sometimes brutal honesty. Features of Moore's novel which are not fully maintained in the film are the heavily scatological nature of the Algonquin and Iroquois speech, and the Indians' cannibalism. What is preserved is the coarse brutality of many aspects of Indian culture and the carnality of the Indians. These are the Indians who initially repelled Chabanel, and therefore Laforgue's struggle to yield to his call is quite real. Likewise, Beresford's greatest accomplishment in *Black Robe* is his re-creation of the physical landscapes of 17th century northern forests and the first settlements in America. Mud abounds, the sky is often grey, and the water is like tin.

The young Father Laforgue must travel 1500 miles by canoe to reach a remote Jesuit settlement in Huron territory, where two other Jesuits are struggling to maintain a mission. He sets off from Quebec in 1634 under the commission of Samuel de Champlain who arranges for a party of Algonquins, led by Chief Chomina, whose beautiful daughter, Annuka, will later become mistress to Laforgue's assistant and translator, Daniel. The Algonquins are hostile to the Jesuits and begin to feel that the "black robe" Laforgue is a demon. They seek counsel with a dwarf shaman named Mestigoit, who convinces the party to abandon Laforgue, which they do. When Chomina has second thoughts and returns to Laforgue, the party is ambushed by a band of Iroquois.

Chomina's wife is slain by an arrow, his son's throat slit before his eyes, and the party tortured. Laforgue's own finger is torturously removed with a sharp shell. However, Laforgue, Chomina, Daniel and Annuka manage to escape and continue the journey to the mission. Chomina eventually dies of his wounds, and Daniel and Annuka leave to live with the Algonquins. Laforgue arrives alone at the mission and finds only one priest, Father Jerome, barely alive, and the Indians racked by a plague, probably European smallpox. He nurses and then buries Father Jerome, and confronts the Indians who want to be baptised to cure them of the plague. Laforgue agrees to baptise them only after the Indians acknowledge that he is a man, not a demon, and obtain from him a confession of his love for them and commitment to stay and help them. A postscript to the film informs the viewer that the Huron were routed and destroyed by the Iroquois after their conversion to Christianity, and that the Jesuit missions in Huron territory were closed.

In his mission to the Indians, Laforgue faces two barriers which make his pilgrimage especially trying. The first is the animism of the Algonquins who escort him to the mission. The Indians follow dreams and believe that spirits haunt the woods. The great soul of the earth speaks through all that exists, and the Indians listen for its messages. Chomina dreams that the black robe comes to him as a raven, and with the black robe is the she-manitou who will welcome him into death. He also envisions an isolated island which indeed becomes the place where he dies.

Laforgue's Christianity is less complex and poetic. God the Father loves the Indians and wants to let them into Paradise through the waters of baptism. To Chomina and the other Indians, this seems not only simple-minded, but also unattractive. Therefore, the Jesuits must be ignorant to think of so black and white a god, and their water of baptism must be magical if it has power to change people.

After the Iroquois' raid, Chomina and Laforgue have a short but meaningful exchange as Chomina lays dying. Laforgue wants him to accept Jesus and be baptised, but Chomina refuses, since his wife and son will not be in the Paradise of Laforgue's God. Yet, he calls Laforgue "friend", and thus acknowledges the sincerity of Laforgue's faith and intent. Interesting in this context is Beresford's handling of Chomina's death. After Laforgue leaves him to continue towards the mission with Daniel and Annuka, Chomina does indeed see the she-manitou who comes to lead him to the place of the dead. How this should be interpreted – as dream or vision, hallucination, fact or strange intervention of God Himself – is left open.

Laforgue's second barrier is the Jesuit religion. The Algonquins are an earthy people with a strong emphasis on family and physical prowess. Laforgue's attempt to convince the Indians to turn from polygamy and warfare and await Paradise was received poorly because of Laforgue's own Jesuit austerity, symbolised by his black robe and perpetual celibacy. Even Daniel turns from Laforgue towards the Indian ways when his faith in God becomes seemingly conditional to his rejecting his love for Annuka. Laforgue's ideal for Daniel is to be a priest, which means a life of relative sterility when compared to the perceived richness of the Indian life. Daniel is willing to make this sacrifice only after witnessing the barbarity of the Iroquois (a barbarity which, in the novel, includes not only the killing of Chomina's son, but also the eating of him). By this time, however, Laforgue has come better to understand the Indians and himself, and he tells Daniel that his duty is to care for Annuka as a wife. (Annuka will request baptism later in the novel.)

The conclusion to these struggles for Laforgue comes in his final confrontation with the Indians at the ruined Huron mission. The Huron chief confronts Laforgue and asks how long he will stay. When Laforgue replies, "All my life", he weeps. The Huron, reasoning that demons feel no grief, asks, "Are you a man?". After Laforgue says "Yes", the Huron says that he must help them. When he asks if Laforgue will love them, Laforgue is confronted with all that he has seen on his trip, and with all the suffering Indians with their children before him. His affirmative reply is a confirmation of his own new awareness of what would break the barriers standing in the way of his success as a missionary. Love breaks the barriers. What the Indians' animistic world lacks is love, a God who is personal and compassionate, and whose messengers are likewise. The dwarf Mestigoit becomes in this context an excellent representative of the great lack of love at the heart of the Indian world-view. Love also becomes the force to conquer the Indians' social and cultural barriers. Polygamy and untamed carnality are wrong because they are ultimately bestial and lacking in love for human partners. Likewise, warfare is self-perpetuating hatred, which can only be stopped by the love which is forgiveness. Laforgue's baptism of the Indians is not a mechanical act designed to barter heaven in the final context, but a seal of his agreement to be the servant of Christ for the Indians. When Laforgue stands under the mission church cross towards the film's conclusion, he has been transformed more into the figure on the cross than into the bearer of it.

Here again, the similarities between *Black Robe* and *Diary of a Country Priest* are striking. Like the young priest of Ambricourt, Laforgue succeeds by failing. While Laforgue confidently travelled by river with the goal of convincing the Indians of his "better" way, he was impotent for the task. His pride kept him from true love. He intends to win the Indians by luring them with gifts and with his superior knowledge, his literacy, but they attribute these strengths to the demonic. Likewise, Bresson's priest is most successful when acting most human – when confronting the duchess about her excessive grief, or when allowing Séraphita to care for him.

Black Robe thus underlines the continuous struggle of Christian missionaries. Typically, those missions and missionaries who have succeeded most through the centuries are those who embrace foreign ways before attempting the conversion of souls. The model of Christ eating and drinking with publicans and sinners, and washing the feet of his disciples, has long been the most difficult to follow. This is what Brian Moore instinctively latched onto in his encounter with Noel Chabanel and in his readings of other Jesuit diaries of the 17th century. Laforgue's personal pilgrimage is to embrace the Indian culture and love the people before attempting to change them.

Alongside this motif is one of power and powerlessness. Laforgue goes with a commission from the powerful explorer, Champlain, and feels confident in the plan for his journey, but throughout the journey he is confronted with his own powerlessness. Firstly, he is tempted by his own lust, seeing Daniel and Annuka having intercourse in the forest at night. He flogs himself and confesses the sin to Daniel, but is forced to confront similar images as long as he stays with the Indians. He is also humiliated and faced with a loss of dignity when he is mocked coarsely as he relieves himself off the side of a canoe. Before the first appearance of Mestigoit, some young girls steal his large black hat and play with it. At one point, he loses his way in the woods and must cry out for the Algonquins to find him. Daniel leaves him to join Annuka and the Algonquins when he is abandoned. The Iroquois humiliate and disfigure him. His companion priests prove ineffectual when he arrives at the mission, and the Hurons thoroughly misunderstand the nature of the Christianity that has been taught them. Laforgue must learn in the end where the source for Christianity resides and what the duty of each man is. The cross which glistens in the sun in the last scene is indeed the final response to Laforgue's powerlessness and humiliation. Strength in the Christian faith comes through weakness, since God is the ultimate mover of men's souls ("My grace is sufficient for you, for my power is made perfect in weakness" [II Corinthians 12: 9]).

Beresford draws these threads together with a subtlety that is reinforced by Lothaire Bluteau's idiosyncratic performance. Like Claude Laydu in Bresson's film or Enrique Irazoqui in Pasolini's *Il Vangelo secondo Matteo* (*The Gospel According to St Matthew*, 1964), Bluteau's Laforgue is a text that needs to be read carefully. His internal trials and temptations are exposed only briefly, as when he prays for God's help when lost in the forest, or when he weeps at the film's conclusion. Beresford's camera, not Bluteau's minimal expression, tells the story of Laforgue's doubt and faith. Although Bluteau's Laforgue appears in virtually every scene in the film, the emotions of each scene typically are prompted in response to his presence, rather than by his character. This type of understated presentation, so typical in the type of sacramental filmmaking under study in this book, can be troubling to viewers unaccustomed to it; Bluteau's performance was predictably criticised in many of the film's early reviews.

The visual mechanics of the film contribute to the difficulty of reading Laforgue's internal crisis. In the first scene of the film, set in Quebec, the camera follows Laforgue from the rear as he walks towards a group of workers building huts. As he walks, he creates distance with the viewer. When he is first seen from the front, his eyes are shaded by his wide-brimmed hat. Throughout the film, the camera tends to maintain a distance from Laforgue. There are relatively few intense close-ups, and those which occur rarely reveal much change in the priest's face. At the moment of Laforgue's deepest crisis, after Chomina's death as he tells Daniel and Annuka to leave together, he confesses: "What can we say to a people whose dreams are real?". As Laforgue leaves Daniel and Annuka, he walks away from the camera which follows him from the lovers' point of view in a gesture identical to the opening image of the film. There is an intentional distance created to preserve the mystery of the Passion that Laforgue plays out in these moments. His ability to carry on against such huge obstacles can only be attributed to his personal mission.

The visual pairing of similar and contrasting images is one device used to underline the contrasting world-views of the Indians and the French, as well as the conflict that Laforgue must fight through. One of the most striking pairings is between the Iroquois camp that the small party barely escapes, and the Huron mission that greets Laforgue. Both are stark and snow-covered. The Iroquois raiding party takes the captives through an eerie graveyard to their camp, which is a nightmarish, chaotic settlement in the snow. The mission is likewise blurred by snow and ice, and inhabited by death and seeming pointlessness. The first sight that greets Laforgue when he enters the mission church is a priest's corpse, hideously positioned on the floor. The viewer is drawn to conclude that Laforgue recognises the similarities in these settings and must face them both with the same resolve. As the snow blinds Laforgue's vision, both the Indians and the French are clouded together in a common mass of human misery. The paradoxical images hint at the salvation which the world needs and which Laforgue symbolically carries. Laforgue's willingness simply to love the Indians and to baptise them indicates his acceptance of life's many incongruities.

These pairings, which have so profound an impact on the film's climax, are signalled early in the film in an interesting montage of images surrounding the initial agreement between Chomina and Champlain to escort Laforgue up river. In a series of cross-cuts, Chomina's elaborate dress is compared to that of Champlain; yet, neither fully respects the other's traditions. When the two men sit down to barter with their aides beside them, the Jesuits sit between them, as it were to mediate. And, of course, this will be the role that Laforgue fully accepts in the end.

The character who seems best to understand the similarities between the two cultures throughout the film is Daniel. He appreciates the advantages of French culture, and would gladly accept a return from Quebec to Rouen to study the priesthood; yet, he is drawn to the vibrant social life of the Indians and to the passion of a girl such as Annuka, even though he idealises the Indians somewhat and faces a shock when confronted with the Iroquois barbarity. His rugged good looks contrast with the more intellectual-appearing Laforgue, making him perhaps the best blending of the two worlds.

The harshest contrast in the film is between Laforgue's experience in the wilderness with the Indians and several flashbacks of his life in Rouen before his trip to America. Visually, the differences between the refined world of the genteel French and the coarse world of the North American wilderness initially make the French scenes seem grossly out of place, but they are necessary briefly to define the context in which Laforgue initially encounters the Indians, or "savages" as he refers to them later. Beresford quickly carries the viewer through these disparate images, not only to provide background for Laforgue's struggles, but also to underline the gritty realism of his North American scenes.

The most startling images in the film, apart from the Iroquois camp and Huron mission, are the shots of the North American wilderness, and the river on which the party travels. The first such image follows the party as it sets out from Quebec. The sky carries several hues of grey, blue and pink, and the water is steely grey. From a wide-angle shot of the horizon, the camera cuts to an overhead view of the canoes snaking their way through the water. This overhead shot forces the viewer to see the party from a divine, objective point of view, which creates a reading of the film that logically leads to the shot of the cross glistening in the sun in the last sequence. Despite the horrors and deprivations which the party will undergo, everything follows a purpose and goes noticed. An older companion priest, Father Bourque, watches Laforgue's journey begin, in a shot reminiscent of an early scene in

Roland Joffé's *The Mission* (1986), in which two companion priests watch a third (played by Jeremy Irons) climb a waterfall to reach a proposed mission. This image of the canoes drifting through the river will be repeated twice more in the film. In one scene, a series of cross-cuts between Chomina and Laforgue emphasises the trial which the priest suffers as he tries physically to match the endurance of the Indians. The cut to the overhead shot closes this short sequence. The final occurrence is when the Indians abandon Laforgue, as does Daniel, and an overhead shot captures the party of Indians followed by Daniel as they paddle back to Algonquin territory. All three shots close key moments in Laforgue's pilgrimage; all three suggest the larger context of Christ's Passion which the priest must play out – his commitment and pilgrimage, his trial, his betrayal and abandonment.

Reinforcing the visual imagery of these three key scenes is a dramatic orchestral score which suggests the transcendent value of these moments and – as in most religious films, particularly those which work upon the audience in a sacramental fashion – signals them as the sacramental moments of the film. Three scenes later in the film use music to signal moments of transcendence. One is the scene between Chomina and Laforgue as Chomina lays dying on the island of his dream. The other is the scene of Laforgue's arrival at the mission. Both scenes mark the success of Laforgue's pilgrimage and, therefore, the triumph of God and the Church. The most striking use of musical cues to signal a sacramental moment occurs as Laforgue baptises the Indians at the Huron mission. Here a boys' choir joins the orchestra to complete the effect; the camera cuts from the baptisms back to the cross glistening in the sun outside the mission, and then to the blank screen and epilogue. Beresford paces these sacramental moments skilfully to lead the viewer to a full participatory experience in Laforgue's final triumph.

Beyond the use of non-diegetic music, Beresford uses a few key montage sequences to underline his purposes. The first is the scene between Champlain and the Indians which sets up the film's primary conflict, the conflicting cultures which prove a barrier to the Jesuits' work. Another is in Chomina's recurrent dream of death, in which a raven, Laforgue, the she-manitou, the winter ice and the death island are woven quickly together. This sequence underlines the Indian view of the world, full of omens, threats and dreams. The last such instance occurs near the film's climax and leads into the final sequence of Laforgue's agreeing to baptise the Hurons. Laforgue has buried Father Jerome, and the camera cuts from the shot of Laforgue's lonely work to a crucifix in the mission, then a closer shot of the image of Christ on the cross, then a cut to Laforgue praying for God's help, then a shot of the mission bell ringing, and finally a shot of Laforgue under the mission cross awaiting the arrival of the Hurons. This last montage strikes an interesting parallel to Chomina's dream. Both are highly concentrated stylistically and thematically,and both suggest the theme of death. However, the earlier montage ends with a haunting barren wasteland, whereas the latter ends with the bell and cross signalling redemption. If there are any doubts about Beresford's intentions to this point in the film, this concluding montage should dispel them.

Black Robe is a sophisticated and effective sacramental picture of one man's pilgrimage towards death for the sake of others. Seen in this way, the film rewards the viewer on several levels, chiefly of which is spiritual. But even without embracing the strong Christian frame of *Black Robe*, viewers must appreciate Beresford's powerful historical and cultural re-creation. Perhaps no other film so effectively portrays the loneliness and struggles of missionary work; certainly very few films so honestly confront the question felt at times by all women and men of faith – where is God in my moment of trial? Yet, Beresford's film is not finally about faith, but about Christ's cross. Laforgue, the black robe, is metaphorically Christ come to America. His black robe is death and duty and devotion. Ironically, as much as the film provides a chronicle of death and failure, it leaves the viewer with a sense of triumph.

Note

[1]   Brian Moore, *Black Robe* (London: Jonathan Cape, 1985): vii-viii.

6 · The Gospel According to St Matthew (Il Vangelo secondo Matteo, 1964)

It is ironic yet fitting that a soul as apparently unsettled as that of Pier Paolo Pasolini should project so brilliant a religious epic as *Il Vangelo secondo Matteo* (*The Gospel According to St Matthew*). It remains the premier Biblical epic on the life of Christ in any language, despite the fact that it is the least known in the United States outside academic and some clerical circles. Its failure to gain wide popular attention there can be traced to a variety of factors: the overall poor circulation of foreign films in the United States; Pasolini's miserable reputation after *Salò, o le centiventi giornate di Sodoma* (*Salò, or The 120 Days of Sodom*, 1975); and the film's rough texture (so contrary to the stylisation of most Biblical epics).

The Gospel According to St Matthew is the only Jesus film that captures the breadth of the Gospels and the potency of the character of Jesus; yet, it is the product of a man who felt Judaism is "basically racist [and] completely mad", and who did not believe Christ's claims about himself.[1] It was not Catholic dogma that propelled the film, despite widespread Catholic approval and the signature of the Vatican within the opening credits.[2] Rather, Pasolini was moved by his own temporary exuberance for the mythic and epic vision of the Gospel of Matthew, for, in a strange way, this vision appealed to his own somewhat religious embrace of the world.[3]

Pasolini came to the project, or it came to him, while he stayed as a guest of the Church in the town of Assisi, awaiting the arrival of John XXIII, who was visiting the area. The Gospels had been placed beside his bed, and, in the spirit of the event, as Pasolini described it in the following letter, he reread them for the first time since his youth:

> Dear Caruso, I should like to explain to you better, in writing, what I confusedly confided to you in conversation. The first time I visited all of you in Assisi, I found the Gospels at my bedside: your delightful and diabolical calculation! And indeed everything went as it was supposed to...I read them from beginning to end, like a novel. And in the exaltation of reading

– as you know, it's the most exalting thing one can read! – there came to me, among other things, the idea of making a film...To put it very simply and frankly, I don't believe that Christ is the son of God, because I am not a believer – at least not consciously. But I believe that Christ is divine: I believe, that is, that in him humanity is so lofty, strict, and ideal as to exceed the common terms of humanity.[4]

Pasolini carried to the film his enthusiasm over what he had discovered in two critical ways. Firstly, he decided from the onset that his *Gospel* would be a retelling of Matthew's Gospel as written, without substantive additions, deletions or interpretive glosses. Secondly, in directing the film, he drew on the same intuition and emotion that had instructed him to begin the project. In other words, the film emanated from a deep and personal, albeit temporary, evangelical enthusiasm.

To Pasolini's credit, he persevered in making *The Gospel According to St Matthew* against several hindrances. The film took long to prepare and was expensive, and Pasolini took great pains to preserve his sense of Christian iconography with the choice of actors. In addition, the film came on the heels of controversy stirred by Pasolini's political and moral radicalism. Two of his previous films, *Accattone* (1961) and *Mamma Roma* (1962), had brought Pasolini to court on charges ranging from slander of public officials to obscenity. His 1963 film, *La ricotta*, was seized for insulting the religion of the state. As a result, Pasolini was sentenced to four months in prison, although the decision was overturned by the Appeals Court in Rome in 1964. Few expected that the Gospels would receive proper treatment from a temperament as volatile and a spirit as irreverent as Pasolini's, and it thus came as quite a shock when the film received warm applause at its premiere during the 24th Venice Film Festival on 4 September 1964. The Organisation Catholique Internationale du Cinéma et de l'Audiovisuel (OCIC) reported: "The author, who is said not to share our faith, has given proof in his choice of texts and scenes of respect and delicacy. He has made a fine film, a Christian film that produces a profound impression".[5]

The success of *The Gospel According to St Matthew* throws into question most traditional approaches to understanding religious film. It cannot be considered religious or "Christian" on the grounds of its author's faith and intention, for Pasolini openly denied this possibility, despite his enthusiasm triggered by the Pope's visit. In a curious way, the film actually grows more out of a deep personal agnosticism.

Pasolini's personal use of religious terms for his own artistic satisfaction explains and informs the film's style, which can best be characterised as one of analogy, from the choice of sets to Pasolini's private view of historical circumstance. Christ and the Gospel accounts are treated as archetypal myth and epic, an attitude that would satisfy only the most liberal of Christian theologies,[6] and yet one which succeeds within the film's overall aesthetic context. For Pasolini, the relevance of the Gospels lay in what they reveal about human potential, as he did not believe in immediate divine activity in human affairs. To display the supernatural work of God was the last thing Pasolini intended to achieve in the film, although, ironically, many viewers appreciate the film most for its believable depiction of the miraculous.

The film defies attempts at the type of organised thematic and structural analysis that is standard with most religious texts. The film narrative follows Matthew's narrative with relative consistency; it is not rearranged, for example, according to the themes of darkness and light or guilt and redemption, nor are there superimposed fictional narratives designed to enhance the scriptural drama, as is the case in so many similar films. Changes that are made in the Gospel account are for the most part matters of narrative continuity.

Identifiable motifs that exist within the film tend to vary, seemingly at the director's whim. Pasolini's camera begins with classic reverential compositions – for example, the first image of the pregnant virgin – but then moves experimentally through a variety of devices that border documentary techniques – the handheld camera sequences which follow Jesus's passage from town to town. Pasolini's Christ remains unpredictable in his subtleties, alternately brooding with anger and energy, as when driving out the money-changers and calling for repentance, and relaxing in placid or childlike moods, as when welcoming children. Most Scripture-based films are far more predictable, especially the Hollywood epics.

Despite this difficulty, it is possible to perform a partial structural analysis of the film that centres on Pasolini's systematic frustration of the spectator's attempts fully to comprehend the divine mystery. For example, Stephen Snyder attempts such a reading in a study of Pasolini's films.[7] Snyder traces within the film narrative a conflict between rational and imaginative perception. In the opening shot, a close-up of Mary shows solemn holiness, while a corresponding close-up of Joseph shows scepticism and fear. This motif is developed in architectural features of their surroundings: Mary in an arch like an icon; Joseph in the rigid grid of a walled road. Snyder argues that the pattern continues throughout the film, most commonly in juxtaposed shots of Jesus and the disciples against the Pharisees and Roman politicians. The believing world is humble and round; the unbelieving is stern and square.

Snyder offers a useful analysis of many of the film's compositions. Most viewers will notice oppositional patterns, for example, in clothing styles: Jesus and the disciples loose, flowing and natural; his opponents tight and affected. Posturing also follows a pattern: the Pharisees and politicians are stiff and always upright; Christ and his followers are more relaxed. It is clear that Pasolini wanted to equate formal law and proud human rationality with a cruel worldliness that will remain blind to divine mystery. Truth for Pasolini is, by nature, incomprehensible.

What Pasolini appreciated as an artist and as a man was exuberance and humility. An illustration might be found, for example, in some lines written by Pasolini about a young Roman named Ninetto, who became his lover at about the time of the release of *The Gospel*:

> Look, here into the orchestra comes a madman, with soft
> and merry eyes,
> dressed like the Beatles.
> While great thoughts and great actions
> are implied in the relation of these rich people to the film spectacle,
> made for him *too*, he twirling one thin finger like a merry-go-
> round horse,
> writes his name 'Ninetto'
> on the back of the velvet seat (under a long-eared nape
> associated with rules of behavior and the idea of the free
> bourgeoisie).
> Ninetto is a herald,
> and overcoming (with a sweet laugh
> that blazes from his whole being
> as in a Muslim or a Hindu)
> his shyness,
> he introduces himself as in an Areopagus
> to speak of the Persians.[8]

Ninetto becomes a model for the exuberant spirit which Pasolini's Jesus displays. He was the real humanity of the lower class in Italy, which Pasolini sought in his notorious and finally fatal late-night encounters. Free from hypocritical airs and politicised erudition, Ninetto had for Pasolini a mythic, heroic beauty. It was this sense of beauty, coupled with a tragic feeling that he would face his own personal martyrdom (as a result of the censorship of his work), that became analogous with the divine vs. human paradox in Jesus's soul.

Snyder's analysis of the structure of *The Gospel*, however, can only go so far in describing the film. He illustrates some of the film's devices, but Pasolini's techniques in the film, as noted, do not remain constant. He himself admitted to great experimentation in the process of shooting the film:

> When I started *The Gospel* I thought I had the right formula all ready, and I started out shooting it with the same techniques and style as I used for *Accattone*. But after two days I was in a complete crisis and I even contemplated giving the whole thing up...Using a reverential style for *The Gospel* was gilding the lily: it came out rhetoric. Reverential technique and style in *Accattone* went fine, but applied to a sacred text they were ridiculous; so I got discouraged...and then when I was shooting the baptism scene near Viterbo I threw over all my technical preconceptions. I started using the zoom, I used new camera movements, new frames which were not reverential, but almost documentary. A completely new style emerged. In *Accattone* the style is consistent and extremely simple, like in Masaccio or in Romanesque sculpture. Whereas the style in *The Gospel* is very varied: it combines the reverential with almost documentary moments, an almost classic severity with moments that are almost Godardian.[9]

The variety in style, as Pasolini maintained, defines the film and diffuses comprehensive readings. One can follow certain tendencies, such as those of costume style or set design, but these remain tendencies, not interpretive keys. There is too much alteration of style and structure in the film to attempt to contain it within a set of motifs. While it is clear that Pasolini is likening unbelief to a certain internal fixedness, the whole film transcends simple thematic questions such as belief and unbelief.

The religious power of *The Gospel* is located not in a thematic or structural motif, but in an *experience* of the film's variety and freshness. To enter the film is to step into the kind of irrational yet tangible aura of spiritual existence that faith yearns after. It requires a Kierkegaardian leap of faith. If, indeed, a true religious film in the Christian sense is to be likened to a spiritual exercise, the liturgical ceremony or private meditation, Pasolini's *Gospel* is the prototypical religious film. It cannot be systematically explained on the thematic level because it primarily operates on the experiential level. It does so for any person approaching the film as it did for Pasolini himself. Pasolini made the film as a form of personal ritual, not to speak to an audience, but to perform a Passion for an audience. He felt that film was a means of evangelism for the poor, and *The Gospel* was his most personal and profound attempt at that. The result is a clear expression of sacramental film form with remarkable evocative power.

The detail of the production that best illustrates this religious mode and which has been the most often identified as the source of the film's compelling effect is Pasolini's direction of the Spaniard, Enrique Irazoqui, who portrays Jesus. In the tradition of neo-realism, Pasolini chose non-actors to perform preconceived roles on the basis of his own intuition of what they were as people. The choice of Irazoqui was particularly intuitive:

> I spent more than a year looking everywhere for someone to do Christ, and I'd almost decided to use a German actor. And then one day I came back to the house and found this young Spaniard, Enrique Irazoqui, sitting here waiting to see me and as soon as I saw him, even before he had a chance to start talking, I said: 'Excuse me, but would you act in one of my films?' – even before I knew who he was or anything. He was a serious person, and so he said 'no'. But then I gradually won him round.[10]

Most critics agree that the mixture of emotions and pure energy that Irazoqui exudes as Jesus keeps the character at the distance that divine mystery necessitates. Some have tried to define that "mystery" as a cloak for some suppressed homosexual or Marxist sub-message,[11] but Pasolini's Jesus, Irazoqui, is better understood as an attempt at the thing as it exists: the Jesus that came to Pasolini in his reading of Matthew's Gospel. Individual elements of character are evident – holy earnest, rage, resistance, authority – but none defines the whole.

The genius of Pasolini's choice of actor is apparent in the elusiveness of Irazoqui's expression. From his first appearance at the baptism and his early command to passers-by that they repent, Pasolini's camera makes Irazoqui's face a mystery analogous to Jesus's divinity. John the Baptist, travellers on the road, and the Apostles all peer into that face with astonishment and fear, and Pasolini manages to keep his camera in the same posture. Thus, the screen image of Jesus becomes more than the religious identifier for the Biblical character that it is for most Biblical epics – for example, Ray's *King of Kings* (1961); it becomes the signifier of the mystery of the Biblical character, the essential theanthropic soul of Jesus. Pasolini holds the spectator in a mystical spell by never allowing the divine mystery to allow rational definition.

This aura is remarkably managed in the concluding sequences of the film when Jesus is tried and crucified. When the nails are driven through his hands into the cross, we hear a cry of agony, but we are denied a view of Jesus's face, as if such a view might solve the mystery in the moment of his weakness. We are always a step behind Pasolini's Christ, or our head is turned at precisely the wrong moment, so that we miss the multiplying of the loaves and fish although gaining the feast, or, in the conclusion, we arrive only to find Christ already risen from the grave. Through the means of his unstable techniques, Pasolini places the viewer in a submissive position. It is this placement that defines Pasolini's sacramental art. *The Gospel* must be absorbed on a level akin to that of the worshipper.

For Pasolini, to attempt to master and own a film – that is, to contain it by way of investigative scrutiny – was precisely the kind of exercise that art must stand against. It is the rigid Pharisaism that crucified Christ. He would equate this methodology with the Western consumerism that had begun to permeate Italy and the rest of Europe. It was a political homogenization that was stripping culture and art of the mythical energy of raw experience.[12] *Mamma Roma* develops the same attitudes. The son of a common prostitute is raised in ignorance of his mother's past so that he might bypass the lower-class life and rise to the petit bourgeois level of clerk. He ends up a common thief and fool with little humanity, for he has been kept from true living by his mother's materialistic obsessions.

Pasolini preferred the viewer of his films to be kept at bay and forced to re-create the truth behind the art by analogy within private experience. In *The Gospel*, the analogy was to direct the viewer to the Gospel experience of the first disciples. An experience of this wonder would lead to the recognition of that same wonder in the present time, since the Gospel, for him, is itself a parable or myth designed to elevate common experience. Pasolini's unique use of rural Italian landscapes as re-creation of the ancient world, including his depiction of local poor as replicas of the ancient Jews, ties the ancient world to the modern in a way that other Biblical-historical epics have never fully been able to achieve, despite elaborate re-creations and huge expense. The viewer of Pasolini's epic is not given the option of accepting or rejecting the historical portrait of the ancient world. For the viewer, Pasolini's southern Italy becomes the ancient world, both figuratively and literally.

By moving from the rational to the experiential in his artistic process, Pasolini takes the spectator into the religious performance. Its design encourages the viewer to gaze at its subject. The face of Jesus is the spot where meditation can be directed. All the essential features of a spiritual exercise are prominent: the careful composition of place through the analogy of present-day southern Italy; the methodical re-creation of the time projected in Matthew's text; and the rotational nature of the text, which follows the seasons of Jesus's ministry.

These latter two aspects might be developed briefly here (even though they logically follow the initial condition of Pasolini's project, which was to re-create the Gospel account as it stands), because the manner in which Pasolini captures the somewhat epistolary nature of the Gospel of Matthew is a chief virtue in the film. There has been substantial discussion among theologians concerning the temporal arrangements of events in the Synoptic Gospels, with most agreeing that the events were related with less concern for chronological accuracy than for religious understanding.[13] There is what might be called a flavour or unction – to use two favourite terms of the Puritans – to the Gospel records that hastens readers and listeners into the ministry of Jesus in a more immediate experience than could be gained through a more meticulous historical account. Pasolini follows this flavour of Matthew in significant ways.

The most prominent narrative technique in *The Gospel* is a form of subtle montage that occurs on both the visual and auditory levels. The visual montage is most evident in the slaughter of the infants of Bethlehem, as Pasolini cuts back and forth from close to longer shots of the soldiers' callous brutality and the mothers' horror. This montage fills a gap in Matthew's text. Matthew quotes a prophecy from Jeremiah regarding the incident rather than describes it, and then immediately proceeds with the narrative of the holy family returning from Egypt after Herod's death (Matthew 2: 17-19). Pasolini describes the incident vividly and then follows this montage with a quick image of the painful death of Herod. The intention would be to underline for emotional effect what Matthew suppresses. Such suppression is, in fact, one of the most integral aspects of the Gospel eloquence, and the Church has long maintained that one testimony to the divine inspiration of the Gospels is the objectiveness and restraint exercised by the authors in such passages, where the temptation to editorialize would normally be too great to resist.[14] Nevertheless, Pasolini's inclusion becomes a powerful scene in the film.

A less noticeable but more ingenious piece of editing occurs in Pasolini's rendition of the Sermon on the Mount. In Matthew's account, the sermon is a continuous discourse, introduced by Jesus's quieting his followers down and opening his mouth to teach them. The form of the text alludes strongly to the Old Testament account of Moses receiving God's instruction on Mount Sinai while the people gather below. Jesus, the God-man, sits before the congregation and teaches them directly what he learned from his Father. In his teaching, he makes constant reference to the transition from the old order to the new: "You have heard it said...but I say unto you...". The effect of Matthew's text is to describe the Sermon as a new law, a kind of new catechism for the redeemed Jew. As such, the Sermon becomes a new meditation. Just as many of the Psalms recite the law of Moses in ritualistic fashion (Psalms 80-100), so, from the early Church to that of the present day, passages from the Sermon have been used for song or written about devotionally.[15]

Pasolini manages to remain in the spirit of Matthew by a unique visual montage that follows Irazoqui's preaching of the text. As the reading progresses, Jesus is lit by different backgrounds, ranging from thunderous night skies to pastoral afternoons.[16] These metaphorically convey the compression of time in Matthew's text, but, more importantly, they convey the atemporality of the new law and the divine authority in Jesus's words. The sequence is not unlike the traditional Signs of the Cross that appear in most Catholic churches, in which the Passion of Jesus is depicted in twelve stages that follow the twelve key moments in the Passion tradition, and that suggest various redemptive qualities inherent in the different acts – i.e. his physical sacrifice; his selfless concern for his mother; his majesty; and so on. Pasolini's various views of the Sermon uphold the contemplative tradition associated with the Gospel law; in particular, his method evokes the ritualistic passing of time around which meditations on the new law have revolved and continue to do so. Pasolini confirmed this intention later:

> I did not want to reconstruct the life of Christ as it really was, I wanted to do the story of Christ plus two thousand years of Christian translation, because it is the two thousand years of Christian history which have mythicized this biography, which would otherwise be an almost insignificant biography as such. My film is the life of Christ plus two thousand years of story-telling about the life of Christ. That was my intention.[17]

Pasolini's auditory montage is best displayed in the diverse soundtrack that he created for the film with the help of Elsa Morante, a poet and close friend from the late 1950s. The score ranges from Bach and Mozart to a spiritual by Odetta and contemporary instrumental music by Leoš Janáček. The music is woven in and out of the narrative, often thematically, as Odetta's "Motherless Child" accompanies the Passion, the slaughter of innocents, and later scenes of Mary, played by Pasolini's own mother, Susanna. The different musical traditions and styles juxtaposed with the historical accounts of the narrative create another feeling of atemporality or mythos in the film. They stress the tradition of meditation that has followed the life of Christ through the centuries, and they compel the viewer into the meditation directly. The selections from Bach and Mozart particularly have this effect, as they come from the liturgical works by these composers, and the Odetta spiritual has the languorous effect of a chant.

Pasolini's concern for the significance of the Incarnation figures into his religious style as strongly as his "evangelistic" motive of trying to elevate the Italian people, particularly the poor, towards an optimistic humanism. According to Pasolini, it is the divinity inherent in all humanity that is perfectly focused in Matthew's Christ. This is apparent in his treatment of the supernatural occurrences in the Gospel.

Pasolini originally shot *The Gospel* to run to almost 2¾ hours. He shot Christ's eschatological sermons and several miracles that were later omitted to maintain the visual intensity of the progression of events leading to the Crucifixion. He did not omit what many American filmmakers have omitted or sensationalized – the supernatural works. Key sequences in the film are the feeding of the 5000; Christ walking on the water; the healing of the leprous; and the appearances of Gabriel and Satan. Pasolini's faithfulness in this regard brought him criticism from the left-wing Italian intellectuals of the 1960s.

Pasolini displays the miraculous through a shot/reverse-shot technique: long take of the leper approaching Christ/shot of Christ blessing him/reverse-shot back to the man healed. The only time the miraculous process appears to be observed is when Christ walks on water, but, here too, Pasolini simulates the occurrence by cutting back and forth from Christ on the water to the amazed disciples in the boat. These camera shifts become metonymic for divine process, and a careful examination of the technique reveals it to be the controlling editing feature of the film, from the appearance of Gabriel to Joseph, and to the final appearance of the angel at the empty tomb.

This metonym of style, the shot/reverse-shot that signals divine agency, plays out in part what Pasolini attempts on a larger scale when he continually draws the viewer to the face of Christ. Throughout the scenes of Jesus's ministry, the camera cuts back and forth from Jesus's activity and that of those around him to Irazoqui's face. Jesus's face begins to shape or create his surroundings, and, although unknowable to a large degree, the mystery and power of Matthew's Gospel, the life of Christ, are sanctified and opened to the viewer in the elusive attractiveness of Irazoqui's face.

As the film progresses, therefore, each individual miracle evokes the larger miracle of Christ's presence. The effect is that there is no one single incarnational moment in the film, but an ever-growing incarnational presence. The trial and Crucifixion, which provide the dramatic climax of the narrative, paradoxically serve more to draw the viewer back into Jesus's incarnate humanity than to lead to the grand Resurrection which proves his divinity.

What Pasolini has accomplished with his subtle link between his editing and his use of the camera is to make the film function as an icon, both in its images and in its processes. The face of Irazoqui becomes the face of the God-man, and the motion and actions of the narrative characters draw us to the divine presence and divine power. Yet, for Pasolini, divine presence and power are finally just a metaphor. Pasolini compels us towards a sacramental experience in *The Gospel According to St Matthew*, but not an encounter with religious fact (that is, actual spiritual presence); rather, he directs us to the human ideal, the myth he found beneath the Christian tradition. The viewer is referred to Christ through analogous means, so that the spirit of Christ, which for Pasolini is the idealisation of human moral and political potential, might elevate the soul.

Notes

[1] Pier Paolo Pasolini, *Pasolini on Pasolini: Interviews with Oswald Stack* (London: Thames and Hudson, in association with the British Film Institute, 1969): 76.

[2] A brief history of the interrelation between Pasolini and the Church in Rome, including key correspondence, is given in Enzo Siciliano, *Pasolini*, translated by John Shepley (New York: Random House, 1982): 266-277.

[3] These attitudes towards human potential and dignity are drawn most clearly in his early novels, *A Violent Life*, translated by William Weaver (London: Jonathan Cape, 1968) and *The ragazzi*, translated by Emile Capouya (Manchester; New York: Carcanet, 1986); see also Pasolini, *Lutheran Letters*, translated by Stuart Hood (Manchester: Carcanet New Press; Dublin: Raven Arts Press; 1983).

[4] Siciliano: 269-270.

[5] Ibid: 275.

[6] Modern discussions of the kērygma of the Gospel as the force of the Gospel mythology would fit: see, for example, Rudolf Bultmann, "The Task and the Problems of New Testament Theology (the Relation between Theology and Proclamation)", in *Theology of the New Testament*, volume 2, translated by Kendrick Grobel (New York: Scribners, 1951): 237-251.

[7]   Stephen Snyder, *Pier Paolo Pasolini* (Boston: Twayne Publishers, 1980): 59-72.

[8]   Siciliano: 284. Emphasis in original.

[9]   Pasolini (1969): 83-84.

[10]   Ibid: 78.

[11]   For example, see Susan Macdonald, "Pasolini: Rebellion, Art and a New Society", *Screen* 10: 3 (1969): 26-32.

[12]   François Bondy, "On the Death of Pasolini", *Encounter* 46: 6 (June 1976): 53-55; also see John Bragin, "Pasolini – A Conversation in Rome, June 1966", *Film Culture* 42 (1966): 102-105.

[13]   Discussions on the nature of inspiration in the New Testament and how this relates to Biblical hermeneutics are multitudinous. Two widely recognised, traditional discussions are Benjamin Breckinridge Warfield, *The Inspiration and Authority of the Bible*, edited by Samuel G Craig (London: Marshall, Morgan & Scott, 1951); and J Gresham Machen, *The Origin of Paul's Religion* (Grand Rapids, MI: Eerdmans Publishing Company, 1925): especially 3-43. For a specific discussion of the Synoptics, see F F Bruce, "The fourfold Gospel", in D Guthrie and J A Motyer (eds), *The New Bible Commentary Revised* (London: Inter-Varsity Press, 1970): 64-70.

[14]   Conservative discussions of canonicity in the New Testament almost invariably discuss the internal integrity or "loftiness" of the Gospel narratives as a mark of divine authority. This aspect of the faith is not emphasised in systematic discussions as much as it is elucidated sermonically. For an example of the kind of treatment traditionally given to the subject, see John Charles Ryle, D.D., *Expository Thoughts on the Gospels: For Family and Private Use, volume 1: St. Matthew and St. Mark* (London: William Hunt and Company, 1887).

[15]   The Beatitudes receive the largest treatment in devotional manuals, both ancient and modern.

[16]   Apparently, this technique was an improvisation by Pasolini. He created the effect by shooting the scene in a studio with Irazoqui seated in front of a dark background that was lit variably. See Siciliano: 274.

[17]   Pasolini (1969): 83.

One of the unresolved dilemmas of Christian practice concerns Jesus's admonition in the Sermon on the Mount to "turn the other cheek" when abused unjustly. The question that arises with this teaching is how far it should be taken. Most Christians recognise personal martyrdom as one of the great testimonials to and privileges of the Christian faith, but opinions differ greatly when the martyrdom to be suffered is not your own, but someone else's. Can a Christian take hold of the sword to protect a family member, a neighbour or a community? The Calvinist answers one way, the Quietist another.

Roland Joffé's *The Mission* (1986) directly addresses this problem through the dramatisation of a little-known incident in the history of South American colonisation and the ministry of the Jesuits in the 18th century. In doing so, Joffé and scriptwriter Robert Bolt provide a context in which to understand the rise of liberation theology in South and Central America – that theology which promotes the prioritizing of the Church's role as social liberator and peacemaker in oppressed countries. But *The Mission* also presents the paradoxical face of Jesus as both fulfiller of the role of Old Testament warrior king, and that of shepherd servant.

In the New Testament, Jesus identified himself several times as the warrior king, the "Son of David". When he was welcomed into Jerusalem before the Crucifixion, he was heralded by shouts of "Hosanna to the Son of David", and in one sense he fulfilled that appellation by driving money-changers from the temple with a whip. He fulfils that role more completely in John's Apocalypse, when he rides a white horse and leads the armies of heaven against the nations hostile to God (Revelations 19: 11-16). However, the face of Christ in the Gospels is more that of the shepherd servant preparing his people for the day when he will offer himself for the world's salvation. Throughout the history of the Church, especially from the time of the Crusades through to the first century after the Reformation, periods of Christian militancy have focused on Christ the righteous warrior, and sanctioned the vocation of the Christian warrior; yet, Christianity has arguably leaned much more in the direction of the meek Christ and passive resistance, following the model of the early Church and, particularly, Christ and the Apostles, all of whom accepted martyrdom – with the exception of John, who was exiled on the island of Patmos.

In *The Mission*, both faces of Christ and the Church are portrayed and, in the end, reconciled. What makes the film particularly compelling is that neither the militant Church nor the passive Church is given precedence, and neither is able to change the negative course of events that the film recounts. Yet, the Church in Joffé's film is powerful, and its power comes through portraying Christ in the consummate sacrifice that concludes the drama. Thus, the power of the Church is in the playing out of the Passion, which becomes a liturgical ritual for the film spectator.

Bolt – whose most conspicuous previous screenplay came by turning his successful play celebrating the life of Thomas More, *A Man for All Seasons*, into the 1966 film – wrote these patterns into the film by emphasising the clear types of the film's characters, and by de-emphasising their psychological development. Joffé takes the film a step further by intensifying the basic conflicts of the story and bringing them together with startling realism and force in the climactic sequences. It is the patterning of the story and its characters that critics have reacted against, despite the film's success at Cannes and Chris Menges's Academy Award® for cinematography. In some corners, the film prompted near hostility for the overtness of its religious message and for its straightforward plot development; yet, these are actually the strengths of the film when the symbolic context is understood.

One of the more intriguing insights into the film comes from an interview with Roland Joffé in which he recounts a conversation with Corazon Aquino, then president of the Philippines, regarding *The Mission* and its development of the role of the Church in political affairs:

> It wasn't that far after Aquino [Benigno] got in his airplane. He said, very movingly, 'If I am shot as I come off the plane, which is probably the most likely, I'm going to try and fall with my arms spread out, so that when they draw around my body on the ground, they'll draw the shape of a man loving his country.' That's so heroic, that's wonderfully heroic. It's in *The Mission*, too. That's why I feel that the film in its own way is optimistic.[1]

Joffé's comments underscore the positive, heroic quality of *The Mission*, which can only be found in the symbolic significance of the martyrdoms which conclude the narrative, since there is nothing else of a positive nature to celebrate. The stretching out of the arms, although not a literal gesture in the film, has always been in the Church (particularly in the East) an expression of Christ's sacrifice on the cross. The loving of country can be taken as the loving of the mission of the Jesuits, which is the evangelization and discipling of the world, and therefore a loving of the work of the Church in itself. If this is the gesture that Joffé recognised as present within *The Mission*, it does not seem implausible to regard the film's primary purpose as the documenting of a peculiarly Christian paradigm.

The story-line of the film derives from a tragedy that befell the work of the Jesuits working among the Guaraní Indians in the lands near the Iguazú Falls in Argentina, lands which border what is now Argentina, Brazil and Paraguay. For nearly two centuries, the Jesuits had evangelized and maintained missions in this region, but, as a result of some concessions made in previous treaties, and of the hostility of the Portuguese Marquis de Pompal against the papacy, the Spanish had agreed to give over these lands to the Portuguese (advancing the lucrative slave trade in the region) if the Jesuits shut down the Indian missions. Failure to agree to this concession would have meant all-out war against the Jesuits in the Americas and Europe.

In the film, Pope Benedict XIV commissions Cardinal Altamirano (Ray McAnally) to examine the situation and instruct the Jesuit missionaries to counsel the Indians to return to the forest. The narration of *The Mission* is framed by Altamirano's voice-over dictation of the letter which he writes to Benedict explaining the situation.

The Guaraní Indians are especially adept as musicians and instrument-makers, and the mission of San Miguel below the Iguazú Falls prospers for its crafts, farming and spiritual vitality. An attempt by a lone Jesuit missionary to establish a mission above the falls at first fails, as the Indians above the falls tie the missionary to a cross and send him down the rapids and over the cascade. The Jesuit who supervised the effort, Father Gabriel (Jeremy Irons), climbs up the rock ledge beside the falls to attempt a new contact. He interests the Indians with the playing of a flute, and in time establishes the jungle mission of San Carlos, which begins to flourish, as did San Miguel.

One threat to the mission comes from mercenary slave-traders who collect slaves for the Portuguese, who in turn sell them to the Spanish, who have supposedly outlawed the trade. The worst of the mercenaries is Rodrigo Mendoza (Robert De Niro), who collects Indian slaves for the Spanish territorial governor, Don Cabeza (Chuck Low). However, when Rodrigo's mistress falls in love with Mendoza's brother, the mercenary kills his brother, Felipe, in a street fight during the festival of Asunción. In grief, Mendoza gives himself over to despair and is committed to the hands of the local priests. Father Gabriel is called in to counsel, and urges Mendoza to accept God's forgiveness, do penance and return to life.

For a penance, Mendoza chooses to carry all his armaments down river and up the falls to the San Carlos mission. Gabriel allows Mendoza to choose this penance, and watches with others in the travelling group as the former mercenary struggles to reach the top of the falls. When they finally arrive at the mission, a young Indian cuts Mendoza free, and he begins to weep and then to laugh in the new hope offered to his life. Mendoza enjoys life at the mission, and in time asks Father Gabriel for the privilege of becoming a Jesuit. The missionaries rejoice in his change and Gabriel confirms him as a novice. At this point, word comes of Altamirano's visit to the missions. Don Cabeza and the Portuguese governor, Hontar, try to convince the Cardinal that the missions are merely blocking profitable land development and fur trade. Gabriel objects, together with Mendoza who provides first-hand testimony of slave-trading in the lands. Altamirano agrees to visit the mission and to follow his conscience in giving directives to the Pope.

What Altamirano sees in the missions of San Miguel and San Carlos impresses him deeply, yet, despite spending time in prayer and agreeing to do as his "conscience dictates", the papal emissary informs the Indians that they must return to the jungle in order to save the overall work of the Jesuits. The Guaraní chief and men who listen to Altamirano's decision question his authority and refuse to return to the jungle, since the missions are their home. They determine to fight. Gabriel, Mendoza and the other Jesuits agree to stay with the Guaraní against the Cardinal's order, and Mendoza and several others determine to join the Indians in arms against the Portuguese forces which will come to force the Indians out. Gabriel orders Mendoza not to fight, yet gives him his own cross to wear around his neck.

The well-equipped European army arrives with the help of Indian guides, and, despite the brave efforts of the Indians and a few Jesuits, begins what becomes a slaughter. The soldiers advance and indiscriminately kill men, women and children. Mendoza is mortally wounded while saving a child. Gabriel holds a benediction service for the Indians who do not fight, but has the mission church torched around him. He is murdered by the soldiers as he carries the host in a monstrance in a procession with many of the Guaraní, who are likewise slaughtered. Mendoza stays alive long enough to see Gabriel coming towards him with the monstrance, and then he is martyred. After the battle, several children take the monstrance and a broken violin from the scene, and leave by boat.

Altamirano rebukes Don Cabeza and Hontar for the slaughter, but they suggest that the world is often this harsh; Altamirano replies that they have made it such. The narrative concludes with the Cardinal regretfully completing his letter to the Pope, after which follows a dark screen with the text of John 1: 5 "The light shines in the darkness, but the darkness has not understood it".

This scriptural subscript to the film furthers the Christian optimism, which, paradoxically, derives from the martyrdom of the two priests and the loss of the missions. Much like the end of John Ford's *The Fugitive* (1947), the suggestion is that the work of the Church will plod on to the end, despite this apparent loss. The children's gathering of the remnants of the mission of San Carlos constitutes a new generation of believers and artists, perhaps even stronger than their predecessors because of this hard experience. In the words of Cyprian, "The blood of the martyrs is the seed of the Church".

The boy who seems to be the leader of the survivors, although nameless, has played a significant role in the story of the San Carlos mission, particularly as it involved Mendoza. He is prominent in shots of the Guaraní children playing, and the camera fixes on his face in significant moments, such as when Mendoza arrives at the mission, bedraggled and mud-caked, and has his burden cut off by the natives. This boy takes Mendoza later to a pig hunt and offers him the opportunity to spear the pig. Later, the boy encourages Mendoza to take his sword to protect the village against the Portuguese-led soldiers. During the slaughter, the boy watches gravely from a distance.

Whether or not the alignment with Mendoza means that this boy, as a new community leader, will take a more militant stand against oppression is an open question. The children also recover the violin which aligns them with Gabriel's gentler Christianity. Perhaps it is best to assume that both perspectives have been understood and embraced by this new generation, and that these children have then seen the light shining in a dark place and will continue its shining.

There are numerous overt Christian symbols in the narrative that further this more optimistic approach to the conclusion. The cross recurs significantly in more than contextual sequences. The narrative, as told by Altamirano, begins with the images of the first missionary priest tied to a wooden cross, which Guaraní children help to carry to the Paraná river which leads to the Iguazú Falls. The dropping of the priest and cross into the river suggests both self-sacrifice and baptism, especially in the spectacular image of the cross dropping upside down through the spray of the falls. When Father Gabriel reaches the top of the falls in his first journey up, he conspicuously makes the sign of the cross in a completion of the sequence that interestingly foreshadows the film's conclusion with the children picking up the pieces left by the missionaries. (Gabriel is picking up the pieces of the work of the first martyred priest.) In a similar way, it is a cross which Gabriel gives to Mendoza when he asks for a blessing on the mission's defenders, and the cross he gives him is that worn by the martyred priest, which Father Gabriel put on before ascending the falls himself. Gabriel is offering Mendoza a share of the succession of martyrs throughout the history of the Church, the martyrdom which he feels Mendoza and the other priests will be resisting by fighting to defend the mission. Mendoza takes it and, as already mentioned, watches Gabriel's martyrdom just before he dies. Yet, his own death takes a share in Gabriel's part, since it is caused when he saves a wounded Indian child and leaves himself exposed to the Portuguese guns.

Another overt allusion in the narrative is the pilgrimage of Mendoza up the mountain path and the falls to San Carlos with his armaments on his back. Like Christian in Bunyan's *The Pilgrim's Progress* (1678/1684), he can only have the burden removed from his back at the foot of the cross, which, in essence, is where the trip up the falls leads him. When another priest, Fielding, cuts the burden from Mendoza and sends it over a cliff, the former mercenary returns to get it and continue his penance. While on the journey, Mendoza predictably falls under the weight of the cross.

Perhaps the most obvious allusion regards the narrative strategy of having Altamirano tell the story, since he ultimately, like Judas, will be responsible for selling the mission work for silver. Before Mendoza's conversion, the mercenary collects gold coins from Don Cabeza as payment for the slaves he captures. By playing up the corruption in the Catholic administration of the colonies – and the camera lingers over the material excess surrounding the Cardinal – the plight of the missionaries is even more strongly aligned with the Passion of Christ. In this case, the Church suggests the Jewish hierarchy in the Passion story, and Spain and Portugal suggest Rome. In Altamirano's concluding words, the hopelessness of his position and actions is underlined as he reflects that he is the one who has died, while the missionaries live on, for "the spirit of the dead will still survive in the memory of the living". Visually, a cross-cut has these final words spoken over the image of the young Guaraní paddling off with what they have salvaged from the massacre. A postscript, preceding the passage from John, indicates that the Indians continue to struggle for freedom, and that many priests have died attempting to help them more recently. History records that most of the Guaraní were forcibly removed from the missions which were all closed within three years, and Pompal succeeded in expelling the Jesuits from the area. Within twenty years, the Jesuits were suppressed throughout Europe. These are further ironies which indicate the powerlessness of the Church to effect positive spiritual change through political means. The power, in Joffé's terms, comes ironically from that cross sent plummeting over the falls.

The three most memorable scenes of the film regard the descent and ascent of the falls. The martyred priest tumbling through the falls is visually impressive, as the beauty of the cascading water creates a kind of radiance around the image of the cross. This shot startles the viewer, since the sequence begins with very tight shots of the Indians, both their faces and their feet as they secure the priest to the logs. Not until the cross is dropped into the river is it fully apparent that this is a means of death, and, as such, it lacks the visual horror one associates with torture and murder. As with the Guaraní sense of music, there is a rightness and balance to this gesture. The camera remains relatively close to the priest as the log cross drifts through the rapids; the nearness of the camera allows the viewer to determine that the priest is still alive, and sets up the sudden cut to the distant shot of the fall through the water. Joffé uses this method of balancing close-ups to more distant shots as a way of establishing the force of events on individuals, while still suggesting a better, broader context in which further to interpret the individual plight. This movement becomes a form of visual metaphor to one of the larger concerns of Scripture and Christian theology – the freedom and accountability of the individual person vs. the foreordained plan and purpose of God providentially developed through history.

Father Gabriel's ascent up the falls carries equal beauty, but adds more emotional force. By an interplay of cuts between Gabriel struggling up the side of the cliff through the spray of water and shots of the Jesuits who watch from the other bank, Joffé builds the sequence to the powerful climax of Father Gabriel reaching the top and making the sign of the cross. Several of the shots in this sequence are as visually riveting as the image of the falling martyred priest. Also in the sequence, Gabriel slips and slides down the rocks a short distance, in a gesture similar to the later scene when Mendoza slips down the ledge while carrying his sack of armaments. The Ennio Morricone score becomes prominent as Gabriel ascends higher and finally reaches his goal, marking this sequence as one of the film's sacramental moments. Gabriel's commitment to the work of the Church and his willingness to sacrifice his own life to perform his Christian calling elevate him to a level of sanctification above ordinary nobility and heroism.

During this sequence, much attention is paid to Gabriel's bruised feet straining to gain a firm hold on the rocks. Earlier, as the Indians had prepared the martyred priest for his death, the camera lingered on the feet of the Indians, particularly the children, thus linking Gabriel with them. As Altamirano states in his narration, he is "a man whose life was to become inextricably intertwined with their own". Yet, ironically, Gabriel – whose name echoes the angelic messenger who announced Christ's impending birth to Mary, and whose own musical ability suggests an ideal beauty and sweetness – inadvertently brings trouble to the Indians. Altamirano suggests in his conclusion that it might have been better for the Indians had the Jesuits not come. Altamirano's comment is not the final word, however, since it is followed by the image of Indian children picking up the pieces of the ruined mission and the text from the Gospel of John. To suggest that the Indians would be better off without the missionaries is to suggest that the world would be better off without Christ, for Christ himself was martyred, as were the Apostles. Altamirano makes the same mistake in this comment as he does in carrying out the papal order to the missions. He assumes that the Church needs numbers and wise politics to succeed. What Bolt and Joffé argue is that the Church is perhaps at its weakest and most corrupt condition when this is its philosophy. The simple communal faith of the missionaries and Indians is the powerful faith that converts Mendoza and produces the "paradise on earth" that proves a stumbling block to the Portuguese and Spanish, who want the missionaries to cooperate with them in the way in which the Roman hierarchy in Europe has.

One of the visual motifs that characterise the development of the film's themes is the contrast between soft, idealised views of life in the mission and several chaotic scenes of life in "the world". Two scenes in particular develop this latter motif. The first is the scene of the festival which ends with Mendoza's knifing his brother. The pipe playing in the streets is heavily rhythmic and repetitive, a contrast to Father Gabriel's melodious playing which attracts the Guaraní. As Felipe and Carlotta, Mendoza's former mistress, walk through the crowd to an evening meeting place, Rodrigo follows and watches from a distance. Around him are whirling dancers and a frenzied crowd. As the scene turns to evening, the rhythms increase, and the glare of torches lends an eerie light to the sky. The camera constantly tracks in and out and around the crowd in an unsettling manner which forewarns of the imminent crime.

The second scene of chaotic movements is the massacre of San Carlos. In a graphic montage blending the fate of Gabriel, Mendoza and the other Jesuits, the rough fate of the missionaries, Indians and Indian children is played out in smoke, blood and the rushing water of the river and falls. An interesting shot in the sequence is the reaction of Mendoza after killing his first Portuguese soldier. The pain in his face is extreme, and leaves just sufficient doubt about the choice he makes to fight, rather than die passively like Gabriel. The music reflects the ambiguity of the question, alternating between the heroic theme that had previously been associated with the building of San Carlos, and the sadder and more threatening music associated with Mendoza's past life and the machinations of the Spanish and Portuguese. It is in the middle of this long sequence that Mendoza asks Gabriel for his blessing and instead receives the cross. Gabriel insists that God is love, not violence. Earlier, Mendoza asks Gabriel if he can renounce his vows of obedience and is told by Gabriel to get out of his tent; thus Gabriel renounces bloodshed in favour of the love of God. That brief scene is cross-cut immediately with a shot of Altamirano travelling by carriage with Hontar and Don Cabeza, a move which perhaps suggests that, while God is love, when the organised Church becomes corrupt He then exercises judgment. The martyrs are not judged, but Mendoza lifts the sword as an avenger from heaven. He dies because he is only a man, but vengeance will one day come when the avenger Christ of the Book of Revelation steps again into history.

The contrast between blissful harmony and chaotic brutality, like the clearly defined character types, further the Christian typology of *The Mission*. Light is light, darkness is darkness. The film polarizes good and evil, yet focuses on the difficult decisions that lay at the grey moral centre – and, of course, it is the role of the Church to choose the lighter side of the grey. It might be argued that both Gabriel and Mendoza do that, while Altamirano does not. Both priests choose life and display an unwavering determination to save the Guaraní. In the climax, they partake of a common communion under the host and with blood.

Yet, of the two priests, Gabriel leaves the greater impression, for he brings music into the community of Guaraní and allows them the means to flourish culturally. After Gabriel reaches the top of the falls, he walks through the jungle and stops to play his wooden flute. The beautiful melody which sounds through the hills initially attracts the Indians, who arrive with arrows and spears, and surround the priest threateningly. One of the older Guaraní takes the flute and breaks it, but a younger warrior picks it up and returns it to Gabriel to mend. Later, the Guaraní will find a way to repair the instrument. This gesture of gathering up the broken instrument provides another link to the end of the film, when the Guaraní children recover the broken violin from the river. Christianity has brought the Indians a higher quality of life than they had known, and that is what they are particularly interested in preserving. It is the sword which threatens that life, and so, in this sense, Gabriel has fulfilled the prophecy of having the nations beat their swords into ploughshares, whereas Mendoza produces the reverse. The first image of Gabriel in the film has him playing the violin with the young Indians of San Miguel. The suggestion might be that, in recovering the violin, the children recover the spirit of Gabriel. They do not recover guns or swords. Furthermore, what is most memorable in the film, after the startling cinematography and ironic ending, is the Ennio Morricone score which provides the kind of spiritual elevation for the listener which the Indians found in the music of Gabriel and in the music which they produced themselves.

The music signifies in part the spiritual and social freedom brought by the missionaries. Entrapment is one of the film's secondary themes used by Joffé to highlight the nobility of what the Indians become and the tragedy of the climax. Mendoza, while performing as a mercenary to line the pockets of Don Cabeza, captures Indians in a net hidden in some brush. That same net captures him metaphorically when, in his jealousy, he murders the brother whom he loves. When Gabriel visits Mendoza in the cell where he hopes to starve and die, the camera remains close to the men and lingers on the bars of the cells and the lone window in the stone wall where Mendoza sits. Mendoza's penance is, significantly, the carrying of the means of his sin in a net. Altamirano is likewise caught in a moral trap between the pressures of the Spanish and Portuguese and his obligations to the Pope on one side, and his sentiments towards Gabriel and the missions on the other. Mendoza escapes his trap when the Guaraní cut his burden free, but Altamirano cannot escape. The determinism suggested by his voice-over narration makes him a doomed character from the start.

The suggestion of this thematic pairing is that the sins of the self-righteous professional clergy are far greater than the worst sins of the flesh committed by the non-religious. This theme runs through the Gospels, particularly in parables such as that of the pharisee and the publican, and in Jesus's choice of disciples and followers. Both Bolt and Joffé criticise the Catholic hierarchy, yet they still praise the spirit of Christianity which Gabriel and the Guaraní embody.

Beyond Gabriel and Mendoza, the heroes of the film are the children whose very presence rebukes any rationale for the closing of the missions. There is no justification for the murder of children, but this is what the papacy, in league with Spain and Portugal, sanctions. The camera pays close attention to children's faces throughout the narrative, and, particularly during the massacre, records their terror and shock at the senseless violence. The small band of children who leave are the heroes, and here again is an echo of the Gospels – unless one becomes as a little child, Heaven will elude him.

The Mission is a parable about the failure of the organised Church to see its own mission, but, more importantly, it is a playing out of the old problem of how the follower of Christ is to respond to injustice. It is the playing out not only of the Passion of Christ, but also of the passion of the individual Christian torn by a world that does not make sense. The blood of the martyrs may be the seed of the Church, but it rarely seems so when that blood is being spilled. Yet, in the end, *The Mission* offers hope by inviting the viewer into the work among the Guaraní, and allowing vicarious involvement in the resistance against the spoilers of the work. Those who die, die for a purpose, and that purpose makes the experience of this film the same kind of celebration that characterises Christian sacramentalism.

Note

[1]   Michael Dempsey, "Light Shining in Darkness: Roland Joffe on *The Mission*", *Film Quarterly* 40: 4 (1987): 11.

Frank Borzage's *A Farewell to Arms* was made during the director's most productive years, in which he successfully produced for Paramount (1932), Columbia (1933-34), Universal (1933), Warner Bros./ First National (1934-37) and Metro-Goldwyn-Mayer (1937-42).[1] Many of the films of this period were anti-war or anti-Fascist productions, most notably *A Farewell to Arms*, *Three Comrades* (1938) and *The Mortal Storm* (1940). All these films posed war as destroyer of love and friendship on a human level, and as symbol of the world's hostility to the things of God on a spiritual level. Resolution in these films, as in Borzage's earlier classics, *Seventh Heaven* (1927) and *Street Angel* (1928), is achieved on a transcendent level, as characters recognise that their earthly hopes will be fulfilled in the new world to come.

Over Borzage's long career, firstly as an actor in the early days of silent cinema, and then as a director after his successful *Humoresque* (1920), he stayed with melodramatic subjects; yet, his films rarely devolve into rank sentimentality. Borzage consistently pushed his melodramas towards a higher plane, away from the maudlin towards a form of religious idealism that merged 19th century Victorian plots with the best elements of Catholic piety. This is particularly evident in his great period of 1933-32 when he directed *Secrets*, *Man's Castle* and *A Farewell to Arms*.

The melodramatic form tends to posit absolutes, "either/or" juxtapositions of good and evil, hope and despair, prosperity and poverty, age and youth. Like most popular forms, these absolutes tend to undercut the artistic value of such works, since the verisimilitude of such narratives is questionable. With Borzage's films, these absolutes maintain their integrity by virtue of their absorption into a transcendent religious framework in which characters find their own lives drifting away from the compromises of actual existence towards Christian ideals of love and holiness and immortality.

Borzage's stylistic tendencies seem totally out of place in the grim and hopeless world of Ernest Hemingway. Yet, in *A Farewell to Arms*, Borzage plays off the *angst* in the novel by making it the counterpoint of his own idealism. In a sense, he takes the Hemingway novel and offers a better version, one equally tragic but less pointless. Instead of Hemingway's indifferent rain and thick darkness, Borzage offers a sacramental rain and a muted darkness (a black backdrop to bright action). Hemingway's characters are desperate, Borzage's are focused; Hemingway's plot is ironic, Borzage's is redemptive.

Borzage's *A Farewell to Arms* is, nevertheless, reasonably faithful to the story of the Hemingway novel. Frederick Henry, an American medic serving with the Italian Red Cross in the First World War, falls in love with an English nurse, Catherine Barclay, who is being pursued by Frederick's closest friend, the surgeon, Rinaldi. When Frederick is wounded, Rinaldi arranges for him to stay in a hospital in Milan, where Catherine is serving. There the two, who have already consummated their love, are married by a compassionate priest. Frederick recovers and is sent back to the front; Catherine deserts her post and moves to Switzerland, sending Frederick letters and waiting until he is released from duty. The letters are intercepted by Rinaldi who is ignorant of the marriage and worried that Frederick is taking the relationship too seriously. Frederick decides to desert and return to Catherine, but he must first find her. In the meantime, the now-pregnant Catherine experiences complications. The baby is delivered stillborn and Catherine begins to die from haemorrhage. Frederick finds her after a long search and arrives at her deathbed only in time for the two to reconfirm their love, which they insist will last forever. She dies in his arms.

Five characters are fully defined in the Borzage film, each serving an important thematic function. Frederick and Catherine, the young lovers, find a meaning to life in their love and commitment to that love. He will desert the Army to find her in Switzerland. She will leave her job for him and for their unborn child, and live in poverty until he arrives. Whereas, in the Hemingway novel, their love provides the only meaning in the midst of the chaos of war, Borzage adds to this the element of transcendent beauty. Their love is beautiful and pure of itself. It wipes away the war and the lovers' scarred pasts. It lifts them to a heroic greatness and makes of Catherine's death a kind of martyrdom to holiness. Catherine dies not because the world denies meaning, but because the happiness that the lovers found must be left for Heaven and immortality.

Two characters stand in counterpoint to Frederick and Catherine: the surgeon Rinaldi, and Catherine's friend, the nurse Miss Fergusson. Rinaldi and Fergusson are both bitterly pessimistic. Rinaldi tells Frederick in response to the news of his love for Catherine: "Sacred subjects are not good for soldiers. Why don't you be like me – all fire and smoke and nothing inside." Rinaldi has a scientific view of life. He tells Frederick of an operation where he held a patient's still-beating heart in his hand; in a way, he holds Frederick's heart in his hand since he becomes the barrier to communication between the lovers upon Frederick's assignment to the front and Catherine's move to Switzerland. Rinaldi despises Frederick's feeling for Catherine, in part due to jealousy, since he wanted her first, but more from a sense of doom, recognising that the war could not tolerate this depth of human commitment and happiness. It would be better prevented. Fergusson, like Rinaldi, assumes that tragedy will inevitably destroy Frederick and Catherine. She warns Catherine that the two will either "fight or die", and refuses to tell Frederick that Catherine has gone to Switzerland. She lacks Catherine's moral and spiritual courage, and so hides behind a cloak of sarcasm and feigned concern.

The fifth character who stands out from the narrative is the priest who marries the lovers and offers his blessing to Frederick when he deserts. Of all the main characters, he fully understands both the hope of the lovers and the despair of Rinaldi and Fergusson. In the narrative, he represents not only the Church, but also divine wisdom, compassion and love. He will not encourage the lovers in their desperate course, understanding its implications, but he will also not give in to bitterness. He offers the sacrament, he prays, he blesses. Easily a potential stock character, the priest develops a presence that looms over the film and makes Borzage's ending both complete and believable.

One more "character" might be examined here – the war itself. The war blankets and litters the screen, from the opening image of a soldier dead on a quiet hillside to the concluding images of bells announcing the Armistice. The war is the villain in the melodrama which swallows up the minor characters, and leads the lovers to their heroic conclusion. Once Frederick and Catherine affirm their love in the face of death and thus prove its invincibility, the church bells ring, signalling the defeat of war. Significantly, one of the concluding images of the film is a dissolve from the bells to a shot of placards on a wall reading "Armistice Declared". The announcements do not indicate the defeat of the Germans or the victory of the Allies; rather, they announce the defeat of war itself, for the film has not posited side vs. side in the conflict, but people vs. violence and chaos.

What the war represents for the people involved is a distortion of hopes and values, and Borzage plays this theme throughout the narrative. At the start of the film, the distortion is part of Frederick's attitudes. He shows indifference to men dying in his ambulance, callousness to women he meets in the hospital, and drunkenness. By the end of the narrative, he is freed from all three. While he sits at a table in a café waiting for news about Catherine, he prays for her health. Earlier, he had mocked the indifference of God, indicating with blandness that his injury by a shell occurred while he was "eating cheese". Rinaldi is likewise freed from his distorted view of love, as he finally sends Frederick off by boat to Switzerland to meet Catherine, and so reconciles with him and offers his own defiance to the war.

Borzage projects a series of distorted images throughout the film to reinforce this aspect of the theme. Interior shots are slightly cramped and dissected by odd visual lines and angles. Subjective camerawork suggests the altered vision of both Frederick and Catherine as they are wheeled through halls on hospital beds. Borzage's camera maintains this visual subjectivity. Frequent use of Expressionistic devices – dissolves, high and low contrast lighting, skewed angles, subjective camera position – distorts any attempt at viewer objectivity, and forces certain sympathies. Frederick and Catherine are shot through filters and lit from above in romantic scenes, a common technique in melodrama yet given a religious context here. The war is always pictured in darkness, particularly in the long sequence of Frederick's journey to find Catherine. The camera closes in on the anguished expressions of both Catherine and Frederick in moments of tension, such as Catherine's viewing of Frederick's departure to the front, or Frederick's anxiety over the absence of Catherine's letters. These intimacies are juxtaposed with more distanced and practical shots of Rinaldi and other soldiers and nurses, with the notable exception of shots of the sympathetic priest who marries the lovers and helps Frederick to desert.

The most striking stylistic feature is the remarkable montage of Frederick's journey from the Italian front to Milan in search of Catherine. Since this sequence symbolises the overall conflict between the lovers and the war, Borzage places great emphasis on it – to the point of making it a visual apostrophe within the narrative, reminiscent of dance sequences within musicals. The dominant features of the montage are the incessant movement of Frederick, both alone and marching with troops and evacuated villagers against a background of darkness and rain. Punctuating the movement are expressive images of suffering and death. A bandaged soldier stands in a slanted doorway, behind which is a large Red Cross symbol, and stretches his arms out to appear as Christ. A graveyard of hundreds of crosses lingers on the screen. Telephone and electrical poles cast a shadowed 'T' over a wartorn landscape. Soldiers march relentlessly forward. Frederick avoids them, falls to avoid exploding bombs, leaps into a river amidst gunfire. The complete procession places Frederick in the position alternately of both the suffering Christ and the persecuted Church. Most of the images are highly Expressionistic, thus suggesting the psychological dysfunction produced by the war. Frederick journeys as Everyman on a pilgrimage through the valley of the shadow of death.[2]

The rain which falls continually throughout the narrative symbolises a distortion of nature in response to the tragedy of war, a distortion with immediate impact on the relation of the lovers. The rain falls at the train station as Frederick leaves to return to the front; it falls throughout his journey to Switzerland; and it falls as he waits at the hospital for word of Catherine's condition. Catherine says, "I hate the rain...I'm afraid of the rain", for in it she sees her own death foreshadowed. A complementary device to this rain is the sound of the exploding bombs which punctuate the narrative. The opening musical theme of the film is interspersed with the sound of bombs dropping, and the bombs continue to fall in the background of most of the exterior background scenes, particularly during the montage sequence. Both symbols find their conclusion in the final scene: the rain overwhelmed by the sunlight slanting through the window of Catherine's death room, and the bombs replaced by church bells.

All the film's visual and audial symbols culminate in the work's final shots, as Frederick lifts Catherine, lit by the morning light, to the open window. The camera reveals this from behind and the gesture becomes a handing over of her body and their love to God. Had the shot been taken from the front, the effect would have been quite different, a lingering on Frederick's loss. This submissive religious gesture is confirmed with a cut to the bells ringing for Armistice, and another cut to the flying doves. Frederick's words of "Peace, peace" with "Liebestraum" playing in the background mix with these final impressions to make it clear that Catherine's death is a release of soul and a freeing of the lovers' devotion, rather than a destruction.[3]

This final scene marks the incarnational moment of the film. The bells which ring for the Armistice suggest the Church's benediction, as it did earlier when the priest married the two lovers in the hospital room. The flying doves relate to the flight of both Catherine and Frederick from the war, as well as to Catherine's release to immortality. It is significant that the rain has suddenly stopped and that trees are visible through Catherine's previously black hospital room window. These overt extra-narrative cues, together with the Wagnerian music, are metonymic for the sacramental nature of Catherine's death and Frederick's devotion. Through the love of the two and the blessing of the Church, death has been swallowed up. The melodrama does not invite pity; rather, it encourages faith and devotion.

In this scheme, Frederick has become Christ-like in his pilgrimage away from the war through the valley of death to the bedside of his bride. Catherine has been washed clean by his love, as has the Church by Christ's love. As she lies in the hospital bed after her surgery, she is encased in white with a nun-like covering over her head. "I'll never stop loving you", Frederick tells Catherine in the last scene, "in life and death we will never be parted". "I believe it", she replies. These Christian allusions to redemptive faith and divine love are further advanced when Frederick lifts Catherine's dead body to the sunlit window, and the image cuts to the bells ringing and doves rising in the sky. As the background music reaches a crescendo, Frederick utters the words "Peace, peace". As St Paul writes, "Therefore being justified by faith, we have peace with God" (Romans 5: 1).

The Christian pattern, once fixed in these last moments, reverberates to other scenes. Just prior to the deathbed sequence, Frederick is eating breakfast in a restaurant. It is literally a last supper, and the antithesis of the meal of wine and bread which he ate when injured earlier by a mortar blast. When it is announced that the war has ended and all the patrons cheer, Frederick, isolated at a corner table, is immobile. The camera moves in to a close-up of his distant expression, and he prays, "Oh God, don't let her die". We assume from the victorious symbols of the last shots that the prayer has been answered in the deepest sense.

The figure of the priest also takes on added significance in retrospect. The priest appears in three key sequences. The first appearance follows Frederick's second meeting with Catherine during an air raid, and immediately precedes the scene of Frederick and Catherine making love in a garden. In a hazy, romanticised composition, the priest is surrounded by medics who mock him, saying that he should not be worried by the bombing because "What is death to a Christian?". The scene has no narrative function except to set the place for the meeting of Frederick and Rinaldi, wherein they make arrangements for their night of pleasure with the nurses – Miss Barclay for Rinaldi and another nurse for Frederick. The centring of it simply states the motif which builds towards Catherine's death – the Christian's redemptive displacement from the world.

The second appearance of the priest is in the hospital room in Milan where Catherine is tending the recuperating Frederick. The priest enters with some useful items for Frederick: mosquito netting, papers and vermouth. In the ensuing conversation, he picks up the true nature of the lovers' relationship from Frederick's mention of children. At this, he pauses and steps aside, the camera again centring him and surrounding him with a romantic haze as he quietly prays the marriage rites in front of a crucifix. A cut back to Catherine and Frederick reveals their understanding of the situation. They awkwardly straighten themselves and clasp hands. Frederick tells Catherine that he regrets the lack of orange blossoms and organ music. She replies: "I can smell them...I can hear it plainly". Here again, the scene is motivated not by plot, but by theme. The realities of the situation are silent and unseen, driven below the narrative surface by the war, a symbol of a hostile world.

The final appearance of the priest follows the same pattern. He is the friend that Frederick entrusts with the news of his desertion. The setting is a dark exterior of the medical camp, with vehicles and soldiers passing ominously in the background. The two are shot in heavy shadow, although light reveals Frederick's face more clearly. The priest hesitantly agrees to Frederick's request that his disappearance is not told until the morning, and that his friends are bid goodbye. Again, the significance of the scene resides in its thematic placement, for the episode triggers the lyrical sequence of Frederick's journey to Catherine. His desertion, when associated with the presence of the priest and the ensuing montage, is forcefully recontextualized as a Christian pilgrimage. He has renounced not the war, but the world, and for a love that has been marked as divinely favoured.

Borzage's smoothly edited, highly filtered images tip viewers off throughout *A Farewell to Arms* that the bleak context of war, with its distortions, corruptions and casualties, will be softened and overwhelmed. The melodramatic romantic score of the film, as well as its handling, likewise contradicts the pain suggested by the narrative. In an early scene, Frederick is in a bar holding a woman's foot and commenting on the beauty of her foot and leg, which are also seen onscreen. After a bombing and the ensuing chaos, Frederick finds himself in a shelter with another woman's foot in his hand: it is Catherine's. The pattern is thus established from callousness to love, from meaninglessness to meaningfulness. Death is swallowed up in victory.

Borzage's camera perfumes the narrative with a compassionate voice which suggests hope and redemption. When Catherine writes her first letter to Frederick from her Swiss apartment, she describes the room in glowing terms, but with each detail the camera sweeps slowly around her to reveal the squalor. The scene is rife with melodrama, but then, as if in response to this audience perception, Catherine speaks to Frederick from afar and tells him of her loneliness and the ugliness of her lodgings. With this twist the scene loses it artificiality and becomes poignant, the compassionate camera again regaining its force, a force which it maintains throughout the film. Each time the soft lens and evocative score drift towards sentiment, Borzage recalls the viewer with a visual or narrative *tour de force* that re-establishes the credibility of the narration – from the early battlefield scenes to the subjective shots of Frederick in the hospital, the lyrical montage of Frederick's journey, and the soft dissolves of the concluding montage after Catherine's death.

Central to the Borzage version of *A Farewell to Arms* is the marriage between Frederick and Catherine. The marriage legitimises their love affair and allows for the religious significance of Catherine's transcendence of death at the end. Idealised love in a traditional Christian sense serves as a metaphor for the love between God and His bride, the Church. The Catholic dogma of the sacramental nature of marriage and the absolute necessity for fidelity (and fertility) grow out of this Pauline understanding. To discover true love and to adhere to it through faithfulness to the sacramental institution are to play out a divine pattern, and thus to unite oneself with the means of grace for salvation.

This sacramental marriage is perhaps the bottom line of Borzage's film. The film celebrates marriage for itself and for its implications as a means of grace, a manner in which the divine love may be better grasped and experienced. When Frederick carries Catherine to the window and the doves ascend, she is made a peace offering, with Frederick's reluctant acknowledgement that the union formed between the lovers must be subordinate to the union of Christ and his people.

Notes

[1] For a comprehensive study of Borzage's film career, see Frederick Lamster, *Souls Made Great Through Love and Adversity: The Film Work of Frank Borzage* (Metuchen, NJ; London: The Scarecrow Press, 1981).

[2] See John Belton, *The Hollywood Professionals: Howard Hawks, Frank Borzage, Edgar G. Ulmer*, volume 3 (London: The Tantivy Press, 1974): 89ff. Belton elaborates at length on the stylistic significance of this scene.

[3] An interesting side-note is that Borzage had created an alternate ending to the film, in which Catherine remains alive, Frederick announcing "Armistice", and she whispering "Peace". It was rightly rejected for too greatly altering the Hemingway original, although the more severe problem was its sophomorism. The symbolism of the circulated ending is sufficiently obvious.

Jésus de Montréal (Jesus of Montreal) is the first film so far approached in this study which presents a theology that many traditional Christians would find unorthodox and unacceptable. Denys Arcand's parable against modern commercialism portrays Christ as an inspiring man in the fashion of 20th-century theological liberalism, whose message of peace and compassion was mythologized by his disciples into the prophetic Word of the Son of God.

The film did not receive any significant criticism for this unorthodoxy either in Canada, where the film originated, or in the United States, unlike Scorsese's *The Last Temptation of Christ* (1989) or Godard's *Je vous salue, Marie (Hail, Mary,* 1984). It did not play much or receive particularly favourable reviews in the United States. Therefore, perhaps the apathy shown to Arcand's portrayal by the American public, at least, is a reflection of the composition of the audience that did view the film. However, *Jesus of Montreal* did extraordinarily well in Canada, particularly in Toronto, upon its release, and therefore a better explanation of the public reaction might be that the film is firstly and primarily a modern-day parable before it is a literal statement about Christ's person.

Arcand received inspiration for *Jesus of Montreal* from an incident that occurred during the filming of his first major commercial success, *Le Déclin de l'empire américain (The Decline of the American Empire,* 1986). One of the actors in the film had played Jesus in a passion-play at the Oratoire St-Joseph in Montreal. The oddity of such a role suggested to Arcand a film about a gathering of skilled actors who decide to rewrite and reproduce a minor performance of Christ's life, basically the story line of *Jesus of Montreal.*[1] The unorthodox picture of the life of Christ derives primarily from Arcand's own religious scepticism, fed by his studies of history at the Université de Montréal. The film's attack on commercialism takes its substance from Arcand's extensive work producing advertisements for Canadian Television before his filmmaking career succeeded.

The film begins with a play within a play. A young actor playing a remorseful murderer in a church drama laments his inability to receive forgiveness, and hangs himself. When the performance ends, he is praised by critics but gives way to an actor who has just arrived at the set, Daniel Coulombe (Lothaire Bluteau), whom he describes as a "real" actor. Coulombe is asked by the parish priest, Father Leclerc (Gilles Pelletier), to modernise and direct a passion-play performed annually for the last 35 years at a Montreal shrine. The traditional play is orthodox, but dry and uncompelling; in fact, almost comic in its artificiality.

Coulombe gathers four actors to work with him, all of whom are in less than ideal jobs while waiting for an acting break: Mireille (Catherine Wilkening), who makes sexually suggestive commercials for her director boyfriend, Jerzy; Constance (Johanne-Marie Tremblay), who is helping with a soup kitchen (and sleeping with Father Leclerc); Martin (Rémy Girard), who is dubbing voices for pornographic films; and René (Robert Lepage), who is narrating a star show at a local planetarium. The four rally around Coulombe, whose talent they obviously admire, and begin to prepare for the work.

The rewritten play becomes a great success upon its first showing because of its immediacy with the audience that gathers on the grounds of the shrine to watch. Following the traditional stations of the cross, the actors provide an history which paints a picture of a much-modernised Christ (supposedly drawn from new archaeological findings and textual research), who wanted to rally the Jews by proclaiming tolerance and love. The players interact with the audience and suggest numerous obvious examples of how the story can be interpreted in a contemporary setting. Particularly effective in the play is Coulombe's own portrayal of Jesus, culminating in a re-enactment of the Crucifixion.

Despite the play's popularity, Father Leclerc tells Coulombe that the Church hierarchy demands that it be restored to a more orthodox version. This conflict leads to the players' rejection of Leclerc's authority, and their insistence that they will not change, but perform the play one final time. Police come during the performance and, in an ensuing scuffle with the crowd of patrons, Coulombe is knocked over while on the cross as Christ. He is rushed to a Catholic hospital which proves to be overcrowded, but, while waiting there with Mireille and Constance, he is temporarily revived and released.

The climax of the film occurs as the injured Coulombe staggers through a subway station prophesying and warning the waiting people of the coming signs of God's judgment. Mireille and Constance look on helplessly as Coulombe exhorts patron after patron until he finally collapses. He is taken to a Jewish hospital, but dies on the operating table. The doctor requests his body for organ donations and is given permission to use it. In the concluding scenes, a heart patient recovers with Coulombe's heart, and a sightless woman receives his eyes.

The most obvious story elements of *Jesus of Montreal* are the many Biblical allusions and parallels. Most of these centre around Daniel Coulombe as Christ and the Gospel accounts of the Passion. By the film's conclusion, these suggestions become incarnational truth, as Coulombe is transformed into a character larger than the film itself, much like Johannes in Dreyer's *Ordet* (*The Word*, 1955).

When Coulombe first arrives in town, he has no home and no notoriety, although the young actor playing the murderer at the start hails him, as John the Baptist hailed Christ, as one truly worthy of the title of actor. It is known that Coulombe excelled at the conservatory, but he is never given a distinctive past in the film; thus, like Christ, Coulombe mystifies his critics by his sudden emergence as so powerful an acting presence.

After receiving a commission from a Father (albeit a poor model for God Himself), Coulombe gathers a small band of disciples, taking them from humble and, in this case, somewhat compromising vocations. Mireille becomes a reflection of Mary Magdalene, with her commercial modelling being a form of prostitution. The play becomes the vehicle of Coulombe's ministry, in which he both preaches and dies on the cross. After the success of the play he is tempted by a lawyer/agent, who praises him and tells Coulombe that the entire city of Montreal is his for the taking, an echo of the temptation in the wilderness. When he attends an audition with Mireille, he is incensed by the contemptuous exploitation of the actors by the talent agents, and turns over tables and lights in a variation on the cleansing of the temple. Coulombe's actual death is caused by a combination force of Pharisees (Father Leclerc), the police, and a mob of spectators. His prophecies in the subway station become part of the Passion. After his death, the use of his heart and eyes – significantly chosen organs – is his resurrection.

These obvious Biblical allusions are reinforced in the narrative by numerous subtler ones. While the actor who plays the young murderer in the first play is taking his bows, the female advertising executive who will later incur Coulombe's wrath at Mireille's audition whispers to a companion, "I want his head" – for an advertising campaign called "L'homme sauvage" ("Savage Man"). This reference to John the Baptist reinforces the actor's acknowledgement that Coulombe is a real actor. In a similar reference later in the film, Mireille says "Behold the Son of God" as Coulombe approaches the shrine for a performance. Before the last performance, the directors get together and share a meal during which Mireille confesses that the group has saved her from a meaningless life. When Coulombe is carried by ambulance to the hospital, the two women alone accompany him, a reflection of the women who were at the cross and at the tomb.

The symbolism is reinforced by Daniel Coulombe's strong Christ-like qualities. He has a mysterious past. He commands complete trust from his friends. He is gentle with children and tolerant (especially when discovering Father Leclerc sleeping with Constance). He draws unqualified devotion, particularly from the women who follow him – Mireille, who falls in love with him, and Constance. When on the witness stand for destruction of property and assault (for whipping the advertising executive across the face with an electrical cord), he refuses to defend himself or seek legal aid. He is without guile and simply spoken in conversation. When in the role of Christ in the play, or when transformed after his concussion, his words have conviction and power.

These narrative allusions find reinforcement in three predictable stylistic motifs that accompany them. The first is heavy use of day/night contrasts to suggest spiritual condition; the second is a related heavy use of white vs. black colour schemes; and the third is the repeated use of height to suggest transcendence, and depth to suggest moral decline.

The performances of the passion-play as well as the initial play at the shrine all take place at night, as does Coulombe's personal passion and death. René's star show at the planetarium likewise occurs at night. All the exterior scenes occur during the day. Thus, night paradoxically becomes the cloak which reveals truth in the film narrative, rather than that which hides it. This irony applies as much to the star show as to the passion-play, for the text of the star show suggests man's inconsequentiality in a cold, impersonal universe. The passion-play is the answer to this modern despair. During the passion-play, René recites Hamlet's "To be or not to be" soliloquy, and thus echoes the despair he proclaimed earlier at the planetarium: however, his soliloquy is answered by the suggestion of Christ's Resurrection in the performance at the shrine. The salvation within all people that the players suggest – the core of Christ's message as presented by Arcand – brings hope that assuages modern fear. The power of the passion-play is largely its immediacy in addressing the needs of the modern audience. In several scenes, members of the audience of the play are visibly shaken by the relevance of the performance; in one, a young woman from the audience runs to Coulombe and says, "Jesus, forgive me". She has to be restrained, and the narrative point is established.

The white vs. black motif is most often associated with Coulombe and Mireille. Coulombe dresses in casual white clothes throughout the narrative. The only exception is when he is naked on the cross in the play, and naked in a bathtub conversing with Mireille in another scene. Mireille first appears scantily dressed in a flowing white garment in a perfume commercial. When she leaves her director/boyfriend, Jerzy, to join the actors, the apartment backdrop is strikingly furnished with white, modern furniture. The white is enforced around Coulombe and Mireille by their dark hair and eyebrows and light complexions. The shrine where the play is performed is likewise mostly white by day. This motif is employed more traditionally than the day/night motif. Beyond the symbolism, it gives the film a neat visual balance and thematic symmetry.

The height/depth motif is more complex. The shrine is located on a hill, presumably on the outskirts of Montreal, and so extensive daytime scenes often foreground the actors with an expansive view of the city stretched as a backdrop. Constance's flat, where the actors gather, is a loft. The legal court is on a top floor of a skyscraper, and so when the lawyer-promoter suggested by Mireille talks to Coulombe outside the courtroom, they have as a backdrop the Montreal skyline as seen through large observation windows. Other scenes similarly emphasise height. Mireille flees Jerzy and gathers her things in an upper level of his apartment, looking down on him. The entrance to the shrine requires the climbing of stairs at the top of which is a statue of Christ. In an early scene when Coulombe struggles to uncover the historical Christ for the play, he stands at the base of the stairs looking up (the camera looks down upon him). He then slowly climbs the stairs and pauses in thought at the side of the statue looking up. Similarly, the passion of Coulombe after the incident takes him, Constance and Mireille down a flight of stairs, then down an escalator to a subway platform. The camera's concluding image is of the same platform seen from a great height.

Here again, the primary suggestions of this motif are easily recognisable; yet, Arcand plays with them in interesting ways as the narrative concludes. Coulombe's ascent to Christ, which should not be seen as a descent into madness, is triggered by a fall from the cross, descent from the shrine to the city, and then to the bowels of the city in the subway tunnel. This movement into death and the grave elevates the narrative to another level of suggestiveness, for the audience recognises that the steady transformation of Coulombe into Christ has become complete. In the subway he "preaches to the souls in prison" before collapsing with arms partly outspread before a large poster of "L'homme sauvage" ("Savage Man"), an advertisement featuring the actor from the first scene of the film. The narrative is therefore elevated by the incarnation of Coulombe, and the audience is elevated also above the superficiality of contemporary life suggested by the poster. This concluding scene in the subway tunnel is interestingly foreshadowed by an earlier scene in a tunnel at the shrine, in which

Father Leclerc tells Coulombe that he cannot take responsibility for the changes in the original play and must notify his superiors. This sell-out is on a par with that of the young actor who ends up on the poster. (When Coulombe first sees the poster, he vomits into a rubbish bin.)

This pairing, suggested by the concluding scene in the subway tunnel, identifies the two antagonists in the film: commercialism and religious hypocrisy. The police, who stand as the Romans in the allegory, also take some subtle criticism for their rigidity and lack of sympathy with the significance of the events they encounter. The "Savage Man" poster, which embodies all that is wrong with commercialism in its cheapening of talent into a kind of soft pornography, finds a match in an interesting cross-cut of Father Leclerc immediately after the scene of Coulombe's death. Leclerc looks at the empty props from the abandoned play through a dark, rain-splattered window-pane at night, with rain beating against the pane, his expression movingly conveying his own spiritual complicity with what is by this time recognised as the murder of Christ.

The attack on commercialism waged in the film is framed by the young actor whose corruption culminates in his image on the "Savage Man" poster. He is the antithesis of Coulombe and his players, who either leave exploitive positions or, in Coulombe's case, openly attack them. Like Father Leclerc – who has prostituted his calling by his liaison with Constance, and refused to choose either her or a chaste life, and whose lack of moral courage leads him to wash his hands of the contents of the play which he intellectually affirms – the young actor is drawn to Coulombe and yet lacks the fibre to resist the temptation of money and exposure offered to him by the advertising agent. When he sees the passion-play, he is troubled by it and angered, but his inner turmoil leads only to a remorse like that of Judas, not to a repentance. In allowing his face to be prostituted, he metaphorically hangs himself spiritually, causing Coulombe's nausea in the climax and thus becoming the player he portrayed in the opening scene.

This movement from the realistic narrative into the internal fiction, the play, mimics what has happened to Coulombe. He has gone into the fiction of the passion-play and become Christ, and then has been incarnated again as Christ outside. The mythologizing of reality suggested here is not unlike that of the liberal theologies which Arcand evokes. Karl Barth, Rudolf Bultmann, Paul Tillich[2] and other influential modern theologians have suggested that Jesus became the myth longed for by his followers, and ultimately created by his closest disciples and their followers. The process of salvation, the concept of being born again, is a private incarnation of the Christ myth. The film thus puts forward a Christianity which suggests an incarnation within a myth.

This is the reverse of the traditional teaching summed up by, for example, C S Lewis, who argued that Christianity was true myth[3] – that is, the language and iconography of myth made real in history by God.

While this modernism is bothersome to those who follow the faith "once passed down", Arcand manages to steer his film away from potential controversy by aiming his primary arrows at commercialism and the corruption of human dignity it inevitably entails, a message which even the most conservative viewers have to acknowledge. *Jesus of Montreal* is itself a myth which uses the symbols and narrative patterns of Christianity to make a statement about artistic integrity and self-respect. In this regard, the film resembles Gabriel Axel's *Babettes gæstebud* (*Babette's Feast*, 1987), a religious parable about a secular subject: artistic integrity.

The images that linger in *Jesus of Montreal* are finally symbolic, of both bad and good art. Beginning with the opening play, the film unfolds as a succession of fictions: Mireille's commercial; Martin's voice-dubbing; René's planetarium narrative; Father Leclerc's hypocrisy; the original passion-play and Coulombe's remake; the improvisational play of the actors; the horrific beer commercial that Coulombe breaks up; the various faces put on by the critics who respond to the performances; the courtroom procedure that Coulombe is thrust into; and the poster image. These bad fictions grow worse as the narrative unfolds. Whereas Martin's voice-dubbing is humorous, the beer commercial is vicious. Arcand's commercial Satan pulls the soul out of his victims and leaves nothing but a flat image of humanity promoting a corrupted sexuality. The lyrics of the beer ad include "nothing is sacred to you but a good glass of brew", "we worship beer" and "you'ld do anything to share my Appalache beer". When the young actress in the performance tells the advertising agent that she could sing the lyrics herself rather than lip-synch them, she is told that her worth is in her bikini – the same response which Jerzy directed to Mireille earlier, and which ultimately triggers Coulombe's rage.

The good fictions surround Coulombe and culminate in his incarnation on the subway platform. It is significant that, on the platform, Coulombe speaks part of the apocalyptic warning of Matthew 24:

> So when you see standing in the holy place the abomination that causes desolation...then let those who are in Judea flee to the mountains. Let no one on the roof of his house go down to take anything out of the house. Let no one in the field go back to get his cloak. How dreadful it will be in those days for pregnant women and nursing mothers! Pray that your flight will

not take place in winter or on the Sabbath. In them there will be great distress...At that time if anyone says to you, 'Look here is the Christ!' or, 'There he is!' do not believe it. (Matthew 24: 15-24)

The full incarnation of Coulombe culminates more in this warning, finally, about the corruption of the culture and end of the world, than in the salvation that comes with his transplanted heart and eyes, which is more a postscript to the story than a climax. Arcand leaves little doubt that his main concern is for pure art in an impure age, and this message, driven home so profoundly in the final play in the subway, overwhelms the theological suggestions he makes along the way.

The film's sacramental mechanics follow this artistic theme. Three times in the film Arcand punctuates the narrative with a suggestive montage of the Montreal night sky overlaid with a synthesizer musical track. The first occurs after a communal meal between Coulombe and his four actors after they have all agreed to go forward with the play and thus turn their backs on their corrupted artistic pasts. The second occurs after Father Leclerc has challenged Coulombe about the play's unorthodox suggestions about Jesus's origins. A sullen Coulombe walks away from the shrine with the four actors, and is then cheered by Constance who says that they need to be happy that night, implying that they need to embrace the immediacy of their triumph as artists. A similar montage punctuates this moment of artistic integrity and communal fellowship. The last such montage occurs after Coulombe's death. The lawyer is trying to convince the four remaining actors to allow him to orchestrate the founding of a theatre group in Coulombe's honour. Mireille excuses herself and walks alone outside, again at night and again overlooking the city, a gesture which suggests her resistance to the commercial temptation of the lawyer (who earlier had told Coulombe that the city could be his if he wanted it). This act of artistic conviction and insight leads to the final skyline montage. The beautiful and evocative sequence of shots marks a contrast with the many fictions within the film. It is a seamless natural art that God has created, and, in a sense, the Gospel that the film finally pronounces.

Another noticeable formalistic intrusion in the narrative occurs as Constance, Mireille and Coulombe descend the stairs and escalator to the subway tunnel. As they descend, the camera lens is filtered and the light diffused around the three characters. Coulombe is positioned below the two women looking up, and so we see him from behind, as it were protecting the women from the descent down into the bowels of the city. The synthesizer score associated with the skyline shots carries through the full action of the scene, making it the culminating address to the film audience, the sacramental moment.

Finally, Arcand introduces and retreats from the incarnated Jesus of Montreal, Coulombe, by way of a sacred duet sung by two young women, firstly in the church where Coulombe originally meets Father Leclerc, and then in the subway tunnel after Coulombe's death. The first appearance of the women singing, a suggestion of the angelic heralds which greeted Christ's birth and resurrection, is worked into the narrative as a transitional device introducing the opening credits of the film, as well as the shift into the church where the narrative will be triggered. The final appearance is more interesting because the women's duet on the subway platform is unmotivated by the narrative. The duet introduces the final credits and adds to the considerable symmetry of the film, and also continues the sacramental movement begun with Coulombe's descent down the escalator. (In fact, the dynamics of the film editing and visual composition dramatically change for the last ten minutes of the action.) The art elevated or redeemed by Coulombe is thus perpetuated metaphorically through the presence of these singing angels, and the film is granted a grand conclusion, which one expects in this sacramental modality.

While an unlikely film for a study of how Christian liturgics have impacted the style of many religious vehicles, *Jesus of Montreal* proves both the versatility and predictability of the sacramental form. Arcand's film recontextualizes the Gospel and redefines Christ in a somewhat idiosyncratic manner, yet still carries the viewer towards a climactic embrace with incarnate divinity, this time not the God who washes sinners, but the God who inspires beauty and who walks in truth, and has the integrity of a character without guile. Arcand's *Jesus of Montreal* is a film of remarkable continuity and complexity, and it offers a conclusion with great visual and emotional force.

Notes

[1] Robert Sklar, "Of Warm and Sunny Tragedies: An Interview with Denys Arcand", *Cineaste* 18: 1 (1990): 14-16.

[2] A good exposition of this strain of modern Biblical criticism can be found in Rudolf Bultmann, *Jesus Christ and Mythology* (New York: Scribners, 1958). For an orthodox response, see George Eldon Ladd, *A Theology of the New Testament* (Grand Rapids, MI: Eerdmans, 1974).

[3] See, for example, C S Lewis, *Miracles: A Preliminary Study* (New York: Macmillan, 1947): especially 132-142.

In this examination of how the Passion finds its way into a wide range of sacramental films, Gabriel Axel's *Babettes gæstebud* (*Babette's Feast*) presents an irresistible subject for discussion. Although one would be hard-pressed to find in the film overt references to the Passion of Christ, Babette, the heroic artist of the film, certainly plays out a passion by sacrificing herself to redeem her community from despair and dissolution, and she does so through the highly improbable yet symbolically apt medium of a communal meal.

It is the connection between a fellowship meal and the redemption of the community which makes *Babette's Feast* a logical choice for inclusion here, since the Eucharistic celebration is the consummate act of the Christian redemption pageant played out daily by the Church throughout the centuries. In films such as Bresson's *Journal d'un curé de campagne* (*Diary of a Country Priest*, 1950), Beresford's *Black Robe* (1991) and Borzage's *A Farewell to Arms* (1932), the spectator/viewer is offered the communal meal of the central character's sacrifice through the metaphor of film spectatorship, while in *Babette's Feast* the viewer participates in the meal immediately or vicariously – through a window in the back of the church, as it were. Therefore, beyond its appealing content, Axel's film provides a good opportunity to consider the intended impact of the communion celebration on members of the Christian community.

All this is not to suggest that *Babette's Feast* is designed exclusively as religious allegory. The film primarily explores the power of art to uplift or redeem, for the cook, Babette, around whom the story pivots, is a self-proclaimed artist and a great one. She is not a saint. In fact, as she herself declares, her great feast is performed largely for herself, for the artist fulfils a personal need, which only as a by-product satisfies a community's longing. However, the story is set in a strictly religious context, and, in developing the theme of artistic efficiency, it enlaces together clearly defined Christian motifs. The art which Babette performs is the liturgical presentation of an incarnation – food which carries not only a spiritual allusion, but also a spiritual presence. It conveys grace by its very nature.

The success of *Babette's Feast* in the international market, particularly in the United States (it received an Academy Award® for best foreign film of 1987), suggests the universality of the theme which Axel tapped. Like Robert Zemeckis's 1994 success, *Forrest Gump*, *Babette's Feast* has an appeal that derives from more than technical merit and fine storytelling. It is at heart a peculiarly religious film, which has resonance for all who are drawn towards spiritual or aesthetic ideals. Axel's film has a poignancy and a power which are infectious.

The story used by Axel is one of Isak Dinesen's most successful, perhaps that by which she is most known after *Out of Africa* (1938). It originated in intriguing fashion. Dinesen had spent an extravagant Venetian holiday with friends in 1949, and came back out of money. She decided to try her hand publishing in the lucrative American market, and a friend, Geoffrey Gorer, made a bet that she would not be able to get published in the popular *Saturday Evening Post*. Dinesen thought she could if she could just understand the American reading market. Gorer told her: "Write about food. Americans are obsessed with food." So Dinesen wrote "Babette's Feast", which the *Post* rejected. Fortunately, the *Ladies' Home Journal* picked it up in 1950. She eventually incorporated it into the collection, *Anecdotes of Destiny*, published in 1953.[1]

Axel adapted the Dinesen tale accurately, with only a few modifications. The location was changed from Norway to the Jutland coast in the director's native Denmark. This allowed him to change the look of the story's village from Dinesen's "grey, yellow, pink and other colours" to a drab whitish-grey suitable to convey the austerity of the inhabitants, particularly in contrast with Babette herself. The characters of Babette and the General Lorens Löwenhielm are also subtly altered. Babette, as played by the graceful Stéphane Audran, has more warmth and soulfulness in Axel's adaptation than the more hard-edged and stoical character has in the original. This particularly comes out in the film's conclusion, but is also suggested in the drawing of character. Babette arrives in the village of Axel's film with no background, except that she has lost her husband and son in the Paris Uprising. Dinesen has Babette reveal in the story that she was a Communard in the 1871 Paris Uprising, who supplied arms to those on the barricade where her husband and son died. The absence of these details in the film depoliticises Babette's character, making her a more universal type for innocent suffering. Likewise, the General Lorens Löwenhielm is made more a melancholic romantic in the film than he appears in the Dinesen story. This adds more impact to his reflective words at the film's conclusion.

The story centres on Babette, but is more principally about two sisters, Martine and Filippa, who are the repressed yet dutiful daughters of a strict pietist father who has founded and maintained a small sect of believers in the barren Jutland off the North Sea. The film's voice-over narration introduces them first, and follows their story from youth to old age, when they are introduced to Babette, and, in essence, saved by her. Both sisters are courted once seriously in their youths, but discouraged from marrying by their father who "was well-respected, and perhaps also a little feared". He advocates an asceticism that denies the flesh, preferring the coming glories of Heaven.

Martine is courted by a lieutenant of the hussars, Lorens Löwenhielm, a somewhat dissolute officer, who meets her after being sentenced by a superior to a three-month stay with his aunt in the Jutland to mend his ways. The aunt is a disciple of the minister, and so Lorenz inevitably meets the beautiful Martine and falls in love with her. However, he finds nothing but a cold piety with the minister's family, and concludes that union with Martine is impossible. He rides off and determines that he will turn from such romanticism to a reasoned pragmatism, and make a career for himself. He pays court to a lady-in-waiting and steadily advances his career.

Filippa is courted by a Parisian opera star, Achille Papin (played by the popular French singer, Jean Philippe Lafont), who goes to the Jutland for an escape from the vanities of stage life. From a distance, he hears Filippa singing a hymn at a church service. Concluding that she will be a great diva, he offers her music lessons. When they begin singing love duets from Mozart, the minister inclines Filippa to stop her lessons, which she does. A crushed Papin returns to Paris.

The story is taken up many years later. The minister has died, and the sisters, both spinsters, take care of the dwindling and aged congregation, which has begun to suffer from bickerings and resentments. On a stormy night in 1871, the mysterious Babette arrives by boat with a letter from Achille Papin asking the sisters to offer her protection and help. Papin ironically mentions that "she can cook", and so Babette becomes servant to the women, allowing them to devote their energies to their ministry and, through her ingenious house management and cooking skill, saving the women financially.

Fourteen years go by with the sisters fully bound to Babette. Then a change occurs when Babette wins 10 000 francs in a Paris lottery. She asks for and is granted permission to make a genuine French dinner for the sisters and members of the congregation who will be gathering to celebrate the centennial of the minister's birth. The meal Babette prepares is extravagant and delicious. Among the guests who attend is the visiting and now General Lorens Löwenhielm who praises the sisters, particularly Martine, and the uniqueness and excellence of the feast. None of the guests acknowledges his comments in this comic sequence, for Martine and Filippa have warned them of their fears that Babette, a Catholic, has somehow been led by the devil to tempt them through the sensuous meal. However, all present are overwhelmed by the "love affair" of the feast. Old quarrels are resolved at the table, and words of genuine humility and kindness expressed by all. As Löwenhielm leaves, he reaffirms his love for Martine and tells her that indeed "all things are possible".

In the conclusion, Martine and Filippa thank Babette, all the while assuming that she will soon leave them, but she informs them that she will be staying. She had been the head chef at the famed Café Anglais in Paris. The meal was her work of art for them and for herself, and she spent the entire 10 000 francs on it. Filippa embraces her and informs her that in Paradise she will delight the angels with her artistry.

In the Dinesen tale, Babette's sacrifice is primarily an ironic victory of art over life's incongruities. Art reveals the beauty and purpose that infuse all life, even the tragic; it allows "righteousness and bliss" and "mercy and truth" to kiss. Babette's meal brings harmony between the stiff pietist sectarians and the disillusioned general, even though they cannot communicate on even the most fundamental level, as the comic mis-exchange of words at the table so delightfully illustrates. It reunites the poor spinster Martine with her worldly, unattainable lover, the young Löwenhielm, and, in doing so, closes the loop by also indirectly reuniting Achille Papin with Filippa, since Papin has sent redemptive art (Babette) back into the community after it had been earlier rejected in his own person. The meal also breaks down class distinctions, albeit comically and temporarily, by allowing three distinct classes to share in the experience – the General, Babette and the rural sectarians.

Babette's meal in the story also provides reconciliation between human choice and divine disposition. The young Löwenhielm and Papin realise that their dreams of happiness cannot be fulfilled because of the subtle tyranny of the minister towards his daughters; moreover, of course, the minister, aligned with Christ during the table conversation at the end (according to an anecdote of the group of believers, they both walked on water), exercises his authority based on his certainty of God's will. Löwenhielm as a young lieutenant concludes from this impasse that "life is hard and cruel". Papin likewise sings goodbye to his love and hope when he is refused by Martine. However, both men recognise in their advanced age that their visions of success and happiness are ultimately vain. Speaking for both at the end of Babette's meal, Löwenhielm toasts the guests with this benediction:

We have all of us been told that grace is to be found in the universe. But in our human foolishness and shortsightedness we imagine divine grace to be finite. For this reason we tremble. We tremble before making our choice in life, and after having made it again tremble in fear of having chosen wrong. But the moment comes when our eyes are opened, and we realize that grace is infinite. Grace, my friends, demands nothing from us but that we shall await it with confidence and acknowledge it in gratitude. Grace, brothers, makes no conditions and singles out none of us in particular; grace takes us all to its bosom and proclaims general amnesty.

The art of Babette, which has reconciled all other incongruities, also reconciles the choices that each of the main characters has made with the inevitable losses they have suffered from those choices. The meal has transported all the players to a transcendent position – if only momentarily and thus as a foretaste – in which they enjoy both what they have chosen and what they have given up. Löwenhielm comes to realise that, while leaving Martine, he has permanently fixed her in his heart and will keep her there until and, by implication, after his death. Martine and Filippa have chosen the ascetic life of their religious duties, but rather than permanently losing their link to love and worldly achievement, they gain it in a more permanent way in the promise of heaven. Certainly, Löwenhielm's idealised devotion to Filippa is greater than the physical consummation would have been, and Martine's lost operatic career has guaranteed her a greater, more exclusive career as accompanist to the angels. (There is significance that *Martine* consoles Babette with the thought that angels will delight in Babette's feasts.)

Babette herself facilitates these closures, and, in Dinesen's original, remains mostly impassive in the experience of them. She rather proudly declares to the sisters that she willingly lost her family in the Paris Uprising, and later declares with the same unabashed confidence that she is a "great artist". Very little attention is given to her psychological and emotional development in the story, as Dinesen, rather in the manner of Maupassant, presses on with the ironies of plot and theme which she delights in weaving. If the original story has a flaw, it is in the two-dimensionality of Babette's own character.

Here is where Axel began his transformation of the tale. In the visually revelatory medium of film, the presence of Babette cannot be trivialised. It is her eyes which view the sisters, the congregation and the town. It is her hands which make the food, and her face which responds to what she has made. And, of course, these are the eyes, hands and face of Stéphane Audran, whose remarkable film presence dominates every composition she enters. Her bearing and manner carry dignity and warmth. Therefore, by virtue of the rules of transformation from printed text to projected image, and given the particular actress chosen for the part, the character of Babette gains a richness and sensitivity in Axel's film that are lacking in the story.

This change also makes Babette's arrival in the sisters' house all the more pathetic. As she sits with Martine and Filippa during the reading of Papin's letter of introduction, she is most evidently a martyr to her circumstances. We see the rain on her cloak and scarf, and the tears in her eyes, and a visual link is thus formed between her circumstances, her exile and the tribulations of the sisters.

Another link regards the loneliness of Babette and that of Martine and Filippa. When Martine loses Löwenhielm, her isolation is conveyed in a scene in which she lies in her bed clutching her pillow. Filippa asks if she remembers the lieutenant. She turns away from Filippa, away from the only window in the small room, towards the camera, and says "Yes". Similarly, Filippa's loss of Papin is likewise conveyed in a quiet composition of the two girls sitting alone at the family table with the minister reading his Bible in the background. A cross-cut shows Papin's boat leaving after a shot of Filippa's sad face. Axel makes the transition to Babette's bitter experiences by following the shot of Papin's boat with a cut to the village in darkness and rain preceding the arrival of Babette by boat. The cook has been carried to the women on the same waves of sorrow that carried away their own hopes.

Babette's isolation and suffering are evoked most poignantly in one of the film's feature compositions, a transitional sequence which allows the narration to accelerate fourteen years to the climactic events of the lottery and the feast. Babette sits with the brown landscape rolling behind her and the sunset over the hills; she is to the right of the frame. She rises, gracefully holding a small basket, crosses left in front of the sun-golden hills, and leaves the frame entirely. The image suggests both the loneliness of Babette and her artistic harmonious presence.

It is the physical difference of Babette that draws out the contrasts with which Axel works throughout the film. Whereas the two sisters are rigid and angular in all their movements, Babette is graceful. She is equally yoked with them in their spiritual exile, but hers is freer and more willing. She moves with an easy purposefulness that is a visual relief from the calculated steps of Martine and Filippa. Compositions around the minister's table particularly highlight this contrast. As older women, the sisters typically sit at the end, motionless although smiling, framed symmetrically by two windows behind them. Babette never sits at the table but moves in and out from it. In this, Babette becomes the antithesis of the minister, who, having died, exists only as a shadow in an oval frame we see in the background of several later scenes. The minister had sat at the head of the table with the sisters on opposite sides and the faithful members of the community flanking them. The symmetrical table compositions are broken whenever Babette arrives. During the feast, the camera circles the table to destroy any sense of compositional balance, and the sisters are often seen in close-up or bending to taste food or drink. The windows no longer frame them.

Windows carry a certain symbolic value in the film. One of Babette's first duties at the sisters' house is throwing water on the windows so that they allow vision outwards, a vision which the sisters have repressed emotionally and by experience. When the sisters are framed by the windows, they are turned away from them. Babette looks out of the window in several important scenes. After learning how the sisters want her to soak fish and make ale bread, Babette sits alone at a table in her room and looks out of the window towards the ocean and towards her old, more glamorous life – someone walks a dog in the field and she watches impassively. The sisters never appear in compositions with anyone apart from the religious fellowship. In a sequence not much later in the film, the sisters are encouraging two members of the sect to be reconciled after one of their quarrels. The scene is indoors but a cross-cut takes the viewer outside, where a glorious sunset lights up the sky – an editing move implying that this is what the communicants need to see. The following shots provide a short montage of Babette's loneliness. A church bell is ringing. Babette sits at her table looking out of the window. Rain beats against the panes which conspicuously suggest a cross, and this rain suggests a visual link to Babette's arrival, and a correlative of her grief at the losses she has suffered. The next sequence has the sectarians quarrelling again. Close-ups show the tension on each face. The sisters, again framed symmetrically by the windows, suggest the singing of a hymn. No measurable effect on the group is achieved until Babette enters with tea, and rebukes the group in a foreshadowing of her later mediation.

What the windows typically reveal from the inside is the distant sea, which in itself suggests both the outside world that burdens the community and the presence of divine grace. Papin and Babette both travel this sea, and in several scenes contemplate it. Papin leaves the village by boat, and Babette arrives by boat; the food for the feast likewise arrives by boat. The sea is the messenger of the grace that Löwenhielm proclaims in his toast: "Our choice is of no importance. We come to realise that mercy is infinite. We need only await it with confidence and receive it in gratitude." Infinite mercy for the sisters had indeed arrived by boat over the sea; firstly, Papin the messenger, then Babette the saviour. The sisters, Löwenhielm and, to a lesser degree,

Papin have chosen against that which they most desired; yet, Babette's feast harmonises all under a benediction of infinite goodness.

The sea holds the mystery which all the characters seem to long after and achieve only, if momentarily, at the end. Papin experiences a melancholy when he arrives in the Jutland to be confronted by "silence and the sound of the waves". His wistful mood is broken by the beautiful sound of Filippa singing in the town's church. The song speaks of the vanity of worldly things and of God's inscrutability: "God is God even if all life were ended". Papin enters the church, and watches from the rear in rapture over Filippa's voice; yet, his desire is to make her a great diva and to enjoy her gifts alongside his own. The irony, of course, is that he misses the message that makes her song and person so alluring; namely, that the holiness that produces unearthly bliss begins with a turning from the world's allurements. As Filippa sings, the camera cross-cuts from her impassive face to a crucifix at the front of the church, with the odd image of a smiling Christ upon it. The smile is in keeping with the mood of benediction that pervades the film, best captured in Löwenhielm's toast.

The expanse of the sea and its sounds fill the opening frames of the film, and thus set both the literal story context, as the camera tracks back to reveal the small village of drab huts clustered together, and the metaphorical, religious context suggested by the many associations of the sea with the divine. The sea holds the answer which Babette seems intent on discovering in her several reveries. It suggests the method in which the righteousness of the sisters and the earthly happiness all seek can be commingled; it evokes beauty and permanence over vanity; in its incessant caress of the shore, it sounds the message that time brings wisdom, and patience brings joy.

This all leads to the feast of Babette. As Löwenhielm dresses before his mirror prior to riding to the sisters' home for the feast, he recites Ecclesiastes (1: 2): "Vanity, vanity, all is vanity". A storm casts shadows outside. Löwenhielm addresses his young self seated defensively in a chair, and insists that "tonight we shall settle our score". His score is, however, more against the sea, the inscrutable wisdom of God who had both led him to Martine and denied the possibility of their union. The scene cuts to the sisters anxiously awaiting the company and praying "God's will be done". The next scene is of Babette quietly and efficiently preparing pastry shells for the *Cailles en sarcophage* which will amaze the General and lead him to his toast.

The food prepared by Babette seduces the General, the congregation, the sisters and the viewer. It is the sequence of Babette preparing the food that breaks the visual style of the film and marks its sacramentalism, especially when viewed as a contrast to the earlier scene of Papin's performing in a stylised manner on a French stage. The performance of Babette is natural and compelling. The kitchen, with its warm brown hues and softly rising steam, invites a kind of visual embrace like nothing else in the film. Babette is at ease. The twelve culinary disciples around the table are awakened. The viewers are made hungry. The food is the synthesis of art and need, style and substance, the spiritual and the material.

After the meal, the General departs willing to live perpetually with only spiritual embraces from Filippa, and the congregation is united for the first time in true, loving fellowship. Around the well in the centre of the town, which is overt in its symbolic significance, the members of the sect join hands and sing a hymn. The stars sparkle in the sky, an almost surreal image cast against the darkness of the village, and Filippa comments, "The stars have moved closer". These embraces of fellowship played out after the meal culminate as Filippa tells Babette she will delight the angels, and then the women embrace. The score of the film becomes prominent and harmonious at this moment of celebration, and counterpoints the lonely melody that opened the film.

What is of particular importance, however, in this last moment is the manner in which Filippa's words to Babette come as something of a rebuke. Babette says: "Throughout the world sounds one long cry from the heart of the artist, 'Give me the chance to do my very best'". These words are Papin's, and Babette uses them rather proudly to explain her importance as an artist and the justification of her sacrificing 10 000 francs. Filippa's words enforce the greater context. Babette's art is rather a reflection of the great art that Löwenhielm recognised, the art of providence, the goodness and mercy of God. Filippa reminds her: "But this is not the end, Babette. I'm certain it's not." Human art is part of the vanity of life that both Löwenhielm and Papin have recognised through time. God's art is what will last – the art of the sea, the songs that the angels will sing and enjoy.

It is almost impossible objectively to analyze *Babette's Feast* and fail to perceive the religious power of the film's climax. To see Babette's meal as a demonstration of art alone is to fail adequately to reconcile the great personal losses of Papin, Löwenhielm and the sisters. It is only when the final meal is recognised as a type of spiritual communion, suggesting the benevolent purposes of God towards those who wait for Him, that the film adequately attains closure.

The Christian Eucharist celebrates the sacrifice that allows for God's mercy towards people. When the Church gathers to taste bread and wine in remembrance of Christ, the Church experiences joy in the union of the material with the spiritual ideal prepared in heaven. The tasting of Eucharistic bread and wine is the tasting of Christ's own sacrificial body and blood, and the tasting of the hope brought about through it. Therefore, it is both remembrance and a future promise.

Babette's Feast functions most effectively when the allegory that links the climactic meal to the Christian Eucharist is recognised. It is not Babette who has led Papin to meet the sisters or invited Löwenhielm to the final meal. Nor is it Babette who has brought the stars to their special brightness following the storm that preceded the General's coming.

This remarkable film moves viewers not only to understand, but also voyeuristically to ingest the goodness of God. Despite the pain experienced by the characters, judgment is overcome through compassion. The sisters are not mocked, but pitied and respected; likewise the general, Papin and Babette herself. In its portrayal of the ability of the artist temporarily to lift the burden from humankind, *Babette's Feast* suggests that the source of the artist's power comes from God and returns back to God. Babette's art tells of a spiritual goodness that invests all of matter, and blesses it. The film offers a glimpse of a passion that suggests joy in the sacrifice, and pleasure in the reception of it.

Note

[1]   This anecdote is more thoroughly told by Judith Thurman in *Isak Dinesen: The Life of Karen Blixen* (Harmondsworth: Penguin, 1984): 329.

Apart from several studies of the Biblical epic, the work which is most often cited as a systematic arrangement of religious films is Paul Schrader's *Transcendental Style in Film: Ozu, Bresson, Dreyer* (1972).[1] Schrader discusses religious films according to their visual and performance style in a manner which, on the surface, bears some similarity to this present study of liturgical patterns in film. However, to explain fully the differences between Schrader's discussion and this study, it is useful to view Schrader's critical model as it works itself out in one of his films.

The Schrader film which most explicitly plays out his theories and a Passion motif is *Hardcore* (aka *The Hardcore Life*). In this film, Schrader combines the three strands which most clearly define his film work: a concern for the dark side of human psychology and behaviour; a highly self-conscious visual and narrative style; and a latent tendency towards Calvinism or philosophic determinism. What makes *Hardcore* unique is the sharp focus of these three concerns in a film with an explicitly Christian narrative movement.

The narrative of *Hardcore* presents yet another variation on the "search and rescue" motif spun out most eloquently in John Ford's classic *The Searchers* (1956), although here we have a peculiarly unsettling one. George C Scott portrays Jake VanDorn, a respectable member of the Dutch Reformation Church in Grand Rapids, whose daughter, Kristin (Ilah Davis), disappears while on a youth retreat in California. VanDorn hires a private detective, Andy Mast (Peter Boyle), to find her. When Mast returns in several weeks with a cheaply made pornographic film featuring Kristin, VanDorn determines to track down the source of the film and rescue her himself. After a seedy journey through the porn underworld of California, he finds Kristin with Ratan (Marc Alaimo), a notorious maker of "snuff films". There is a climactic altercation between VanDorn and Ratan, which ends with the shooting of Ratan by Mast who has followed VanDorn to protect him. VanDorn then confesses his failures as a father to Kristin and pleads for her to return, but she hesitates to go home with him, explaining that she chose to do what she is doing. These confessions, however, produce a new sympathy between father and daughter, and Kristin finally agrees to return. The film ends with VanDorn offering help to a prostitute who led him to Kristin (she refuses) and Mast urging him to "Go home, Pilgrim".

Hardcore's indebtedness to the plot of the Ford film seems overdrawn and at times gratuitous, with allusions such as Mast's reference to VanDorn as "Pilgrim", John Wayne's nickname for the Jeffrey Hunter character in *The Searchers*. However, Schrader's reference is purposeful in that it provides a generic context for the interpretation of Kristin's return home in the climactic scene. The Natalie Wood character, captured by the Indians and sought by Wayne and Hunter in the Ford classic, was found corrupted and nearly beyond redemption as a result of her captivity. Cousin Ethan (Wayne) attempts to kill her before being dissuaded by her brother, Martin Pawley (Hunter). This fitted the larger generic syntax of the western, in which the wild could never be assimilated into civilisation. In Ford's epic vision, the frontier was conquered, but not without a loss of moral innocence, as well as a significant personal loss. Kristin, on the other hand, is brought back to civilisation despite her defilement, and without protest from VanDorn, who is ready to forgive all. Although her corruption becomes intensified by her own complicity with the pornographers, her redemption is firmly secured, due to VanDorn's mystifying capability in a society totally alien to his own, and Kristin's sudden reversal of sympathy at the last moment.

An equally important allusion in the film that may largely be missed due to the time that has elapsed since its release in 1979 is the striking resemblance of Kristin to Patti Hearst, the kidnapped heiress-turned-revolutionary in the bizarre, highly publicised case of the mid-1970s. The dark-eyed, dark-haired and sullen-featured Hearst, displayed nationally when a criminal in a widely circulated newspaper photo, is here suggested by Schrader in VanDorn's daughter. Schrader later made a biographical film on the Hearst case, *Patty Hearst* (1988). This allusion gives a further undercurrent of meaning to the film's search and restoration. Again, in *Hardcore*, Kristin (alias Joanne, the name she adopts) is restored to her family and culture; Patti Hearst (alias Tania) never regained her former standing in the eyes of the public. In addition, because of the association of the Hearst legacy with Charles Foster Kane in Orson Welles's film, not only is the unredeemable daughter here redeemed, but also the unredeemable father here becomes the redeemer.

These allusions with Schrader's idiosyncratic modifications underline the Calvinist thematics operative in the film. Both within and through the narrative, *Hardcore* illustrates the doctrines of election and reprobation that are a feature of the Reformed faith. These doctrines are addressed directly in several interchanges between VanDorn and Niki (Season Hubley), the prostitute who leads him finally to Ratan. Niki professes herself to be a Venusian – VanDorn confronts her at one point as having a life entirely absorbed by sex, which he acknowledges as being "not very" important in the long run. When she asks what he believes, he tells her that he believes in "TULIP", the acronym for the five points of Calvinism. Neither, of course, can understand the other's position. VanDorn obligingly explains "TULIP", but then dismisses the subject as one which she is incapable of understanding. She counters that they are equally "fucked-up" in their beliefs, for his apparent absence of sexual desire is as alien to her as her philosophy is to him. (In terms of Schrader's own Calvinist perspective, one is either elect or left in a state of total depravity.) In the final sequence, VanDorn's offer of salvation, accepted by Kristin, is scorned by the reprobate Niki. According to the search motif suggested by the allusions, salvation is impossible for the defiled; Calvinism, on the other hand, presents salvation as a possibility regardless of individual worthiness or unworthiness – purity or defilement, wisdom or folly. It depends instead on the seemingly arbitrary good pleasure of God. Kristin can be redeemed even more gloriously after her fall when her heart is miraculously softened to receive the offer of salvation presented to her. When she does, her election is manifested; she is found indeed "Kristin" or "In Christ". Thus, Schrader's irrational ending, in which Kristin decides to return home (while Niki refuses), is the result of sovereign grace in the context of the film.

A brief explanation of the five principles of Calvinism will shed light on the implications of the film's search. The acronym "TULIP", which, as VanDorn tells Niki, emerged from the debates at the Council of Dordt between the Dutch Calvinists and the dissenting free-will clergy in the first decade of the 17th century, defines the five key principles in Calvin's theological system. The T signifies the *total depravity* of people since the Fall. It is impossible for a person ever fully to avoid doing evil, or even repent and believe the Gospel, unless given a new attitude of heart by the work of the Holy Spirit; all people are thus sinners awaiting damnation. U signifies *unconditional election*, the pre-creation decision by God to save some souls according to His own pleasure. L signifies the manner and extent of this atonement: it is the *limited atonement*, limited to the elect, made effective through the substitutionary sacrifice of God Himself in the person of Jesus Christ. I signifies the *irresistible grace* of God, which changes the heart of the elect person from one bound to sinful rebellion incapable of repentance and faith, to one mortified by inner corruptions and so inclined effectively to receive the offer of salvation given in the Gospel. P signifies the *perseverance of the saints*, the certainty that those who are elect (the aspect of the system which is the most elusive) will remain in the way of grace by virtue of the immutability of God's original decree and the efficacy of the work of Christ applied to the elect person brought by God to conversion.

God conducts a search in Calvinism, and it leads to both salvation and damnation. The parallel moments of stasis in Schrader's film, which convey, respectively, Kristin's agreement to return home and Niki's rejection of VanDorn, illustrate these polarized consequences of selective grace in a fallen world. From a position within grace (VanDorn tells Niki that the doctrines make sense once you believe them), the film, as one reviewer saw it, presents a moving and heroic picture of paternal love,[2] a shadow of divine love and, interestingly, the shadowy source of the romantic love that has been Hollywood's staple diet. From a position outside grace, *Hardcore* is, in the words of another reviewer, "the most perversely priggish movie in the history of the American cinema".[3]

VanDorn's "holy pursuit" of his beloved daughter finds visual expression in Schrader's characteristic journey into the bowels of the city sequence, which has VanDorn venturing into progressively darker worlds: from "high-class" porn shot on high budgets in comparatively business-like settings, to popular porn sold in bookstores on the strip in Los Angeles and in sex shops that take MasterCard and Visa, to kinky bars with peepshows, to backroom screenings of snuff murders, and to sadism specialists. This car ride into hell, which recalls the Schrader-scripted *Taxi Driver* (1976) and *American Gigolo* (1980), culminates in VanDorn breaking into a sadism shop and diving through a series of perversely illustrated wall partitions to get at the shop's operator, Tod (Gary Rand Graham), the last link to Ratan. VanDorn punches and muscles Tod down a hill of a San Francisco backstreet, into poles and over rubbish bins, all in an eerie evocation of the journey down the levels of the Inferno. Similarly, the search through the underworld has VanDorn discover evil in increasingly colder and more professional forms. Ratan, when found, sports a cool white suit. He acts with vicious decision, but never speaks. When shot by Mast, his true corruption spills out grotesquely as large red stains expand on his coat and trousers. He falls awkwardly beside the ticket-booth of a porn theatre, with a poster over his prostrate body advertising a film of "ultimate" sex and love.

All Schrader's allusions are unified around the Calvinist thematics in the narrative syntax of *Hardcore*. Yet, as in all his work – especially *American Gigolo*, *Mishima* (1985) and his screenplay for *Taxi Driver* – Schrader adds an interpretive gloss to the narrative with a unified formalistic structure that imitates in modified form the transcendental style of Bresson, Ozu and Dreyer. Through highly contrived visual and auditory techniques, Schrader creates a distance between the world which the spectator accepts at the opening of the film, and the world which the spectator is led to look back and see in the light of the stylistic and thematic development of the plot. Through this technique, Schrader takes the spectator out of the comforts of a static belief in the mundane and commonplace (although, as he will imply, highly artificial and affected) virtues of existence to a more dynamic awareness of the dramatic tensions that threaten to break through the common at any moment. This progression to a new level of awareness constitutes a transcendental journey for Schrader, the meaning of which he freezes in dual moments of stasis within the narrative as it reaches its own climactic, dramatic resolutions. The spectator thus has his world-view challenged and – if one allows Schrader to have his way – replaced by one more in line with the spiritual truths that govern existence.

The film's opening sequence projects images of home, family and childhood innocence – children playing in the snow at Christmas-time in Grand Rapids. The traditional spiritual, "Precious Memories", accompanies the montage. The camera then moves indoors to the VanDorn living-room, where the same apparent purity and simplicity are on display. The men sit in a side room and talk theology; the women prepare food; the children watch television. All appears normal to small-town American life: common virtues in the common world of Grand Rapids. The camera lingers on the various icons of this existence – the television; the table of food – and on other evidences of domestic tranquillity in the home up to the point in the narrative when Kristin leaves by bus for the Youth Calvinist Convention (a Schrader parody of the annual Young Calvinist Conventions of the Midwest Dutch Reformed churches). But two small hints of a potential imbalance are detectable, largely in retrospect. The first occurs in a short segment when Kristin and her girlfriend, Marsha, talk about boys in anticipation of the society that this convention will bring for them; the second occurs following Kristin's departure, as VanDorn, unaware of his daughter's disappearance, makes a subtle play for an interior decorator hired to redesign his office. Neither scene offers any direct threat to the placidity of existence established in the opening sequences, but they have significance in the larger scheme.

Both hints articulate a dynamic of repressed sexuality under the surface of provincialism of Grand Rapids. This power explodes into the open when Mast, a character whose vulgarity in itself forms a break from the mundane, takes VanDorn into a Grand Rapids porn shop to show him the film featuring Kristin. Such a startling exposure of so potent a threat opens the door through which VanDorn will pass into the pornographic underworld of the West coast. It poses a contradictory reality that threatens to be more real than the comfortable images we were originally led to accept. Moreover, the narrative development suggests that the two worlds have created one another. VanDorn is found to be not a widower as initially assumed, but a cuckolded husband, his wife having run out on him. Kristin is found to be anything but a well-adjusted child. The father-daughter relationship evidently lacked the very basics in communication; in fact, all the relationships set up at the beginning become tenuous – a later scene between Wes DeJong, a Grand Rapids friend of VanDorn, and VanDorn reveals the stifling superficiality existing between the two men, as DeJong appears ignorant of what might prompt VanDorn to take such high risks to find Kristin. By the film's resolution, the seeming peace and purity seem an evil parallel to the seedy underworld.

The visual stylistics of the film become more complex throughout this development. The soothing daylight of the early scenes increasingly gives way to variations in lighting effects, which progress to the eerie artificiality of the neon-cast, night scenes that mark the end of the narrative. The camera likewise becomes more animated in its tracks, zooming as it speeds to keep pace with VanDorn in his journeys and pulling back to expose the variety and extravagance of the West coast strips. Earlier shots in Grand Rapids occur with much less motion: in one typical composition, the camera lingers sleepily on the VanDorn living room after VanDorn has left it. The sets in the two worlds are also polarized. Grand Rapids is natural and traditionally domestic – snowy playgrounds; tidy bedrooms; porches with swings. The West coast is highly artificial – film studios; neon signs; the false walls of Tod's shop which VanDorn will destroy. For VanDorn to succeed in his quest, he needs to don a false outfit with a wig and play a role. Colour motifs similarly move from cool blues and earth tones in Grand Rapids to the surrealistic blurs of pink, red and black on the strips. The musical score shifts from "Precious Memories" to strident electronic rock.

Counter to the common, conventionalized world of suburban Protestantism, therefore, is the potent evil of exploitive sexuality, largely defined in terms of cruelty, which broods as a false Gospel under a thin coating of repression. The other-worldly reality behind the religious form is threatening in this film. When Mast takes VanDorn to the Grand Rapids porn parlour to see the stag film that features Kristin, he warns him ominously that it exists "even here".

However, VanDorn's heroic pursuit, both in its theologic implications within the syntax of the narrative, and as it leads formalistically to the dual moments of stasis at the end, reveals a

Diary of a Country Priest (*Journal d'un curé de campagne*, 1950)

The Word (*Ordet*, 1955)

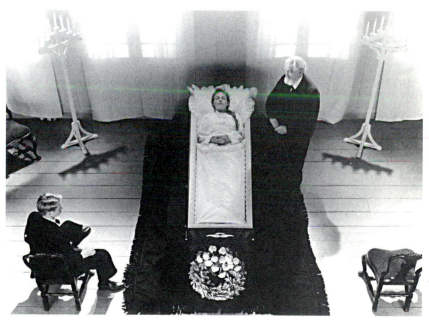

Andrej Rublëv (1966)

Rome, Open City (*Roma, città aperta*, 1945)

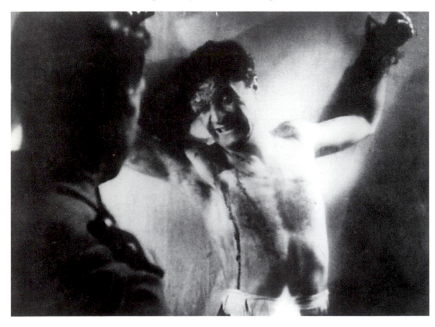

Black Robe (*1991*)

The Gospel According to St Matthew (*Il Vangelo secondo Matteo,* 1964)

The Mission (1986)

A Farewell to Arms (1932)

Jesus of Montreal (*Jésus de Montréal*, 1989)

Babette's Feast (*Babettes gæstebud*, 1987)

Hardcore (1978)

Gallipoli (1981)

On the Waterfront (1954)

You Only Live Once (1937)

The Last Temptation of Christ (1989)

Chariots of Fire (1981)

spirituality of greater substance and power than this evil. In this heroic role, VanDorn has become Christ in pursuit of his sheep, the hound of heaven in pursuit of the lost soul. He is instrument of a greater good, despite his plunge into the underworld, since he is ultimately carrying out a grand redemptive intention through this moral passion journey.

There is a curious circularity in Schrader's transcendental ending to the film. It is clear that the cold determinism of Calvinism is a motif that Schrader believes deserves parody and denial, since it shrouds the potent forces that make life a constant tension in a web of scholastic rationalism that disavows tension, and so leaves the weak and innocent unprotected when confronted by this tension. We do not want to live in Grand Rapids. But nor do we want to move West. Furthermore, the redemption that is finally revealed comes from Grand Rapids, both in the agency of VanDorn (and he and Kristin both go home in the end) and in the God of the Grand Rapids's theological construction. It is the codification of Christianity by Calvin and the subsequent social constructions created, albeit indirectly, by this faith that drive Niki from home and into the throes of the menace. But Calvin's God also saves her.

This conflict separates Schrader from the transcendental stylists whom he emulates. His characteristic doubling of focus – between Kristin and Niki in the end – which serves to underline the parallel doctrines of election and reprobation, equally a part in the Calvinistic plan of redemption, points to the individuality of Schrader's work. The "Other" of Schrader's transcendentalism operates within the framework of a fixed rational system. What is irrational for Schrader is not the essential nature of the being and force of the Other, but the disposition of that Other's will and the direction of its force. Moreover, this is not only pure scholastic Calvinism, but also pure materialism. All occurrences and personalities in the world fit a mechanistic model.

Schrader's analysis of what he terms "the transcendental style in film" grew out of his own considerations of how to create an American version of a religious style that he discovered in the works of Bresson, Dreyer and Ozu. Most of his films fit into the pattern that he lays out in his book-length analysis of the three directors, *Transcendental Style in Film*.[3] In that study, Schrader defines transcendental style in film as a technique that strips away conventional interpretive devices or "screens" evoked by filmmakers to propel their narratives to higher ideas – the "heavenly choir" suggesting divine presence, for example – and replaces them with narratives that reduce to simple ritualistic formulas which reveal large transcendent ideas when experienced by the viewer. He compares this film style to medieval church iconography: a sparse surface, made flat and typical, comes to evoke a rich spiritual dimension that inspires awe in the sensitive observer. As with such iconography, a discernible set of conventions is associated with transcendental film style:

> [T]ranscendental style chooses irrationalism over rationalism, repetition over variation, sacred over profane, the deific over the humanistic, intellectual realism over optical realism, two-dimensional vision over three-dimensional vision, tradition over experiment, anonymity over individualization.[4]

Schrader illustrates this technique in the films of Ozu, which evoke the Zen belief in life processes; the films of Bresson, which evoke the concept of redemption through the trials of an individual soul; and the films of Dreyer, which isolate spiritual forces at play within and around damned and holy souls. Schrader places the creators of the Hollywood religious epic, who conjure holy feelings through abundant displays of meaningful religious characters and symbols, in contrast to these stylists.

Schrader divides the transcendental film into three components. Firstly, there is a careful presentation of the ordinary world, "a meticulous representation of the dull, banal commonplaces of everyday living".[5] The transcendental stylist creates a recognisable person(s) in a recognisable situation with few options and a predictable future, an Everyman in an everyworld. Secondly, there is an entrance of some element of disparity in this common world, "an actual or potential disunity between man and his environment which culminates in a decisive action".[6] The tension becomes the centre of narrative development, moving the plot forward until a climax occurs which forces the everyman into participation with the disunity in the world. Such participation concludes in a moment of unresolved but recognisable disparity, "a frozen view of life", or "stasis", "which does not resolve the disparity but transcends it".[7] The stasis allows for an embrace of both the commonplace and the tensions built into it, and so projects both the film subjects and the spectators to a position that transcends the initial position – the contemplative position of possible and permanent resolution. The stasis shot in the transcendental film thus compresses the film into a single, profound frame.

To adapt transcendental style to a given culture, Schrader argues that the director must locate "the spectrum at which the Transcendent is most successfully expressed".[8] The director must be able to identify the screens of his or her own culture, in order to be able to present reality in its bare details without interpretation, given the particular historical moment. Points of contact, whereby both the common and

124

the holy are introduced, need to be carefully tailored to a specific audience:

> A motion picture, from its first frame, has great potential empathy; one of the functions of transcendental style is to use that empathy as *potential* and keep it at that level. The audience has a natural impulse to participate in actions and settings on screen; a film-maker employing transcendental style can use these given abundant means, this natural empathy, to hold the audience in the theater as he gradually substitutes sparse means for abundant. In transcendental style sparse means are, to a large degree, simply a refusal to use the available abundant means.[9]

For a transcendental film to succeed, therefore, the portrayed commonplace reality must be perceived as such: a typical scene conveyed in a typical way. In addition, the subsequent presentation of conflict and removal of screens should be jolting by contrast, even though the move is towards less rather than more. How this is achieved depends on audience expectation, but it is manufactured by the perceptions which a director enforces.

According to Schrader's theory, after the film-goer senses the conflict in ordinary existence (the mountain is more than a mountain in the Zen metaphor he uses), he is to be taken to a place where reality exists above the ordinary systems of experience, and thus encompasses all systems (the place where the mountain is a mountain, after all). This is his interpretation of the effects produced by Ozu, Bresson and Dreyer. The conflict that the transcendental heroine or hero faces, whether it is St Joan or a Japanese businessman, threatens her or his natural and rather ordinary existence, but the resolution of the conflict makes the irreconcilable a norm within existence, and therefore tolerable on a transcendent level.

The logic of Schrader's conclusions upsets the transcendental balance of his own film work, and has left his harsher critics calling him hypocritical (Fascistic, in one case).[10] Whereas the concluding resolutions of Bresson, Ozu and Dreyer remain largely ambiguous on an interpretive level, Schrader's filmic resolutions consistently fit a rational Calvinistic model that operates according to a materialistic depiction of God's justice and mercy. This religious materialism can be traced to Schrader's own religious upbringing in the Calvinistic Christian Reformed Church, and his subsequent departure from Christianity.

The result of the conflict between Schrader's films and his theory is firstly to separate Schrader's own tendencies from those he emulates. On the theoretical level, Schrader's materialism compromises his defined transcendental style, for he places all natural and supernatural occurrences within a rational system, and thus all identification of truth must occur within the context of an interpretive screen. Bresson, the Catholic mystic; Ozu, the Zen Buddhist; and Dreyer, the Lutheran pietist – all plug into the defined formalistic cinematic system that Schrader creates. The elements of their individual religious philosophies give visual and audial substance to the code of transcendental form, which then carries those under its spell to a higher mode of consciousness. The power of Bresson, Ozu and Dreyer resides in their formalistic incantations, therefore, not in the specifics of the messages inherent in each film and the skill of execution. The different symbols of these directors reflect their differing philosophies, which are themselves results of their different social and religious milieux. The truths of the philosophies depend upon their effectiveness within the larger system that leads to transcendence. For Schrader, God is essentially nameless, although known to humanity by a multiplicity of names. The role of artists is firstly to identify the name of God suitable to their context, and then to use that name as incantation within the effective system.

Although it takes a certain stretch of the imagination to see Buddhism, Catholic mysticism and Lutheranism as similar religious codes, Schrader is easily able to do so on a metalinguistic level: one can view all three as defined religious systems, and then fit the terms of each system into fixed categories (i.e. what is believed about God, what explains evil; where salvation can be found; and so on). Schrader, a product of a private religious college (Calvin College), would have been exposed to such metagories, since this is the way in which Calvinists (and other sectarians) tend to evaluate other systems of thought. But, useful as such a categorisation might be for a simple understanding of world religions discussed in a survey, it can be misleading in the search for the key elements of a particular religion. It is all too possible to assume that the metacategory used to clump the systems together and distinguish one from another is integrally built into the structure of individual systems. That is to say, it might work on paper, but it is naïve to think that one can understand the mysticism of Bresson by asking what he believed about God, sin and salvation. This is the source of the tension in Schrader's own films, and it is the problem in his definition of transcendental style.[11]

The discussion of sacramental form presented in this study of the Passion in films therefore fundamentally differs from Schrader's in scope. Liturgical patterns offer a system of organising and understanding a much larger body of religious films, and are much more historically and culturally based than Schrader's mega-system. The field needs to be limited to films that follow in the Christian tradition if one is to be theoretically consistent. Secondly, not all religious films can be reduced to the elements of sacramental form; it is rather a strong tendency, or a genre, that has evolved – as have all film genres – according to certain acceptable cultural patterns. Thirdly, sacramental form cannot be viewed as a criterion for evaluating filmic quality or religious profundity. It is simply a key to understanding the religious mechanisms of a large group of films by tracing patterns of narrative style and relating those patterns to existing patterns of Christian liturgy and devotional practice.

Most of Paul Schrader's films work out his idiosyncratic approach at a transcendental style, and sometimes with measured success, as in *Mishima*. In *Hardcore*, the style is less effective in producing a transcendent moment of stasis at the end than in illustrating the odd comparison between Protestant provincialism and American moral corruption. In this respect, Schrader's perspective is more like that of David Lynch than that of Bresson.

Yet, *Hardcore* does offer an interesting view of a different kind of passion-play, one written with the scholastic pen of American Calvinism. This is the liturgy of Reformed rationalism, a faith which has filtered Christian sacramentalism down to a rigid theological system placed over Scripture and tradition. Underneath is the intensely passionate pursuit of the lost sinner by the loving Saviour, while on top is a highly propositional liturgical experience which examines the nature and pattern of the pursuit.

Notes

[1]   Paul Schrader, *Transcendental Style in Film: Ozu, Bresson, Dreyer* (Berkeley: University of California Press, 1972).

[2]   Richard Schickel, "Porn Scorned", *Time* 113 (19 February 1979): 59.

[3]   David Denby, "What Fools These Moralists Be", *New York* 12 February 1979: 84.

[4]   Schrader: 11.

[5]   Ibid: 39.

[6]   Ibid: 42.

[7] Ibid: 49.

[8] Ibid: 168.

[9] Ibid: 160. Emphasis in original.

[10] Robin Wood condemns Schrader for his attitude towards homosexuality in particular, and for his moralism in general. See Robin Wood, *Hollywood from Vietnam to Reagan* (New York: Columbia University Press, 1986), and also Ken Eisen, "The Young Misogynists of American Cinema", *Cineaste* 13: 1 (1983): 31-35.

[11] See my more complete discussion of Schrader's style in "*American Gigolo* & Transcendental Style", *Literature/Film Quarterly* 16: 2 (1988): 91-100.

Among the Australian director Peter Weir's many fine achievements, one film stands out as a small masterpiece: his third major film, *Gallipoli*, a tragedy based on a notorious historical incident central to Australian national consciousness. In this film, Weir threads his main philosophical concerns of romanticism, mysticism and fraternity into a poignant story of two young Australian track athletes who find themselves at one of the most tragic battlegrounds of the First World War. One of the men, Archy Hamilton (Mark Lee), has joined the Australian cavalry, the Light Horse, for the glory of defending the world against the Germans and Turks. The other, Frank Dunne (Mel Gibson), joins the infantry out of friendship for Archy and three of his other "mates". Neither of the two young men is prepared for what they find in the trenches on the battlefield, and the horror of the one-sided and misguided campaign makes their idealism and innocence appear futile.

It is this futility, the inexorable procession of a highly tragic event, that Weir underscores by counterpointing the story with suggestions of Christ's life and Passion. The sacramental moment of Weir's film, a stasis shot of the death of Archy as he runs defenceless into Turkish machine-gun fire, has no redemptive value in the context of the film, and thus creates an emotional hollow for the viewer that has great force by virtue of its undermining of the expectations usually generated in a Passion narrative.

The events at Gallipoli were part of an Anglo-French operation against Turkey in 1915, which was intended to force the channel of the Dardanelles and move British troops towards Constantinople, ostensibly to knock Turkey out of the war. A large military force, heavily weighted with Australian and New Zealand troops ("ANZACs") was assembled and trained in Egypt under the British General, Sir Ian Hamilton. They began to land on the peninsula on 25 April 1915, but were able to advance little against the Turkish troops led by Mustafa Kemal Atatürk. Over 200 000 British Commonwealth troops fell in the battle, including battalions of ANZACs, many of whom were easily mowed down by Turkish gunners before they were able to advance far from their trenches.

The Gallipoli campaign was horribly bungled by the British, and led to the resignation of then-First Lord of the Admiralty, Winston Churchill, and Prime Minister, Henry Asquith. However, beyond its significance as an English blunder and as a wastage of young Australian men led into a war of little consequence for their own country, Gallipoli came to symbolise the "ANZAC spirit" of noble sacrifice and indomitable courage. When Weir sought a good First World War story to film after *Picnic at Hanging Rock* (1975), Gallipoli became the obvious choice due to its epic quality and spiritual resonance.[1]

Weir wrote the original story for the film with the intention of following the entire campaign from 1914 to the evacuation completed in January 1916, based on accounts taken from the official history of the battle written by C E W Bean. He went to David Williamson for help with the draft, and the two eventually decided to tell the story from the point of view of the two fictional runners, Archy and Frank. This simplified the narrative and allowed Weir to build towards the emotional climax of Archy's death, an event with powerful Christian undertones.

In some measure, the Christian patterns that Weir weaves into *Gallipoli* are a concrete development of his interest in trans-historical, spiritual agency in the world. *Picnic at Hanging Rock* is a good example: the story of a small group of girls who inexplicably disappear on a strange rock cliff while on an outing with their school.[2] The film suggests some paranormal explanation for the occurrence, but never defines it. *Witness* (1985), perhaps Weir's most popular film, hints at a similar theme in its context of Amish spirituality, but does so more in its concluding sequence which quotes from the end of Carl Dreyer's masterpiece of dark spirituality, *Vampyr: Der Traum des Allan Grey* (*Vampire*, 1932). *Gallipoli* suggests some brooding cosmic spirituality in several scenes set in the Australian desert and in Egypt, but the spirituality most referenced in the narrative is Christian.

Gallipoli opens with the handsome young Archy Hamilton training with his uncle Jack for a run at the world record for the dash. The seventeen-year-old Australian athlete is intent on proving his manhood, firstly by racing barefoot against a man on horseback to answer a dare, and then by secretly joining the Australian Army to fight against the Germans and Turks. Archy accomplishes the latter by going off with his uncle to run in an important local meet, and then not returning. At the race, he meets and defeats the rather cynical Frank Dunne, who is physically and spiritually his opposite. Archy is blonde, sociable and idealistic, a rural innocent. Frank is dark-haired, cocky and cynical, a tough, streetwise product of the city of Perth.

Archy tries to convince Frank to enlist with him, but Frank does not understand Archy's sense of the importance of this kind of patriotism. However, things change when Archy is not allowed to join the cavalry after the meet because of his age, and so he and Frank hop on a train bound for Perth to try there. The train (poorly chosen by Frank, a foreshadowing of the tragic conclusion) leaves them at the edge of a desert, and the two youths walk 50 miles across it to get to the city, an experience that enforces their fraternal bonds. In Perth, Archy joins the Light Horse, and Frank tries to follow, but is rejected since he cannot ride. The two are separated, and the story follows Frank through his enlistment in the infantry with three of his former mates, and through their training in Egypt. Beyond training, the four friends pursue some amusements in the bazaars of Cairo, which provide a sharp contrast to the final sequences on the battlefield at Gallipoli. Archy and Frank are then reunited during a mock battle, and allowed a short time in Cairo to enjoy this twist of fortune.

The day before the climactic battle, Archy is chosen as a runner by the regiment commander, Major Barton (Bill Hunter), but he convinces the Major to allow Frank to run instead, since Archy has got Frank involved in the war and is far more courageous, or foolish. The narrative then turns to the futile ANZAC stand against the Turks played out in all its bitter horrors, as rows of men are shot down at the orders of the British Colonel Robinson (John Morris), who orders Major Barton to continue to rush the Turkish trenches to give the navy a chance to establish its positions. Major Barton decides to go over Colonel Robinson's authority to stop the slaughter, and sends Frank to run to General Gardner (Graham Dow) to secure a cease fire. Frank runs heroically at great personal risk and gets the order, but arrives back in the trench a moment too late as Major Barton is forced by Robinson to again blow the whistle to start a charge on the Turks. The line of ANZACs is massacred, including Archy who runs bravely into the enemy fire.

The impact of this concluding scene is profound, as Weir allows not only the war, but also the cruellest caprice of fate, to intersect at the moment when Frank collapses after arriving too late to save his friend and the other young soldiers. Although Archy seems doomed from the opening scene, when the audience is given a close-up of his handsome, innocent face as he prepares to run a practice sprint for his uncle,[3] the tragedy of his death is so devastating to experience after all that has preceded it that Weir's concluding stasis shot takes the viewer's breath away.

Perhaps it is the personal force of this moment that led Weir and Williamson to reach for the Christian motif of the Passion. Archy's physical beauty and innocence, coupled with his athleticism and goodness, make him a character rather larger than life. He runs to death fearlessly with his head thrown back, as if welcoming the bullet that stains his white shirt red, and it is this fearless idealism that helps the other young men in the trench, as well as Frank, to find the confidence to obey the terrible orders given them. When Barton prepares to blow the whistle for the final time, he encourages the fighters to "remember who you are". Archy embodies "who they are", the golden youth ready to lay down vocation and life for a cause greater than his own. It is the pattern of Christ dying as the perfect sacrifice for his people, yet here the sacrifice and martyrdoms which it inspires ring hollow. Weir's stasis shot is followed by no redemptive resolution. We do not see the community picking up the pieces with a renewed conviction as in *The Mission* (1986), nor hear the testimony of the saint pointing to a greater hope as in *Journal d'un curé de campagne* (*Diary of a Country Priest*, 1950). In Shakespearian terms, the rest in *Gallipoli* is silence. The screen goes blank.

Weir builds the sacrificial pattern early in the film. The opening scene of Archy training foreshadows the conclusion, as Archy hears his uncle drill him with a verbal play in preparation to run: "What are your legs? Springs, steel springs. What are they going to do? Hurl me down the track. How fast can you run? As fast as a leopard. How fast are you going to run? As fast as a leopard. Well, let's see you do it." The uncle wears a military-style hat, and blows a whistle to start his young protégé, the same style of whistle which Barton blows to send his men out of the trenches to certain death. Archy breathes deeply and submissively takes part in the game before running his sprint in a record-setting time.

Two aspects of this scene particularly enforce its symbolic context. The first is the camera's intimate look into the faces of Archy and his uncle. Uncle Jack (Bill Kerr) is grizzled and harsh as he prepares Archy; he is a type both of the war machine, exemplified by Colonel Robinson, that crushes the young men, and of the apparent ruling presence of the universe which engineers the complete gambit. If Archy is a young god, Uncle Jack and Colonel Robinson are each in some measure the father who sends, and thus the universe is more sinister than good. All the fathers in the film – with the exception of Barton, who is as much a victim as are Archy and the rest of the ANZAC troops – are depicted harshly. Archy's father is a rancher, indifferent to his son's athletic skill and waiting only for him to return so that his property can be fully managed. Frank's father is a crude drunkard, who impotently watches as his son prepares Archy to look older and pass the military enrolment officer at Perth. All the military officers are harsh or, as in Robinson's case, indifferent marionettes.

The second aspect of the scene that stands out occurs on the auditory level. With the exception of Archy's breathing and the exchange between him and Uncle Jack, the scene is silent. The ambient sounds that one would expect even in the desolation of the Australian ranch are missing, and the haunting score that accompanies the credits and returns in the final sequences, Albinoni's Lenten "Adagio in G minor for Strings and Organ", stops abruptly after the opening credits, scripted in red-tinged Gothic characters, are complete. The credits, appearing over a black background with the Albinoni score, set a liturgical context that is unmistakable, particularly when followed by the eerie, silent ritual of Archy sent running towards a finishing mark by his uncle.

That Archy and Frank are runners furthers the religious patterning, for St Paul equates the foot race with spiritual pilgrimage in his often-cited analogy in the Epistle to the Corinthians: "Do you not know that in a race all the runners run, but only one gets the prize? Run in such a way as to get the prize." (I Corinthians 9: 24). The idea is found several times in Scripture in both Old and New Testaments, and is highly recognisable among Christians. An obvious cross-reference might be *Chariots of Fire* (1981), which follows a similar narrative development as *Gallipoli*. In the large context, both Archy and Frank run the race of faith to Gallipoli, which Frank loses and so is spared. Archy's victory paradoxically rewards him with a bullet to the heart, which again suggests that the determining will behind this Passion is not intent on "working all things for good".

Archy's desire to enter the war follows his desire to step from young manhood into full manhood, a passage which never quite finds fulfilment, for Archy eventually comes full circle to the place of the obedient son, not the enlightened adult. As Martin Green has pointed out, Archy "shows no real promise of manhood. He is entirely ephebic, with his broad-brimmed hat and loose-limbed gestures and loping, sloping gait – defined by the contrast with Frank's cocky swagger".[4] When Frank prepares Archy for the enlistment officer at Perth, he has to glue hair on Archy's face. The war is the adventure that Archy believes will initiate him to the stature of his Uncle Jack, who has been on the Barbary Coast, and to that of the men he admires from newspaper accounts of the battles. But Archy cannot become a man, for he is too naïve and pure by nature. As he awaits the whistle that will sound his own death, he composes a letter to his parents: "Everyone is terribly excited. There is a feeling that we are involved in an adventure that is somehow larger than life." The simple-hearted sentiments of the letter fly in the face of the anguish and fear of the men in the trenches around him, who prepare for the worst in their own ways, as well as Frank, who is seen in cross-cuts dodging enemy fire and struggling to make it back in time with the command to cease fire. Archy seems to be made for another world, and, in a ritualistic sense, he is.

Weir plays on this theme throughout the film. Early on, Uncle Jack reads to Archy's younger siblings the description from Kipling's *The Jungle Books* (1894-95) of Mowgli's tearful parting from Bagheera to enter the realm of men. Archy enters the room as his uncle completes the story. In the subsequent sequence after a cut, Archy stands at the gate of the ranch looking out over the rugged terrain, and Jack goes to him and puts an arm on his shoulder. Obvious in this scene is the suggestion of the boy's wanderlust and his uncle's sympathy. Less obvious is the counterpoint which the landscape provides to Archy's dreams. The terrain is harsh and desolate, and the only prominent sound is the hollow, incessant whistling of the wind.

This wind, distinct in several early scenes, has some associations with the echo in the caves of E M Forster's novel, *A Passage to India* (1924): it represents the eternal question of existence. Archy pays no heed, but Frank will fear it. The sound recurs in the desert scene, as Frank and Archy walk to Perth. Archy is confident, and compels Frank to attempt the trip; throughout the trek, Archy leads, using his watch to determine direction, and Frank reluctantly follows. Several overhead shots emphasise the futility of the journey as the two young men appear in incidental spots on a glaring white landscape. It is pure coincidence that saves them from death, as Archy finds tracks in the sand at the moment when all hope appears lost. The tracks do not belong to a hero, but to an old desert vagabond who is completely unaware of the war and mystified as to why Archy and Frank would concern themselves with it.

The same motif is translated visually in the training sequence outside Cairo, as the men play rugby at the foot of the pyramids. The visual contrast is striking, as the game and players seem anachronistic and thoroughly out of place within the setting. Weir reinforces the symbolic importance of the pyramids in a later scene, when Archy and Frank race to the base of them and then climb them at night. A brief cross-cut of the pyramid looming above in the darkness punctuates the scene, as did an earlier brief shot of the Sphinx sandwiched between shots of Frank and his other mates buying cheap goods in the market, and shots of an officer helping the men to understand how to avoid venereal diseases.

When Archy and Frank are reunited in the mock battle, again the hollow wind provides the auditory context. By the time the ANZACs cross to Gallipoli, the viewer is conscious of this brooding, enigmatic force that threatens the players, and Archy in particular. Frank is aware of it and rebukes his friend for always being so cheerful; at the time, they are together in the trench with shells exploding nearby.

The passage of the troops into Gallipoli at night, perhaps the most riveting visual sequence of the film, begins the ritual that will make this spiritual reality known. It is, of course, a passage through water and fire, an apocalyptic baptism that dispels any question of where the narrative is leading. Fog rolls over a dark sky. There is no ambient sound and no musical track. The boats, full of young soldiers, cut through the fog, guided by a single light, until shells explode and add their glow. Then the Albinoni Adagio begins again, for the first time since the opening credits, and serving as a foreshadowing of the final scene in the trench. The Mass initiated, silence again takes over. A subsequent scene has a group of young soldiers, including Archy and Frank, run naked into the sea with shells exploding around them, and the water slowly tinting red from the first wounded man. The echo of St John's Apocalypse is unmistakable: "The first angel sounded his trumpet, and there came hail and fire mixed with blood, and it was hurled down upon the earth. A third of the earth was burned up, a third of the trees were burned up, and all the green grass was burned up. The second angel sounded his trumpet, and something like a huge mountain, all ablaze, was thrown into the sea." (Revelations 8: 7-8)

Of Frank's three mates (all of whom worked together on the railroads outside Perth) the weakest is Billy (Robert Grubb), a pale blonde youth with poor teeth who barely makes it through the medical examination during enlistment. He is a Christian who refuses to join the others when they visit a brothel in Cairo; yet, his faith seems insubstantial in the trenches. After Frank discovers from one mate, Snowy, that another, Barney, is dead, he searches for Billy and finds him badly wounded. Rather than offering Frank consolation, Billy quietly gives him his few possessions to pass on to his parents. This gesture cues the Albinoni score for the third time, signifying the triumph of the tragic, and thus again foreshadowing what will occur to Archy.

The final sequence, like all sacramental moments in film, changes the tempo of the narrative, and introduces a variety of interpretive signals that invite spectator identification and response. The camera tracks in extreme slow motion through the trench, and bits and pieces of dialogue form into a montage which concludes with Archy's internal narrative of his letter to his parents. Significantly, this is the only glimpse into Archy's thought life allowed to the viewer. The camera lingers on the objects which the soldiers place in the trench to be found after their deaths – notes, photos, knives and, finally, the stopwatch (a packed symbol in itself) which Uncle Jack left Archy, and the ribbons Archy won for his earlier race. This slow eulogy is then cross-cut with Frank's frantic run back from General Gardner, and with the static conversation between Major Barton and Colonel Robinson over the telephone, both men seemingly frozen in their peculiarly tragic roles in the pageant. The camera as narrative presence, together with the highly subjective auditory accompaniments, becomes the prominent player in this climax, and to resolve the incongruities, as it were, between rapid motion and slow, youth and death, purposefulness and chaos, the camera freezes Archy as he runs towards the enemy guns, and as the bullet stops him conclusively.

Archy is grossly out of place in the concluding sequence. He has no fighting experience. His speed on foot serves to make him an easier target for the Turks. He is forced to charge with a bayonet with the rest of the ANZACs – a useless weapon against the machine-guns of the enemies. Yet, he has been strangely out of place in the entire film. His physical beauty contrasts sharply with the rough terrain of his father's farm and with his co-workers, a dark-skinned friend named Zac, and a crude hand, Lenz. Zac disappears from the story after Archy leaves for the race. Lenz ends up in the same portion of the trench as Archy, who recognises his terrified friend just before the end. Likewise, Archy is out of place with his Uncle Jack. Although he may crave the adventure of his idol, he does not seem to have the same grit, and therefore has no business following the call to Gallipoli. Finally, Archy, as already mentioned, stands in sharp relief to Frank, who is older and more prepared for the battle by virtue of his instinctive understanding of what it will cost.

These themes, focused in Archy, resonate throughout the film. Both Archy and Frank are grossly out of place in the middle of the Australian desert, which they reach by hopping onto the wrong train. At Perth, Archy must alter his appearance to fool the enlistment officer about his age. Frank likewise tries to convince the officer that he can ride for the Light Horse, but he is unable to get his horse even to move in the trials. When Frank does enlist in the infantry (not his choice) with his friends, they likewise have to strong-arm their way in after the medical examiner questions Billy's teeth. In Cairo, Archy and Frank's light-hearted banter hardly fits the looming presence of the pyramids and the Sphinx. Later, Archy and Frank will find a way to sneak into an officer's ball prior to the expedition to Turkey. Major Barton discovers this last ruse, but allows the two friends to continue dancing, since he has received orders of the next day's mission. Barton will also see through yet another ruse – Archy's use of the last name "LaSalle", forged by Frank on a false birth certificate. Barton recognises Archy as the notable young runner, Hamilton, already well-known in parts of Australia. By these recognitions, Barton is established as the only character who sees the full tragedy that unfolds at the battle, although he is impotent to stop it, for Robinson insists on continuing the foolish campaign due to false information he has received about ANZAC troop successes.

There are more illusions and contrasts in the narrative, but these examples are sufficient to establish the point. Visually, the camera likewise alternates between scenes of great movement and business (the fair where Archy and Frank run; the Egyptian bazaar; the officers' ball; the trench) and scenes of stillness and open expanses (Archy's father's ranch; the desert; the Egyptian landscape; the field between the trenches of the ANZACs and Turks). On the audial level, the Albinoni Adagio is a striking contrast to the pulsing synthesizer score of Brian May which follows the parallel running scenes of Archy's barefoot race, Archy and Frank's run to the pyramids, and Frank's run to General Gardner.

All these devices underscore both the duplicity of the English who engineered the futile war effort that would leave so many Australian and New Zealand youths dead and wounded, and the folly of man's attempt to defy the forces of destruction and death. The former is historically the principle lesson to be learned from the failed military campaign. But Weir ups the stakes by suggesting that the historical tragedy is simply one instance of the larger tragedy played out through time by a grim fatality that cannot tolerate youth to linger or beauty to maintain its lustre; nor can fate abide good to conquer evil in every case. Archy is the sacrifice to this avenging power. Like the knight in Bergman's *Det sjunde inseglet* (*The Seventh Seal*, 1957), he plays a desperate chess game with death, yet he seems unaware of the game until the very end, when he hangs his uncle's stopwatch on the side of the trench. Time has allowed Archy to shine in near perfection, but only to take him as expiation at the last instant. Archy's almost welcome embrace of this role is evident as he prepares himself for the run with his uncle's verbal game, and as he rushes out of the trench and into the gunfire.

On the other hand, Frank must live on, knowing that one or two more seconds of speed may have saved dozens of lives. And Barton must live on, as the one witness to the events who fully shares in the audience's grief. Barton's sympathy is made evident in several scenes, most notably that in which he bids goodbye to his wife as he boards a ship bound for Egypt. This incidental scene does little to advance the plot, except to show, by virtue of the manifest love between Barton and his wife, that he will be different than Robinson and some of the other British officers who direct the troops. On the night before the assault on the Turks, Barton sits in his quarters sipping wine given to him by his wife, and listening to a Bizet opera on a phonograph. He closes his eyes in a reverie at the music and at the poignancy of his own situation, which he senses; at the entrance to his quarters, two soldiers look in at the Major with some perplexity. Their vision, like those of Archy and Frank, is more limited. That Barton should blow the whistle to send the troops to their death doubles his role in the tragedy with that of Archy's Uncle Jack, who has proven as insightful and yet impotent to ward off the progression of events – in his case, Archy's decision to leave home to join the Light Horse without his parents' knowledge or consent.

The physical and temperamental differences between the two men constitute a further subtlety handled by Weir and Williamson. Jack is a hard-edged adventurer who treats Archy like a benevolent drill sergeant. His choice of reading is Kipling's exotic Indian tale. Barton is depicted as softer and rounder in features, a more sensitive spirit. He sees through the relationship of Frank and Archy, and so gives in to Archy's request to allow Frank to run, and he treats his troops with understanding. Instead of Kipling, he listens to the more passionate Bizet. Both men have apparently experienced the things that Archy and Frank pursue, and both see the folly of such pursuits. Family ties are for them the epitome of human experience. Jack is more concerned for Archy and his siblings than their own father is. He has come back from his adventures to the desolation of the ranch, apparently for the family. Barton's primary concern is for his wife.

All this furthers the bad father/good father paradigm of *Gallipoli*. In addition, the connection of this model with Christian dogma and liturgical practice is useful for the larger discussion. Not only is Scripture laden with bad and good fathers, but also redemptive history can be seen as the development of a kind of family drama. The bad pseudo-son Lucifer rebels against God, who must send His only begotten son to defeat him. Lucifer becomes the bad father (of unrighteousness and darkness) in the fight, dragging many pseudo-sons like himself into the losing battle. Christ fulfils the duty of the perfect son and rightful heir by nobly sacrificing himself to claim many legitimate heirs for his father, and he fulfils the Father's prophetic words that the "seed of the woman", the legitimate son of God, would crush the head of the serpent, the illegitimate son/father. This is accomplished paradoxically on the cross. A foreshadowing of this cosmic story is found most specifically in the two books of Kings, a chronicle of the good and bad royal sons and fathers of Israel, and particularly the account of David and his bad son, Absalom. The Eastern branch of Christianity emphasises this narrative thread of Christian soteriology more than the West does, as it bases theological discussion and liturgical models most typically on the notion of Christus Victor, Christ the conqueror (over the evil son/father, Satan).[5]

The Christian overtones of Peter Weir's masterful film are unmistakable and provide force for the tragic conclusion. However, Weir subordinates these traditional patterns and symbols to a larger, more sceptical view of an ill-fated universe. Archy's death, Frank's tardiness with the crucial message, and Barton's inability to convince Robinson of the folly of the military campaign – all work together like the dismal events of a Thomas Hardy novel, in which players find themselves pawns of a larger sacrifice to be offered not on the altar of a Christian church, but on a Druidical table. It is the Passion story played out for a deaf and blind congregation, and to a silent, enigmatic and ultimately faceless god.

Notes

[1] "Peter Weir on *Gallipoli*", *Literature/Film Quarterly* 9: 4 (1981): 213-217.

[2] Gary Hentzi addresses Weir's New Age tendencies in "Peter Weir and the Cinema of New Age Humanism", *Film Quarterly* 44: 2 (1990): 2-12.

[3] As Martin Green has eloquently written, he is "too good to be true, too exquisite to merely survive, too fine to be allowed to coarsen, harden, toughen with experience" ("The Cult of Young Manhood", *Commonweal* 109 [March 1982]: 181-184).

[4] Ibid: 182.

[5] See Gustaf Aulén, *Christus Victor: An Historical Study of the Three Main Types of the Idea of the Atonement*, translated by A G Hebert (New York: Macmillan, 1969): especially 36-61.

Elia Kazan's *On the Waterfront* is one of the happy accidents of film history. Born out of the painful aftermath of the House Un-American Activities Committee (HUAC) hearings in Hollywood, and beset by lawsuits upon its release, in many regards it should not have risen above the kind of preachy message films that look terribly dated ten years after the fact. The remarkable performance by Marlon Brando as ex-fighter turned longshoreman, Terry Malloy – a performance which inspired Sylvester Stallone's *Rocky* (1976) and all its sequels and spin-offs, Martin Scorsese's *Raging Bull* (1980), as well as countless other films and actors – could easily not have happened. Kazan's original choice for the part was Frank Sinatra, while producer Sam Spiegel wanted Montgomery Clift. Neither opted for the role, so Kazan, as an afterthought, chose Brando whom he had directed in the Actors' Studio in New York.

On the Waterfront remains arguably among the top ten best Hollywood productions of all time. As powerful and moving 40 years after its release as it was when it swept eight Academy Awards® in 1954, this surprise masterpiece has all the resonance of the most personal and controlled of independent productions, and all the technical merit of the best Hollywood films. When Leonard Bernstein was initially approached to do the score for the film, he hesitated; but, when shown the original print of *On the Waterfront*, he was overcome by enthusiasm.[1] It is said that he viewed the film over 50 times in order to create a score fully to complement Kazan's conception.[2] Similarly, the film has remained an appealing choice in smaller art house cinemas, and for showing in colleges and film classes. Two of the most remarkable and often-quoted scenes are the initial courtship scene of Edie Doyle (Eva Marie Saint) and Terry Malloy, and the climactic conversation in the back of a cab between Terry and his brother, "Charley the Gent" (Rod Steiger), with Brando's "I could have been a contender" monologue. Interestingly, both scenes contained interpretive gestures by Brando that were largely spontaneous, and yet these tend to stay most firmly in the memory – the putting on of Edie's dropped glove in the first scene, and the pushing away of Charley's gun in the second.

These two famous scenes from the film point to one of the central features of the narrative: its Christian pattern. Terry puts on the glove of virtue through the mediation of Edie Doyle and the tough priest, Father Barry (Karl Malden), and pushes away the gun of vice held by his brother, Charley, a lackey for the corrupted longshoreman's union and its mob boss, "Johnny Friendly" (Lee J Cobb). The connection may be made here to *Casablanca* (1943), in which Rick (Humphrey Bogart) undergoes a type of spiritual renewal through the mediation of a woman, Ilsa (Ingrid Bergman), that enables him to make a supreme sacrifice with similarly strong Christian overtones. In the climactic scene, Rick tells Ilsa that she cannot go where he is going, a reworking of Jesus's words to his disciples prior to his death; he sacrifices himself that she may be "a pure bride". In *On the Waterfront*, Terry's change of heart leads to an equally overt sacrifice, as he leads the union workers in a stand against Johnny Friendly that gets him rejected by all his old friends and nearly beaten to death.

The Christian patterning in *On the Waterfront*, however, is more consequential than in the subordinate theme played out particularly at the end of *Casablanca*, so much so that Kazan's film deserves attention as an example of the sacramental style, and, more particularly, as an overt development of how the Passion drama finds a central place in liturgical cinematic narratives. Terry Malloy does more than experience a moral make-over by the end of *On the Waterfront*. He walks his last steps into the yawning entrance to the dockyard as the incarnation of the Saviour, whom Father Barry has told the workers "is down here on the waterfront". He walks into the darkness of death "to lead captivity captive and to bestow gifts on men" (Ephesians 4: 8). In addition, this final procession employs a subjective camera to encourage and enhance our participation in this Passion. The film builds this drama from its opening sequence, when Terry unknowingly sets up Edie's brother, Joey, for a mob hit, and is troubled by the guilt and shame of the blood on his hands. It is this Passion drama of Kazan's film, so convincingly developed in its overall conception and brilliant individual performances, that mostly explains the remarkable power of the film. Reflecting on the film's success, Kazan himself drew the same conclusion: "My guess is that it's [the film's power is] the theme, that of a man who has sinned and is redeemed".[3]

Yet, it is not just a redeemed sinner who leads the longshoremen in a revolt against the mob bosses; it is a saviour, for, until Terry picks up his hook and staggers to the dark entrance, the men have no heart to fight the corruption. The echoes are unmistakable – Terry staggers forwards, with his hook a kind of cross to fulfil the instruction of the Father (Father Barry); he is ministered to by a woman, Edie, who wants to keep him from the journey; he falls, but gets back up; and, as he proceeds, Johnny Friendly is pushed into the harbour (an apocalyptic reference to Satan cast into the pit).

Before proceeding further along these lines, however, references should be made to the events that originally led Kazan and scriptwriter Budd Schulberg to the material, since these seem to have played a large part in the original design of the drama. Firstly, there was the testimony of Kazan and Schulberg (and of Lee J Cobb, who played Johnny Friendly) before HUAC in the early 1950s. Both men had been active members of the Communist Party in the 1930s, and both subsequently rejected the dehumanizing subordination of will demanded by the Party. When they were called before HUAC, they readily confessed their previous associations with Communism, and implicated others in the film industry who were involved. For this, they incurred the wrath of many within the Hollywood rank and file, an experience which seems to have given birth to the film's theme of public confession as a two-edged sword, dividing men from their fellows, yet providing personal regeneration and peace.

The second significant event leading to the creation of *On the Waterfront* was the publication of New York State Crime Commission findings on corruption in the docks of New Jersey harbour. The links between organised crime and the running of the New Jersey docks in the 1940s and 1950s were unmistakable – extortion against freight carriers; bogus union elections; fraudulent book-keeping; bullying tactics. The Commission exposed many of the practices by coaxing certain workers to "rat" on the mob bosses, and then providing them with police protection (with marginal success). The character of Terry Malloy was apparently based on Anthony (Tony Mike) De Vincenzo, who collected over $25 000 in an out-of-court settlement against the filmmakers for invasion of privacy. De Vincenzo had informed against Michael Clemente, the boss of ILA Local 968 (and a prototype of the Johnny Friendly character), a mobster with close links to the powerful Vito Genovese family of New York, which profited off the docks. De Vincenzo claimed he was "proud to be a rat".[4]

Schulberg travelled to Hoboken, New Jersey, to do research for the screenplay, and decided with Kazan to shoot the film on location, using the corrupted dock practices as a context for the narrative's more personal concern, the psychological drama of Terry Malloy's journey towards integrity. While in Hoboken, Schulberg made the acquaintance of Father John Corridan, a priest who had entered fully into the life of the docks as his parish, and who thus became the model for the film's

Father Barry, a dynamic and earthy man whom Schulberg had originally doubted could be a priest. Some of Father Barry's sermon to the dockworkers near the end of the film was a paraphrase of Father Corridan's own published admonition to the workers in Hoboken and their employers: "Some people think the Crucifixion took place only on Calvary...Christ goes to a union meeting".[5]

The events in Hoboken provided a more focused and dramatically tight narrative frame for the redemption story that seemed to be suggested by Kazan and Schulberg's HUAC experiences. Here was a way not only to illustrate the virtue of informing for the good of society, but also to make the agencies of good and evil more identifiable for the average audience, and thus more universally appealing. Unlike other films triggered by HUAC's examination of Hollywood, such as *The Front* (1976) or *Guilty by Suspicion* (1990), *On the Waterfront* does not suffer from veiled anger and biased, historically-blinded preachiness. The historical moment of Kazan's film and its connection to his and Schulberg's personal experiences as "informers" simply put flesh on the larger, overtly Christian drama of sin, redemption and self-sacrifice centred in the character of Terry Malloy.

The story-line of the film is sufficiently simple. Terry Malloy sets up a dockworker named Joey Doyle to be killed by thugs employed by crooked union boss, Johnny Friendly. When Joey is killed, thrown from his apartment roof, Terry is grief-stricken, having thought that the plan was simply to rough Joey up; Joey was about to testify against the union to the New Jersey Crime Commission, and Johnny Friendly had to silence him. Joey's sister, Edie, recently home from a Catholic girls' school, urges a local priest, Father Barry, to get involved in the workers' lives to find Joey's killer and to do something to end the corruption. Father Barry calls a meeting of disgruntled workers, which gets attacked by Johnny Friendly's men. One of the workers beaten for attending, Kayo Dugan (Pat Henning), agrees to testify against the bosses. In addition, Terry begins to sympathise with the workers and to fall in love with Edie. Father Barry urges Terry to testify, and, conscience-stricken and driven by his love for Edie and by an awakened moral sense, Terry agrees to do it. As a result, his brother Charley is killed by Johnny Friendly. Terry plans to revenge his brother's death with violence, but Father Barry convinces him to do it before the Crime Commission, which he does. As a result of his testimony, Terry is shunned by many close friends and at the docks during the "shape-up" when jobs are distributed. Terry confronts Johnny Friendly at the docks and begins to beat him in a fist fight, but Friendly's men step in and together beat Terry viciously and leave him semi-conscious on the ground. Again, Father Barry steps in and urges Terry to get up and lead the workers on the docks in open defiance of the corrupt union bosses. He does so and Johnny Friendly is humiliated before all the workers.

The most prominent thematic pattern in this film is that of public confession, of the union practices on the one hand, and of personal guilt and complicity on the other. Throughout the film such confession is considered "ratting" or "stooling"; yet, it is the only hope for a cure to the problems, the only hope for social and personal peace. The symbol most used to suggest this message is the pigeon. Both Terry and Joey keep pigeons. Terry sets Joey up by telling him that he found one of his pigeons, and is sending it up to the roof. The pigeon is released, set free by Terry, and Joey is killed. By this act, Terry is caught in the web of waterfront crime. So the bird tends to represent both the captivity of the characters and their means of freedom.

When Terry confronts Johnny Friendly about Joey's death, Johnny pays him off in cash and by giving him an easy job on the docks "in the loft". In the following scene, Terry is on his own roof tending his and Joey's pigeons, which he keeps in a square cage on his roof. He tells a young boy, Tommy, who helps him, that pigeons have it easy, since they only have to eat and sleep. Thus, Terry is caged by his guilt like the pigeons, and unable to break free to fly and enjoy life. When Terry is confronted with a possible subpoena from Crime Commission agents, he asks: "How do you like them mugs takin' me for a pigeon?". When Edie enters Terry's life, she joins him on the roof, and he shows her his prize pigeon. During the scene, he is on one side of the mesh cage and she is on the other, for he is unable to share her freedom, due to his complicity in Joey's death. When Terry finally confesses to Edie, their relationship is fully established and he is set free from the influence of the Johnny Friendly gang. In anger, Tommy kills all the pigeons and throws Terry the prize bird, calling, "a pigeon for a pigeon". The death of the birds ironically frees Terry from his past and reverses the conditions at the beginning, when the losing of the bird spelled Joey's death and Terry's bondage to guilt.

Images of freedom and captivity run through the whole film. One of the strongest visual contrasts in the film is between the open space of the Hoboken waterfront and the dark enclosure and brick wall of the dockyard. Johnny Friendly and his men gather in a small crude shed on the edge of the pier, a structure grossly out of size with the expanse of water behind it and with the huge forms of the men who gather inside. When Friendly's men storm the church where Father Barry initially attempts to rally the workers, these workers, together with Terry, Edie and Father Barry, must flee the trap by running in all directions. Terry and Edie break free and step out into a street scene that again is extremely wide and expansive. As they walk towards the waterfront, the screen space opens out even more. Likewise, Terry's rooftop loft creates a wide open space that greatly contrasts with the claustrophobic settings of other parts of the film – the billiard hall; the back seats of cars; Edie's apartment; the tavern where Terry takes Edie on their first day together. When Terry confronts Charley in the back of the cab about Charley's mismanagement of Terry's life, Charley wants to take Terry to a ball game at the stadium, a wide-open space. Instead, Terry is let out of the cab, and the driver, a plant, takes Charley to Johnny Friendly, who has him murdered and pinned to a wall in a dark and narrow alley.

The theme of confession, and these contrasts between wide-open, free spaces and deathly enclosures, blend with the larger Christian pattern of sin, confession, and the freedom of forgiveness and peace. Terry complains to Father Barry: "If I spill [confess], my life ain't worth a nickel". The priest counters: "And how much is your soul worth if you don't?". A little earlier, Terry tells the priest that his guilt is "like carrying a monkey on your back". Father Barry again replies aptly: "It's a question of who rides who". As the Christian faith teaches, unconfessed sin produces bondage of the will and death to the soul. "We know that we are the children of God", John writes, "and that the whole world is under the control of the evil one" (I John 5: 19). Freedom comes when the shackle of guilt is removed through forgiveness. When Terry finally confesses to Edie, it is on a hill at the water's edge overlooking the harbour. Although Kazan uses a ship's whistle as an overlay that prevents the viewer from hearing the whole of Terry's admission – and thus intensifies the emotional force of his words on Edie and the magnitude of his crime – the visual relief created by the waterfront background, together with the subjective distance in which the camera mostly maintains the perspective of Father Barry who watches from a distance, imply the freedom that this confession will ultimately bring. As Father Barry watches Edie run off, signalling to him that Terry has unburdened himself, the camera lingers in an unusually interpretive close-up of the priest's face, catching his sense of relief and gladness as he lights a cigarette.

Terry's awareness of his own guilt comes by degrees. After Joey's death he tells Johnny Friendly, "I think I should have been told" about the intention of the set-up. His manner is awkward and his glance is sheepish. Johnny is able to convince him temporarily of what a good friend he ("Uncle Johnny") is to him. He even spars with Terry in play, a foreshadowing of the final scene. As Terry leaves Johnny and his men, and walks through the door of the billiards hall, he disappears through a veil of smoke. Smoke or fog will continue as a visual motif throughout the film, particularly in the scenes in front of the dock, and when Terry first walks Edie home after the altercation at the church. This haze suggests Terry's moral blindness, as well as the corruption of the city. Significantly, when Terry finally sees clearly and confronts Charley in the back of the cab ("There's more to this than I thought"), the camera is stable and the image of the two men crisp. Before this new vision, however, Terry must fight himself and put up with the urgings of Father Barry and Edie, neither of whom are particularly easy on him. Father Barry refuses to hear his confession at first, and Edie will tell him in the tavern, "No wonder everybody calls you a bum".

That Terry is a bum troubles his conscience. He denies it to Edie, or at least urges her not to say it. Later in the cab, he will admit it to Charley, although forcing his brother to recognise the part he played in Terry's failed life. When Terry has confessed and decided to go to the docks for work and ultimately to confront Johnny Friendly, he tells Edie: "They always said I was a bum. Well, I ain't a bum, Edie." Due to the social agenda of the film – Terry's confession is for the good of society, at least according to Father Barry – Terry's sinful guilt is given a social context. He is useless in society, a bum.

The moral battle which Terry undergoes is conveyed metaphorically by his boxing. He had been a fine middleweight, almost a contender, until Charley told him to throw a fight so that Johnny Friendly and his friends could get rich on the odds. As the film begins, Terry is an ex-fighter. When Johnny Friendly spars with him in the billiards room, he half-heartedly plays the part. It is not until his conscience is awakened, during Father Barry's sermon after Kayo Dugan's death, that Terry actually strikes out, decking one of Johnny's men who heckles the priest. And, of course, at the end, he beats Johnny before the men step in. Terry's moral impotence, created by his complicity with the dirty union, matches his physical; and, as he is renewed, he becomes more physical. This is also true in other instances. Because of his association with Edie and the priest, he is forced by Johnny Friendly to work loading cargo instead of laying in "the loft". He breaks Edie's door down to tell her of his love after his confession to her. Then he breaks a window to save them both from a truck sent to run them down by the mob. He intends to kill Johnny Friendly with Charley's gun, until Father Barry knocks him down with a punch (an extension of the spiritual strength/physical strength motif). Then he throws the gun into a portrait of Johnny Friendly and the "Mr Big" behind the union bosses. At the Crime Commission investigation, he answers aggressively, and in the final scene his activity – staggering to the dockyard to lead the workers in – saves the men.

As Kenneth Hey has pointed out,[6] the film's narrative centres around three ritualised scenes, each of which furthers the Christian context. The first is that of the "shape-up" when "Big Mac" distributes job assignments to a large crowd of desperate workers. The second is Father Barry's sermon over the dead body of Kayo Dugan. The third is Terry's testimony before the legal authorities brought together by the Crime Commission. Each scene receives extended play in the drama and stands as an apostrophe within the main action.

In the shape-up segment, the smirking union stevedore tosses job assignments onto the ground for the last workers to scramble after. It is a scene of cruelty and subjugation which underlines the depths to which the mob has brought the men. When Edie scrambles after a job coin for her father, Pop Doyle, Terry confidently grabs it and playfully holds it away from her, positioning him with the leering stevedore and the exploitation brought by the union. When he finds out that Edie is Joey's sister, his attitude changes abruptly, since she represents both what he has lost and what he wants to retain.

In the second ritualised scene, Father Barry delivers a powerful sermon for all the workers to hear over Kayo Dugan's body, crushed by a load of boxes intentionally dropped on him to keep him from testifying. During the sermon, Father Barry urges the men that "everyone who keeps silent is just as guilty as the Roman soldiers who pierced the flesh of our Lord". Terry is particularly struck by the words, and the camera reveals his fixed attention in several reaction-shots. Terry is thus linked with the common workers, Kayo and Edie vs. Johnny Friendly and Charley, both of whom look down upon the men from a greater height.

In the third ritualised scene before the Crime Commission, the courtroom setting seems entirely out of place with the *mise en scène* of the remainder of the film. It is too orderly and populated by outsiders. Johnny Friendly and his men are fenced from the rest of the court in a separate seating area, Terry is boxed in beside the bench, and the spectators and reporters are seated neatly (until the end of the scene, when Johnny Friendly threatens Terry for his confession).

The three scenes suggest a liturgical progression from the acknowledgment of sin to the proclaimed message which condemns the sin and points to the way of salvation to the confession and response to that message. Terry is a central figure in all three, which together form the grounds for his alignment with Christ in the final action. The uniqueness of each scene as a set-piece serves as a cue for the spectator to the prominence of them in the complete narrative. When the camera takes Terry's subjective viewpoint as he staggers towards the dockyard opening, the sacramental nature of these narrative gestures is fully realised.

A visual set-up for this sacramental pattern is the up vs. down positioning of the actors and the camera throughout the narrative. Terry calls Joey from a street below his window; then Joey ascends to the roof and is thrown down. Terry climbs to his loft to brood over his troubles, then descends to Father Barry and confesses his guilt to Edie who walks along the shore (with Father Barry watching from above). Father Barry's initial meeting with the workers is in the basement of the church. Then he preaches from below in the sermon over Kayo Dugan. Johnny Friendly tends to be positioned to look down on those around him. When Terry breaks into Edie's apartment, she cowers from him on the floor under a crucifix. When she runs, he grabs her and they fall to the floor in an embrace and kiss. The camera follows the same pattern, shooting Big Mac from below to emphasise his size and authority, and shooting Terry in several scenes from a position above him to emphasise his smallness. Within the larger ritual, this pattern tends to emphasise powerlessness vs. power; individuals at the hands of the corrupted system; sinners at the hands of a greater evil; and men under the providential watch of God. In the final scene, Terry is beaten down by Johnny Friendly's men, and he lays in a pool of water on the pier where Edie and Father Barry coax him to rise. On his walk to the entrance, the camera views him from the front and slightly below level. Pop Doyle then knocks Johnny Friendly into the harbour, and, as the men follow Terry, the camera glances back to the union boss from a height, diminishing his importance.

This last shift against Johnny Friendly's authority is entirely motivated by Terry's ascendency in his ritualistic alignment with Christ. As Peter Biskind has argued,[7] the film is largely about shifting power arrangements; yet, the final appeal to power is to that of God. If there is some ambiguity regarding how effective a solution Terry's confession has brought to the union problems on the waterfront, there is little ambiguity to the suggestion that, regardless of the social alignments, Terry has transcended them through his "conversion". The way of the Cross becomes the way to freedom and change.

Kazan sprinkles the film with visual suggestions of the cross, not unlike Borzage's many images of the icon in *A Farewell to Arms* (1932). The most noticeable of these images are on the rooftops near Terry's loft, where antennas and their braces look like a series of crosses on the buildings. When Edie first visits Terry on the roof, she is positioned conspicuously beside one such structure. The image is reinforced when Terry talks to her from inside the cages, behind the wire mesh, a posturing that suggests a confessional booth. The previous scene had Pop Doyle reprimanding Edie in their apartment for being with Terry. On the back wall, often centred in the frame during the exchange, is the household crucifix. Pop Doyle tells Edie of his own sacrifice to send her to the convent school. One arm is longer than the other from swinging his hook, so he reminds her of the cross he has born for her and the family. She seemingly carries that cross to the roof when she meets Terry, for her plea to him, as she will tell him in the tavern, is "Help me if you can, for God's sake" to find her brother's killer. The only way for Terry to help will be to give himself up and incur the wrath of the mob. Father Barry preaches to the men that "killing Joey Doyle and Kayo Dugan is a crucifixion". When Charley is killed, Johnny Friendly's men pin him to a wall by his hook, which is aligned with the cross by Pop Doyle and in Terry's final walk to the dock.

A similar visual image prominent in the film is the fence or mesh grate. When Terry first sets up Joey, he calls him from behind a spiked iron fence. When the workers fill the church, several are beaten against a fence. When Terry takes Edie home, they stop by an iron fence similar to that at the beginning, and Terry opens up a little of his past to her. The mesh of the pigeon coop becomes prominent in several scenes in which Terry alone is on the inside; however, after Tommy kills the birds, Edie enters to give him sympathy. When Father Barry watches Terry confess to Edie, he stands behind the iron fence, which Terry passes around to meet her. Again, in the courtroom scene, Johnny Friendly and his men are fenced from Terry and the crowd. The imagery, as with the crosses, seems rather obvious in the larger patterns of the film. Terry is fenced from Joey and Edie and all that is worthwhile by his moral bondage, and broken free from these fences by his confessions. The concept of moral bondage appears frequently in the New Testament, especially in the highly theological letter to the Romans, in which Paul appeals to Jewish legal practices to explain the significance of Christ's death and the Resurrection: "Therefore, there is now no condemnation for those who are in Christ Jesus, because through Christ Jesus the law of the Spirit of life set me free from the law of sin and death" (Romans 8: 1-2). The usage in *On the Waterfront* is somewhat standard within a Christian context, and the images of enclosures also further the oppressive atmosphere of the visual environment. All the men are in a social and moral bondage. All have been rendered "D-D", deaf and dumb for the sake of the union.

The overall feel of the film's visual planes is one of loneliness – men huddled in small groups before the dock entrance, hoping to get work; indigents staying warm in front of smouldering rubbish bins; small figures, such as Terry and Edie, in large spaces playing out the important rituals of their lives. The fog and smoke; the blowing of ships' whistles in the distance; the excess of concrete surfaces – all suggest modern alienation and *angst*. Leonard Bernstein's score shares the same mood, especially the minor-keyed melodies that open and close the film. This is the little man in the big city mood that characterises so much of film noir in the 1940s and 1950s; yet, here the main character lacks the aggressive self-confidence of the players in that genre. Terry is very much lost in a void, searching for meaning. When he shares his life philosophy with Edie in the tavern, he shares the primitive law of tribal bands, "Do it to him before he does it to you". This is an almost conscious parody of Jesus's words to "love your neighbour as yourself" or, in the popularized version, "Do unto others as you would have them do to you".

It is interesting that this mood of urban loneliness is perhaps the aspect of the film that most influenced Avildsen's *Rocky*, especially since that film quite consciously mutes the Christian overtones of *On the Waterfront*.[8] There is a strong feeling of moral isolation in both films, and both protagonists overcome their loneliness through the love of a woman and a form of ritualised self-sacrifice. Both men suffer to redeem themselves, but Terry Malloy also provides a model to redeem the community. Rocky's act becomes a symbol for a kind of fanciful wish-fulfilment, best seen in the development of the film's sequels and its spin-offs, such as *Flashdance* (1983) and *The Karate Kid* (1984). It is specifically the Christian liturgical characteristics of Kazan's and Schulberg's film that keep the narrative familiar, and therefore emotionally resonant and spiritually affecting.

On the Waterfront succeeds just because it seems so familiar, especially for those who have experienced urban life. Its redemptive conclusion has, for this reason, the force of truth. As in Eucharistic celebrations, the power of the Incarnation manifested far transcends the power of words and propositions. Father Barry's sermon within the narrative may succeed in turning Terry towards moral courage, but it is Terry's journey with his cross, which we experience vicariously in those subjective moments at the end, which turns the film viewer towards moral courage in the world of real women and men.

Notes

[1]   Leonard Bernstein, "Notes Struck at 'Upper Dubbing,' California", *The New York Times* 30 May 1954, Section 2: 5.

[2]   Kenneth Hey, "Ambivalence as a Theme in *On the Waterfront* (1954): An Interdisciplinary Approach to Film Study", *American Quarterly* 31: 5 (1979): 666-696. Besides the useful historical information in Hey's article, the author presents an excellent comprehensive look at the narrative themes and visual patternings of the film.

[3]   Elia Kazan, *Elia Kazan: A Life* (New York: Alfred A Knopf, 1988): 528.

[4]   Cited in Edward Murray, *Ten Film Classics: A Re-Viewing* (New York: Frederick Ungar Publishing Co., 1978): 101.

[5]   Cited in Hey: 679.

[6]   Ibid: 677-681.

[7]   Peter Biskind, "The Politics of Power in 'On the Waterfront'", *Film Quarterly* 29: 1 (1975): 25-38.

[8]   Maurice Yacowar compares the two films at length in "Dick, Jane, Rocky and T. S. Eliot", *Journal of Popular Film* 6: 1 (1977): 2-12.

When Fritz Lang fled Hitler and Nazism and came to the United States in the late 1930s, he made three "social consciousness" films in succession, *Fury* (1936), *You Only Live Once* and *You and Me* (1938). Each carried the moral concerns of Lang's earlier German successes – such as *Metropolis* (1926), *M* (1931) and *Das Testament des Dr Mabuse* (*The Testament of Dr Mabuse*, 1932) – more strongly in the direction of societal criminality and guilt over that of the individual. The child murderer in *M* accuses his underworld tribunal of hypocrisy when they seek to punish him without appreciating the negative influences that created his warped desires. In *Fury*, Lang takes this idea further in describing how a small-town mob slowly forms around a false idea, and then turns to murder to complete the folly. Joe Wilson, a single man en route to his own wedding, is stopped by a rural police officer and brought into the station for suspicion. The police decide that he fits the description of a murderous fugitive and lock him up. Word gets around town that Joe is the murderer, and a mob surrounds the prison and burns it down; however, Joe escapes and brings murder charges against the town. This shift from the guilt of the individual towards the guilt of society against the individual is what is most striking about Lang's first American films or, perhaps more aptly put, Lang's post-Hitler films. Lang seemed to find in the rise of National Socialism confirmation of his belief that the law of the mob is far more heinous than the licence of the mob's scapegoats.

You Only Live Once has a story-line not far removed from that of *Fury*. Eddie Taylor (Henry Fonda), a three-time loser, is released from prison through the intercession of his fiancée, Jo (Sylvia Sidney), who works for the public defender, Stephen Whitney (Barton MacLane). Eddie and Jo marry, and Eddie gets a job through Whitney at a local trucking company. The two find a dilapidated cottage for sale and decide to buy it; however, just before closing the deal, Eddie is unjustly fired by his boss who is prejudiced against him for being an ex-con. Eddie is then framed for a bank robbery and murder by another former con named Monk Mendall, and convicted on the circumstantial evidence of his hat being found at the scene. He is put on death row, but escapes. As he tries to leave the yard with a prison doctor as hostage, word comes over the wire that Monk's body has been found with the getaway truck and that Eddie is innocent. The prison chaplain, Father Dolan (William Gargan), a good-hearted man who has helped Eddie in the past, tries to convince Eddie that he is a free man and to stop him from fleeing. Eddie kills the priest and manages to escape, although he is wounded by gunfire. Jo meets him and nurses him back to health, and the two go on the run, sleeping in shanties on the way to the Mexican border. On the way, Jo gives birth to a son whom she entrusts to Whitney and her sister, Bonnie. Shortly before reaching the border, Jo is recognised while purchasing cigarettes, and the police trap the two on the road and fire through the car's rear windshield. Jo is mortally wounded and dies in Eddie's arms as he carries her towards the border. A sniper kills Eddie moments later, but, as Eddie dies, he sees a light in the sky and hears Father Dolan saying, "You're free Eddie. The gates are open."

From the first moments of the film, Lang reverses the terms of justice to prepare the viewer for the sympathetic treatment he will give Eddie, even after killing Father Dolan. The scene is set in the public defender's office, and a cheerful Jo, preparing to go to the prison to see Eddie, is being confronted by a local apple-seller who complains strenuously and somewhat comically that the beat policeman who is supposed to watch his stand keeps taking apples to eat without paying. As the scene is played – since the later developments of the plot are hidden – the apple merchant seems a crank, and the viewer sides with Jo in dismissing him. But, at the conclusion of the scene, after an exchange within the inner office between the DA and Stephen Whitney, the camera returns to the apple-seller who watches in dismay as the beat policeman he had been accusing enters the office, takes another of his apples, and begins to eat it without concern.

This early incident, unrelated to the fate of Eddie and Jo, prepares the viewer for the injustice that Eddie and Jo will suffer through the narrative. Tipping this connection off is the film's visual leitmotif, a close-in shot of an object or group of objects, which then opens to a larger shot of their place within a context. The introduction to the apple-seller and his plight is just such a close shot of a group of apples on a counter. The apples have no significance at this point and little throughout the scene, until the end when the viewer recognises the injustice of the beat policeman and the significance of the apples to the vendor in the face of this injustice. The subsequent scene opens with the same gesture, this time a close-in shot of a suitcase being packed. The camera pulls back to reveal Jo busily and happily preparing for her reunion with Eddie and their ensuing marriage. Given the way the first scene plays out, one expects the suitcase to take on a similar significance – which it will, since the centre of Eddie and Jo's life together will be their flight from the police with little possessions beyond what she can stuff into this suitcase. Ironically, after Eddie and Jo escape the police following the murder of Father Dolan, local gossip attributes to them every crime committed in the areas through which they travel. Lang, at one point, cuts to a man who suggests to a companion that the two fugitives must be living it up somewhere. In truth, as another cut reveals, they are cold, hungry and desperate. Therefore, together with the importance of context established in these opening scenes, Lang suggests perception or interpretation of objects in their context as a crucial element in the story. Just as the viewer is led to misevaluate the apples and is left guessing about the significance of the suitcase, so the viewer will be demanded to analyze carefully the primary objects on display, the two ill-fated lovers.

With the elements introduced, Lang dissolves from Jo's preparations to the prison where Eddie will be viewed for the first time. The camera fixes Eddie's face, predictably, as it had on the apples and the suitcase. The warden recaps the man's criminal history, and encourages him to make a new life. Eddie replies in bitter words, which makes his figure an unlikely match to the bubbly Jo: "I will – if they let me".

The scene is followed by one which again forces contextualization and interpretation. Some inmates are playing baseball and an umpire behind home plate makes a call that the players hotly contest. The umpire gruffly dismisses their yells and catcalls, and leaves the players to join Eddie who will be leaving the prison. When the umpire takes off his mask (a device used later in the robbery sequence), the viewer notices the flash of a white clerical collar. This glancing image again reverses expectations as the tough figure of the umpire seems incongruous with the garb of a priest. Within this minor revelatory moment lies hidden another, noted by critic George Wilson: "Among the crowd are two prisoners who are playing draughts surrounded by their own small audience. When this group turns its attention to Father Dolan's faulty umpiring, one of the players, unnoticed by the rest, makes a cheating move. We have another lesson in audience attention."[1] When Eddie is encouraged by Father Dolan as he leaves the prison, the priest tells him that he does not look happy. Eddie again replies bitterly: "I cheered the first time I got out – they rammed it right back down my throat. They're not all like you on the outside." Again, the viewers expectations are reversed. Not only is Eddie not a suitable match for Jo, at least based on speech, but also he is not behaving with the attitude we would expect of a man in his position, let free into the arms of a beautiful woman. Furthermore, his comments cast suspicion on the role of the warden and the priest.

Those who represent society's view of Eddie and Jo throughout the film are consistently flawed. The warden's view of Eddie is proven shallow when he goes from accepting Eddie's guilt and corruption on the evidence of Eddie's hat found by the police, to his instant and nearly absurd proclamation that Eddie is innocent, based on the one-line message passed over the ticker-tape, a message which he feels Eddie will readily embrace. Whitney gets it right when he tells the police inspector later in the narrative: "The law condemned him to death. They found out they'd made a mistake – and they thought they could straighten it out just like that." Likewise, the police treat the couple with a kind of cynical pleasure in their misery. The gunner who wounds Jo jumps into the highway and indiscriminately fires a machine-gun through the car window. Then a sharpshooter fixes the couple in his rifle sights and calmly fires to finish the work. The image of the couple seen through the cross-hairs of the rifle is synecdochic of society's attitude towards criminal scapegoats.

Three other scenes play this out in more particular detail. When Eddie and Jo arrive at the Valley Tavern, a small resort that Jo has found for their honeymoon, the lovers experience a few moments of bliss outside by a pond, complete with two frogs sitting together and flowers all around.[2] The owners, a pinched husband henpecked by a waspish wife, throw the lovers out of their room in the middle of the night when the husband recognises Eddie's picture from a crime magazine. The hypocrisy of the gesture – a soured dysfunctional couple of "middle-class respectability" condemning the happy lovers for Eddie's past crime – makes Eddie's previous and subsequent anger seem justifiable.

In the second such scene, Eddie confronts his boss at the Ajax trucking company to plead for his job. The camera captures the callous owner from above, suggesting the distance between his position as a "respectable" business-owner within the environs of his workplace, and the pessimism Eddie has begun to undergo. While Eddie leans across the desk and implores the man to reconsider his decision to dismiss him, the boss talks on the telephone to his wife, deciding who should come to a poker party at their house. He turns in his chair away from Eddie to speak in genteel fashion to his wife, then puts his hand over the phone and speaks hard words to Eddie which convey an attitude of loathing.

The third scene of this nature opens with the leitmotif of the camera lingering in close-up on a newspaper pinned to a wall. The headline reads, "TAYLOR FREED IN MASSACRE!". When the camera pulls back the viewer sees three newspapers, the other two with headlines, "TAYLOR

JURY DEADLOCKED!" and "TAYLOR GUILTY!!". An editor slouches at his desk waiting for the call that will decide which paper should be run on the day after Eddie's trial for robbery and murder. This new context again underlines the need to view the thread of Eddie's life from an appropriate perspective, and suggests the vicious indifference of the "respectable" citizens who hold the couple's fate in the balance. Justice on earth is skewed and fallible.

Lang weaves these threads together most tightly in the climactic scene when Eddie kills Father Dolan. Present with Eddie are all the antagonists who seem bent on his destruction – the warden, the police, the respectable doctor as hostage, and, of course, the priest, who stands for the moral compass of society (he is the prison chaplain, after all), despite his sympathy towards Eddie. Eddie is below in the prison yard shrouded by a dense fog, and lit by a spotlight which creates an eerie Expressionistic atmosphere, reminiscent of chiaroscuro shots in some of Lang's German films. The warden, flanked by two prison guards with rifles, tells him to give himself up. The camera looks down on Eddie and up to the warden, the reversal of the attitude which the camera has led the viewer to adopt. When Father Dolan enters the scene and goes down (a symbolic move) from the bridge to talk with Eddie in the yard below, the fog literally envelopes him in a cloud and thus suggests an authority beyond time and place. Behind the priest, light flows through the bars of two prison windows whose symmetrical design and position suggest a fixed way of seeing and, thus again, moral perspective. Eddie's murder of the priest is in this way placed in a context that in some measure makes the crime if not understandable, at least logical. The priest has been aligned with the forces of law and respectability from the start, and thus also with their limitations and hypocrisies. The mist which envelopes him suggests both the moral ambiguity of his character in Eddie's eyes, and the social quagmire out of which he operates. At this point in the narrative, Lang drops the blinkers from the viewers who know that Eddie is indeed free and the priest honest, but Eddie is still down in the Expressionistic fog of *angst* and impaired perception. When the priest is shot, he hides the wound and assures the warden that Eddie has missed him, thus allowing Eddie to escape the yard and begin his life on the run with Jo. This furthers the viewer's impression that Eddie is still worth saving – Father Dolan apparently thinks so – and that, from some transcendent point of view, he is even divinely favoured; Jo loves him, after all.

This brings the viewer to the question of what function Eddie serves in the narrative, beyond the kind of star-crossed romantic protagonist of a film such as Borzage's *A Farewell to Arms* (1932). The conclusion can only be recognised within the film's overarching context, set up in the opening and closing moments and intermittently along the way. The film opens with a shot of a building with a sign inscribed "Hall of Justice". It ends, not with justice – for Eddie and Jo's deaths so near to freedom are a cruel caprice of fate – but with a kind of divine mercy. The lovers are killed, but Father Dolan's words announcing Eddie's entrance into a true freedom "through the gate" suggest that justice has been superseded by divine mercy. This movement from justice to mercy reflects the heart of Christian teaching regarding salvation and the liturgical rehearsal of that salvation. This is the larger context in which the viewer is urged to evaluate the drama, and the sacramental entrance of the "heavenly choir" and the resonant voice-over of Father Dolan punctuate the message. There is a God who sees all and whose compassion is more permanent even than a woman's love (Jo's).

Yet, Eddie is not playing the tragic part simply to spell out the Christian moral to the story. Within the liturgical procession of the narrative he acts out the central role of the ritual scapegoat. On him are heaped the sins and shame of society. All manner of crimes are falsely attributed to him; he is condemned and banished from the camp; and, once across the border, he is executed. *You Only Live Once* is not a morality play, but a Passion narrative. The viewer/participant is less instructed intellectually than carried into the experience of Eddie's ritualistic procession towards his appointed death. Evidence of this is the way in which Lang pulls the viewer into the same guessing game that Eddie finally loses when he kills Father Dolan.

This play on viewer expectation carries through the examination of objects apart from and then within their context, to a gradual distortion of the film's visual imagery as the narrative progresses. This occurs on two levels: the first regards the concept of reading and misreading, or vision and blindness in the narrative; the second regards the use of the camera by Leon Shamroy under Lang's direction, which gradually forces the viewer to interpret the visual imagery on multiple levels.

The use of objects apart from their context – the apples; the suitcase; the newspapers; and so on – prepares for the interpretation of Eddie himself as an object. After leaving his former boss in the trucking company, Lang sets the viewer up for the hold-up scene in which Eddie will be assumed to be the criminal perpetrator. The camera opens on Eddie's room in town with a close-up of his hat and picture on a bedside table. Prostrate on the bed is a man whom we presume to be Eddie; however, as the camera tracks back, it becomes clear that Eddie is at the room's window, and it is his former criminal partner, Monk, on the bed. This little gesture foreshadows the robbery scene, in which again the camera will reveal Eddie's hat on a case of explosives and two eyes peering through the back window of a car. Lang never allows the viewer to identify those eyes, since the robber will put on a gas mask before leaving the car, but the viewer assumes, based on the standard grammar of film narrative, that they belong to Eddie, given that he is the logical antecedent. When Eddie shows up at the cottage carrying a gun and looking wild and desperate, that conclusion is reinforced. When Jo refuses to believe that he was involved after his claim of being set up, the viewer finds some hope, but it is not until the robbery car is dredged from a lake and the message comes to the warden that Eddie is innocent that the viewer receives confirmation. Although the camera has foreshadowed this moment through the patterns already discussed, the conclusion that Eddie is guilty is easily drawn.

Thus, Lang forces the viewer into the same posture of those who falsely blame and condemn Eddie – from the owners of Valley Tavern, the warden and his wife, the police inspector, the public that harasses him outside the courthouse and eagerly awaits his execution, and to the police that gun the couple down. Like the growing bleakness of Frank Capra's great trilogy of *Mr Deeds Goes to Town* (1936), *Mr Smith Goes to Washington* (1939) and *Meet John Doe* (1941), Lang has darkened his vision progressively from *Metropolis* to *M* to *Fury* to *You Only Live Once*, until he manages in the final film not only to challenge the viewer to understand polemically the nature of societal evil, but also momentarily to be drawn into that very evil.

There are countless images of eyes and mirrors throughout the film which hint at Lang's intention. The eyes in the mirror; Eddie's cold eyes as he stands in the death cell prior to his escape; the eyes of Jo as she looks at Eddie through a visitation room window in the prison (a curious image, as a covering that opens over the window has been pulled up and reflects the couple from above); and the eyes of the sharpshooter capturing Eddie and Jo's images in his sights – all force the issue of vision vs. blindness, and thus reading vs. misreading. By the end of the film, we are led to question whatever we see. It is a sly move on Lang's part that the man who will recognise Jo as she buys cigarettes wears glasses and sees her through a window. After a first glance, he squints and checks a wanted poster on his wall to match it with her face. Of course, what he sees on the poster is a terrible parody of the actual woman who stands before him. Jo has just given her baby over to Bonnie to care for until she and Eddie can find a safe haven – a touching and heroic gesture – whereas the face on the poster is purported to be that of a cruel monster.

Lang supports these narrative devices with an array of visual manœuvres which serve a similar purpose. On the simplest level, he blurs the screen in the moments when either the viewer's or Eddie's vision is most impaired. In the robbery scene, rain falls heavily and adds to the viewer's inability to mark the identity of the robber. When Eddie shoots Father Dolan, a thick fog blurs the vision of the whole prison yard. When Jo finds Eddie in the railway yard wounded during his escape, it is in the darkness of a boxcar at night. During the car journey to freedom, rain again distorts the view of Eddie and Jo as they travel.

More interesting are Lang's Expressionistic images of Eddie and Jo in the latter part of the film. The film's early scenes are shot in a straightforward manner, with only a few exceptions, such as Jo's first appearance at the prison to see Eddie when we first see her from the other side of the prison bars, a foreshadowing image which suggests her own captivity to the consequence of their love. (Bars and barriers are other common images weaved through the film's visuals.) After the robbery scene, the film's images grow darker and more complex. A much-discussed image is that of Eddie's death cell. According to Lotte Eisner,[3] Lang visited San Quentin and Alcatraz while researching the film, and re-created the death cell of San Quentin. A bright lamp hanging from the ceiling over Eddie within the cell casts shadows from the cell which fan out eerily over the floor of the entire room. This Caligariesque image seems to trigger a complete change in the film's visual grammar throughout the escape sequence. Together with the previously discussed scene in the prison yard, the scene in the railway yard is particularly striking. As Jo walks Eddie towards safety outside the yard, again a bright central light within the yard glows off the lines of the train cars, and creates a series of reflected lines that seem to capture the lovers in a deterministic web. The scene of Jo and Eddie in the shanty after Jo has given birth has similar overtones, as the room is barely lit from within, and the cluttered area with numerous non-parallel lines all pull in around the characters to make them seem trapped.

One scene provides a unique visual relief from these claustrophobic concluding images: a brief reverie with the lovers refreshing themselves by a pond in some woods. The pastoral quality of the scene shot in soft focus as Eddie brings wild flowers to Jo, with their baby softly crying in the distance, provides a short break from the surrounding images of Eddie and Jo's car ride towards sanctuary. The function of this juxtaposition is twofold – the pastoral love scene near the end reinforcing the brief moment of bliss the couple experienced at Valley Tavern, and the scene elevating the love of Eddie and Jo to a transcendent level (much like what Borzage accomplishes in *A Farewell to Arms* or *Seventh Heaven* [1927]). This latter function closes the narrative loop regarding viewer expectation. There is no question during this moment and the surrounding sequences of the love of the young couple as to where the camera wants sympathy to lie. These sympathies are essential for the impact of the sacramental conclusion when Eddie and Jo are both killed and welcomed into Paradise by Father Dolan. If there are indeed any lingering doubts about Eddie, which his murder of the priest in the prison could certainly raise, they should be dissipated, particularly when his own victim blesses him in the end.

It is precisely because Eddie is a victim throughout the film, the sacrifice to society's double-mindedness, that Lang arouses such sympathy for him and Jo. Eddie fights to be free continually throughout the narrative, but the bars that hold him are not the steel bars of the prison. Lang's Expressionist shot of the death cell in particular suggests that something larger and more sinister is at work. From inside the cell, however, Eddie is unable to see the full malevolence of that place. He is impassive and immobile, looking straight through the bars and almost into the camera. This is his posture when he tears a tin cup and slices his wrists as a means of gaining access to the gun hidden in the prison hospital by another convict. As the camera looks in, he is an appropriately docile victim, the blood dripping from his wrists between his legs and to the floor, a foreshadowing of the death awaiting. As he looks out, he misses the point, due to his position within fate's net. He is as blind to his own context as the viewer had been to the significance of the vendor's apples, and he actually looks blind by virtue of his unblinking stare throughout the sequence. Apparently, Lang worked extremely hard with Henry Fonda to achieve the appropriate expression in this and other scenes, and antagonised the star to a certain degree. The position of the viewer outside Eddie's bars places him/her into the role of the law which cannot see Eddie's actions in anything but black and white. The law is not cruel, but limited. It only sees apples on a table, a suitcase on a bed, a hat marked "E.T." or a convict in a cell. This viewer positioning is most fully realised when for a moment both Eddie and Jo appear in the cross-hairs of the officer's rifle. The point of view is again personal. The viewer is forced to see its victim for the scapegoat that he is and then pull the trigger to put an end to this bearer of sins. What makes the moment palatable is the concluding romantic images of Eddie and Jo comforting one another and reaffirming their love in death. In addition, as Father Dolan's voice comes to Eddie out of the glow, the incarnational quality of the moment is signalled by the overt insertion of the heavenly choir over the images. Eddie looks again directly into the camera, again with a frozen expression, but this time with more softness and with the light of the divine presence reflected off it.

Prior to Eddie's break from prison, a brief sequence captures a part of a conversation at the warden's home between the warden, his wife and Father Dolan. The wife chides the priest, "I still can't understand your feeling for the Taylor boy. I think he was born bad!". Dolan answers: "Every man – at birth – is endowed with the nobility of a king. But the stain of the world soon makes him forget even his own birthright." The warden comments in return: "Well, I hope when Taylor dies tonight he won't be born again. He's caused enough trouble in this world." Interesting in this exchange is how far afield each comment is from what the camera reveals, even Father Dolan's comment. Eddie is clearly not as devoid of moral conscience as the warden's wife implies. In fact, we learn that he was first incarcerated for beating a boy who tortured a frog. Eddie has not caused so much trouble, as the warden suggests, as he has given society a victim to blame and thus assuage the fears of the respectable society in the areas through which Eddie and Jo travel. Father Dolan's comment is limited as well. The stain of the world is the stain of the individuals in that world, including Eddie and Jo. Eddie's murder of the priest is, after all, a wilful decision on his own part, even in the given circumstances. He tells Jo that he "can still see Father Dolan's face" when he shot him. There is a greater evil in the world than that hinted at by the romanticism of Father Dolan, an evil that is individual and must be expiated. And this evil is in the criminal and respectable person alike; in Eddie's case, in fact, he is clearly better than those who scorn him.

Scapegoats are necessary to remedy universal culpability and guilt. Father Dolan's words might suggest that the world needs better to understand the nobility that is slowly lost through life's bitter experiences, the Wordsworthian "clouds of glory" that trail behind and are slowly dissipated. However, the liturgical movement of the film which places Eddie in the position of the sacrificial offering trivialises the priest's words. When the priest takes Eddie's bullet and covers his wound to keep Eddie alive, he even trivialises his own sentiments. In Lang's conclusion, Eddie has taken the role of more than victim and societal martyr. He has entered into the place of Christ in the Passion, at least in a very fundamental sense:

> He was despised and rejected of men, a man of sorrows, and familiar with suffering. Like one from whom men hide their faces he was despised, and we esteemed him not. Surely he took our infirmities and carried our sorrows... (Isaiah 53: 3-4)

Notes

[1] George Wilson, "*You Only Live Once*: the Doubled Feature", *Sight and Sound* 46: 4 (autumn 1977): 226.

2   Lang apparently spent a significant amount of time trying to bait one of the frogs with flies to get it to jump into the pond and so create a symbolic disturbance in the pastoral moment. Cited in Wilson: 179.

3   Lotte H Eisner, *Fritz Lang* (New York: Oxford University Press, 1977): 177-190.

15 · The Biblical spectacular

The tradition of religious film in the United States is almost exclusively Christian.[1] Where other religious groups find a place within some productions, they typically become assimilated within a larger "Christian" context, their ethnic difference often symbolising narrative tensions.[2] In the popular American cinema, Christianity both forms a narrative backdrop for the resolution of private conflicts, as in the films of John Ford (*The Grapes of Wrath* [1940], *The Fugitive* [1947]) or of Leo McCarey (*Going My Way* [1944], *The Bells of St Mary's* [1945]), and poses as the complete stylistic and structural principle.

The Hollywood Biblical film has an history as long as American filmmaking. In 1901, a version of *Quo Vadis?* was attempted, and, as Griffith and others experimented with epics on a large scale in the 1910s and 1920s, Biblical and traditional Christian material became an obvious source for a variety of thematic concerns (Griffith, of course, with *Judith of Bethulia* [1913] and *Intolerance* [1916]). The continuing viability of the genre was evidenced by the number of remakes produced. *Quo Vadis?*, for example, was made at least three times. *Ben Hur* was made in 1907, 1926 and 1959; *King of Kings* in 1927 and 1961; *The Sign of the Cross* in 1914 and 1932; and *The Ten Commandments* in 1923 and 1956.

In its evolution, the Biblical spectacular came to be defined as much by style as by content. It employed the grand style of long takes, boom shots, theatrical internal sets, and intrusive and large non-diegetic musical scores. The 107-foot crane shot of the Exodus in Cecil B De Mille's *The Ten Commandments* (1956), and the melodramatic musical pauses of Nicholas Ray's *King of Kings* (1961) underline the stylistic standards of the genre. These films tend to focus on the religious struggle of one character of torn allegiance. The crisis will be melodramatically highlighted by the close attention of the camera, usually on facial gestures and expressions. The character will invariably convert to an orthodox religious position in a moment which the film will celebrate with grand stylistic gestures – blunt and often obtuse examples of the type of sacramentalism discussed in this study. Often the conversion will be foreshadowed throughout the film through subtle or not so subtle Christian allusions – images of crosses; prayers; suggestive dialogue; and so on. And, of course, the spectator of the film is encouraged to embrace the celebration.

The Hollywood epic became major box-office fare in two decades, the 1930s and the 1950s. The 1930s saw the release of three large epic productions – *The Sign of the Cross* (1932), *The Crusades* (1935), and *The Last Days of Pompeii* (1935). The 1950s are notable in that six of the era's biggest box-office attractions were religious epics: *Samson and Delilah* (1949), *Quo Vadis?* (1951), *David and Bathsheba* (1951), *The Robe* (1953), *The Ten Commandments* (1956) and *Ben Hur* (1959).

The sociological reasons for these two outbursts of religiosity in Hollywood seem apparent. As Gerald Eugene Forshey has pointed out, the post-crash 1930s saw a great revival of moralism and community consciousness with the popular influence of Roosevelt's "New Deal" policies, and Hollywood followed the popular current (*I Am a Fugitive From a Chain Gang* [1932], *Wild Boys of the Road* [1933], *The Grapes of Wrath* [1940], and so on). In the 1950s, Cold War neurosis and McCarthyism created a similar revived moralistic and familial spirit. Hollywood responded with new westerns, musicals and family melodramas. The religious epic, building upon the traditional literary and rhetorical myth of America as God's holy nation, provided a format compatible with both social milieux. The Christian community in the films of the 1930s could be seen allegorically as a buffer zone for the kind of new sensibility needed to correct the social evils popularly attributed to the wild and licentious 1920s. The Christians in the 1950s films were seen as prototypical peacemakers whose simplicity and virtue under Roman oppression exemplified American values against the power of Communism.[3]

So it was represented in the religious epics of these two eras. In the 1932 version of *The Sign of the Cross*, directed by Cecil B De Mille, Rome was seen as sexually corrupt and fully hedonistic, while the Christian martyrs were poor and chaste. The film details many of the martyrdoms that arose from Nero's reign, after he placed blame for the burning of Rome on the Christians – a gesture which the film depicts as growing out of his mad guilt, which grew in proportion to the meekness of the Christians. The conflict is played out in the narrative in the subplot of a romance between a Roman officer, Marcus (Fredric March) and a Christian girl, Mercia (Elissa Landi). The officer attempts to win the girl and later to seduce her, but, despite her affection for him, she refuses him because of his atheism. He cannot believe in God in a world as riotous as his own. Nevertheless, when the girl is finally captured and given to die as a martyr, he chooses to die with her and so become like her. This resolution bears a strong suggestion of the social Christian tone of the "New Deal" era: sacrificial, moral and family-oriented.

In the 1950s, the conflict shifts from the arena of sexual morality to that of political power. In William Wyler's 1959 version of *Ben Hur*, it is the atheism of Rome that is represented as the driving motivation behind their conquests and for the conflicts that separate the two friends, Messala (Stephen Boyd) and Judah Ben Hur (Charlton Heston). Messala encourages Ben Hur to leave his Jewish allegiances and join the Roman forces, because "Roman law, architecture and literature are the glory of the human race", and because they live in an "insane world" where the only sanity is "the loyalty of old friends". Ben Hur refuses, and, through a series of accidents, becomes the enemy of Messala and Rome. After a long period of slavery, drawn in parallel to the Jews in Egypt, Ben Hur is brought into a rich man's house where he gains new status and wealth, and is afforded opportunity to avenge himself upon the Romans in the famous chariot race. This he does, but he is saved from acquiring the spirit of a revolutionary when his family is converted to Jesus. He eventually converts himself, after seeing Jesus's passiveness and suffering at the Crucifixion. Thus, the film allegorically links hearth and home (and some wealth) to the peace of Christ that conquers oppression and arrogance. Again, such a political figuration reified the American ideal of prosperity structured around the upper-middle class in the 1950s.

The Hollywood religious epic provided a perfect environment for continuing the American garden myth in the popular imagination. As long as such nationalistic optimism could find new social forums for revival, and as long as Christianity retained its popular authority in America, the Hollywood religious epic could succeed as a viable genre.

The popularity of the genre in the 1950s made its continuance through the 1960s an apparent certainty. When John F Kennedy became President in 1960, and spoke of a new freedom in his 1961 inaugural address, the country reached a high point of political optimism. Kennedy embodied a central ideal projected in the 1950s. He was prosperous, handsome, family-oriented (or so it seemed), formally religious, and liberal-minded. One Hollywood epic was released conveniently in that inaugural year, and it went to the pinnacle of the Christian tradition – the Jesus story. This was Nicholas Ray's remake of the classic *King of Kings*.[4]

In *King of Kings*, Jesus's mission of peace becomes dramatically highlighted. To draw out this motif, Ray, together with producer Samuel Bronston and scriptwriter Philip Yordan, decided to develop the ministry of Jesus (Jeffrey Hunter) in contrast to a fictional account of the affairs of the Jewish revolutionary, Barabbas (Harry Guardino), who is mentioned in the Gospels as the criminal whom Pilate released instead of Jesus. The team also chose – as is the practice in Biblical epics – to displace blame for Jesus's death from the Jews to the Romans.[5]

King of Kings follows the Synoptic accounts of the birth and early life of Jesus, as well as the calling of the Apostles and baptism by John. However, it includes certain fictional insertions to set the stage for the Jesus-Barabbas contrast. A Roman officer named Lucius (Ron Randell) is introduced and placed in proximity to all the events of Jesus's early history. He is a doubter, but he is against the barbaric tendencies of Roman rule, such as allowing Herod's massacre of the innocents of Bethlehem. He meets Mary and Jesus while taking a census, and chooses not to probe deeply into their history, after discovering that Jesus should have been killed with the other infants in Bethlehem. He is later assigned to Pilate's court, and becomes the officer in charge of the forces trying to suppress the revolutionary activities of Barabbas. Lucius's activities form the centre around which the ministry of Jesus and the revolts of Barabbas circle. When Barabbas is finally crushed in his attempt to overthrow the Romans, it is inevitable that Lucius will be fully aligned with Jesus. He watches the Crucifixion with Pilate's wife, and, when the sky darkens at Jesus's death, Lucius tells her: "He must have been the Christ". The evangelistic gesture reinforces the film's emphasis on Jesus's peaceful mission.

Another striking feature of *King of Kings* is its subtle Catholicism. Great prominence is placed on Jesus's mother, Mary, played with extreme sweetness by the Irish actress, Siobhán McKenna. Mary is always portrayed in somewhat beatific posture and expression, and remains the only character able fully to comprehend Jesus's character and sacrificial mission. In addition, the film incorporates bits of Catholic tradition avoided by most Protestants, such as the Veronica cloth (a woman wipes Jesus's face with a cloth on his way to the Cross), the names of the wise men, and the motif of Jesus's "sacred heart" of love.

The boyishness of the teen idol who portrays Jesus in the film, Jeffrey Hunter, accounts for the comic trade name often given to the production, "I Was a Teenage Jesus". When Jesus's divinity is evoked, director Ray typically closes in to lingering shots of Hunter's blue eyes. This is particularly apparent in a key scene when Jesus comes to the imprisoned John the Baptist to reassure him. John, played by "tough guy" actor, Robert Ryan (a casting curiosity that further adds to the image of the soft and approachable Jesus which the film intends to portray), asks Jesus if he is the Christ and is answered by a long stare, the camera cutting back and forth between the eyes of each. John is satisfied with this. The beautiful appearance of Jesus-Hunter is testimony in itself.

These particularities of *King of Kings* suggest its political undertones as Kennedy myth. The Messiah is peaceful, blue-eyed, Catholic and beautiful to behold. Such a political rearrangement is characteristic of the genre's evolution to this point. As the American myth continued – the country as garden of innocence; her people as God's community under siege, but divinely protected – the Hollywood religious epic could continue as an arena for the display of redemptive socio-political ritual. The Biblical epic told of America's continuing fortune. It is thus inevitable that, with the breakdown of the American myth in the mid-1960s and 1970s, triggered in large part by Vietnam and Watergate, the genre itself would begin to break down and find new formal and thematic modes of expression as it passed through the 1970s and 1980s.

The dominant popular religious form in 20th-century America has been the Baptistic or evangelistic style of Protestantism that developed out of the revivalism of the 19th century and the Bible School movement of the first three decades of the 20th century.[6] In the 1970s and 1980s, this variety of Christianity underwent a new revival of its own when Christian television networks began to emerge in major metropolitan areas across the country. The culmination of this new exposure came when the Reverend Pat Robertson, the President of the largest network, Christian Broadcasting Network (CBN), and an Assembly of God minister, entered the Republican presidential primary contest in 1987. Although Robertson was easily beaten by the successor to Ronald Reagan, George Bush, his ability to challenge the field in the national election symbolised the new, if short-lived, popularity of evangelical Protestantism.

Characteristic of American evangelical Protestantism is a tendency towards religious decision and a Gospel of prosperity. True believers come to their faith and find assurance in it by virtue of a conversion experience, whereby they suddenly hear the message of God's love through Jesus and realise that this love was meant to be their personal salvation. It is a highly subjective and potentially self-focused manner of faith that, nevertheless, found a large audience in the fast-paced neurosis of the hi-tech era. Together with the conversion experience, many high-profile evangelical preachers have taught a prosperity Gospel, similar in substance to the popular versions of the American good life in the 1950s, and based upon the idea that faith is rewarded by God in tangible ways – i.e. financial security, popularity, or emotional and psychological fulfilment. The prosperity Gospel made celebrities of athletes, actors and businessmen whose wealth and prestige could be termed a sign of blessing if accompanied by public profession of a "born-again" experience.

The effect of evangelicalism on American Biblical films and on those produced overseas for the American market, primarily in Britain and Australia, has been to allow for the full secularization of the genre. The Hollywood religious epic had previously stuck to canonical figures and events. These defined American Christianity, although each character and event could carry a symbolic meaning that was suitable for the day. The religious aura associated with the Biblical epic was stylistic, related to the stiff and artificial style that seemed to appeal to the religious tastes of both devoted and nominal Christians; for example, the previously noted angelic chorus that marked climactic moments, or the supposedly solemn sound of trombones played in a minor key. The new religious films, following the drift of American pop Christianity, could maintain these stylistic elements, but modify the thematic core and subject-matter of the films; that is, they could move in the direction of subjective experience, the internal religious moment, without necessarily having to maintain the traditional canonical and historical religious frame. In addition, since religious motives in the doctrines of the prosperity Gospel were now outwardly aligned with materialism, religious experience could be retold from a secular perspective.

The post-evangelical Hollywood epic could take the new arena of national tension, which in the 1970s and 1980s became America's loss of value and integrity, and integrate it with the generic religious text without having to protect the overtly Christian narrative material. The tensions of the post-Watergate era could occur within the religious community, within religious heroes, without redemptive resolution, for the popular mood was to allow the sacred to be absorbed within the secular. An illustration of this shift can best be introduced by reference to the one large-scale attempt in this period to revive the Biblical narrative. The attempt was made by the Australian director, Bruce Beresford (*Breaker Morant* [1979]; *Tender Mercies* [1982]), who found as his subject the Old Testament figure of David, and attempted a psychological epic relating the trials of David as King with those of his predecessor, Saul. The film was entitled *King David* and released in 1985, only to die quickly at American theatres and find circulation exclusively as a videocassette.

In its attempt at realism, *King David* emphasises the gore and passion of the early years of the Israelite monarchy. The film begins with the prophet Samuel confronting King Saul (Edward Woodward) and cursing him for not carrying out God's plans to "utterly destroy" the Canaanite people. Saul has spared the King of the Amalekites and considered a treaty with him. Samuel takes a sword and beheads the Amalekite King himself, and then throws the head in Saul's direction.

Although the camera does not show the beheading, the image of the severed head is revealed in great detail at the moment Samuel gives it to Saul. Such sensationalistic devices characterise the film's "realistic style". The emotional centre of the film, for example, occurs in a sequence where Saul and his son, Jonathan, are brutally killed in a bloody battle that David sees in a vision while awaiting for a runner to arrive with news. Realism thus becomes equated with the gruesome quality of the film's special effects, a physical or visual realism that reduces the concept to a single sensational shot or series of shots – ironically, a method previously associated most often with horror and pornographic filmmaking.

Beresford's film evokes an aura of social relevance with a similar reduction. Both Saul and David are shown to succumb to the temptations associated with power: luxury and voluptuousness. Saul attempts to kill David, who has been anointed by Samuel as his successor, because he cannot bear the loss of prestige – the women now sing of David, and cast their eyes at him, while the men celebrate his exploits in stories. In addition, David marries Saul's daughter, Michal, a cool beauty with royal bearing. But David as King gives in to similar proud attitudes when he murders his soldier Uriah in order to take his beautiful wife, Bathsheba, whom he has seen bathing in the nude. David then angers God by designing a grand temple for the Arc of the Covenant which God had not requested.

The parallel drawn between the two appears to propel the drama to the dimensions of classical epic, but it instead takes the heart out of the Biblical narrative of David. David, by the parallel to Saul, is made a man at war with God, as was Saul. On his death bed, David tells his son Solomon to follow the instincts of his heart if he is to be true, and then he expresses a hope finally to see God's face. The plea is met by a blackened screen and the introduction of the film's credits. This device casts a cloud of despair over the entire narrative, as the trouble has come precisely because Saul and David followed the instincts of their hearts and longed to reach beyond their appointed limits. Such an ending refocuses the film to allow the Biblical history to meet the needs of a modern era that has lost faith in traditional figures of law and in traditional religious accounts. In the Biblical narrative, King David is drawn in polarity to Saul (even with his failures), and made a prototype for the coming Messiah in his zeal for faithfulness to God's decrees.

The film's lead is the American actor, Richard Gere, while its other players are mostly English and Australian actors of some prominence. The choice of Gere, who is painfully weak in the title role, follows the tradition of the Hollywood epic (which follows the typical Hollywood star-casting policy), in which "holy" heroes are chosen for their physical beauty: for example, Charlton Heston, Victor Mature, Jeffrey Hunter, Jennifer Jones. The boy David has distinctive Jewish features. After God's call and a fast-forward through his teen years, he emerges as the blandly handsome matinee idol, Gere. The physical beauty of Gere is made a vital key in the passage of events when he dances in a loin cloth through the streets of Jerusalem ahead of a procession carrying the arc into the city. It is this dance that first impresses Bathsheba, played by the glamorous South African-born actress, Alice Krige. When David sees Bathsheba bathing, the two are linked erotically through mutual voyeurism and sensuality, just as the viewers of the film are voyeuristically drawn to both of them. The mechanics of this union follow the typical Hollywood romantic pattern, especially in its modern formulation. The generic devices seem to force the film's conclusion, in which David fails as Saul had failed. He must fail, for within the bounds of the popular tradition, the film's secular generic form, David cannot resist the beautiful Bathsheba, and cannot fail to love the voluptuousness and luxury that has determined his own screen image.

Beresford's *King David* illustrates the difficulty of maintaining the form of the Hollywood Biblical epic in the changing popular mind of the 1970s and 1980s. As weak as the older epics were, the source Biblical texts were given a marginal authority, as was the tradition of orthodox religious fiction in the West. Cecil B De Mille could tamper with the details of the Book of Exodus to allow for popular tastes and the need for romantic subplots, but the primary direction of the Biblical text could not be altered: Pharaoh would have to let the Israelites go, and the Law would be cut into stone by the finger of God. Popular taste was for the gist of the story. But in the context of the shift to evangelical subjectivism, the focus moved to the psychological and spiritual heart of the story – David's struggle with faith and despair in *King David*. Popularize or secularize this side of the Biblical story and the religious centre is bound to crumble. Beresford maintains a narrative accuracy in many of the details of the Biblical accounts, but, because his David is drawn according to the image of the popular hero, the character is left wandering confused and out of place within the film itself, and his spiritual struggle is thus made trivial. The "realistic" methods of the film appear to have outgrown the power of the Biblical text, and thus of the Hollywood epic, to hold them in.

The inevitable consequence of these shifts, as with all generic transitions, is the replacement of the traditional text with one more suitable to evolving popular styles. The dominance of the Biblical spectacular in the popular conception of what makes a film religious made the shift awkward, however, especially given the sensitivity of religion as a subject in film. Even when Hollywood has brought in directors such as Borzage, Lang, Murnau and Renoir, whose previous work revealed a spiritual depth, their American projects have not featured exclusively religious subject-matter. The major American Catholic directors – Martin Scorsese, Alfred Hitchcock (by adoption), Francis Coppola and Leo McCarey – have produced works in which their Christian heritage can be identified through recurrent thematic motifs of guilt, redemption and sacrificial love; however, none of these directors has attempted to work within a distinctive religious style.[7] The closest thing to a true religious filmmaker, both in terms of style and content, that America has produced is Paul Schrader, whose better-known films include *American Gigolo* (1980) and *Mishima* (1985). However, as discussed earlier, Schrader's film work has not achieved large popular appeal, nor uniform critical praise.

The point to make here, before proceeding to the transitional phase of the genre, is that the older genre was less defined by content than by style. Beresford's *King David* marks a turning away from the older genre towards a new form of popular religious filmmaking, in which the older style begins to integrate with new narrative types. This is interesting for an understanding of many of the new heroic and epic films that emerged particularly in the 1980s.

A religious film which met with a great deal of adversity at its release, and which did so precisely because it suggested a new era of American religious films, is Martin Scorsese's *The Last Temptation of Christ* (1989). Scorsese set out to update the Gospel narrative, especially its language, in a fashion similar to the pop films, *Godspell* (1973) and *Jesus Christ Superstar* (1973). However, instead of directing the film to youths through the rock musical format, he aimed his film at the mainstream audience by using the outer form of the old Biblical epic.

The film goes even further in the secularization of the genre than does Beresford's *King David*, in that Scorsese chooses to tell the story of Jesus through the fiction of Nikos Kazantzakis's novel, *The Last Temptation*, instead of through the Gospel record. The film centres on a fictional temptation that Christ undergoes while on the cross, a temptation to leave his suffering and opt for a normal family life with Mary Magdalene. But Scorsese follows Kazantzakis's lead in fictionalising many other aspects of Jesus's life, such as his inner struggles with God's call and his years as a carpenter.[8] The resulting film narrative is the closest thing to New Testament apocryphal literature that has ever occurred on film.[9]

As a tampering of the canonical tradition in such a popular format as the Hollywood religious epic, *The Last Temptation of Christ* drew a violent public reaction. In scenes reminiscent of those around showings

171

of Griffith's *The Birth of a Nation* (1915) and Riefenstahl's *Triumph des Willens* (*Triumph of the Will*, 1935), crowds of picketers surrounded theatres where the film was originally released. Outside the Biograph Theater in Chicago, some picketers shouted The Lord's Prayer at those who crossed the line to enter the theatre. The film was labelled "blasphemous" by both Catholic and Protestant leaders, and anathematized as if it were a satanic manifestation.

Scorsese inadvertently challenged the authority of a weakened Church in America, and embarrassed popular evangelicalism by attempting a form of popular evangelism according to evangelicalism's own subjectivist and materialistic tendencies – yet without the approval or authority of the Church. He had also demythologized the holy aura that surrounded the old Hollywood epic. Some evangelicals, in particular, reacted to the film with such intensity that they in turn aided the film in its popularity. One major Christian television network, WCFC Channel 38 in Chicago, urged viewers to avoid the Scorsese film altogether and screened a counter-film. That film, *Jesus* (1979), sponsored by an evangelical student organisation, Campus Crusade for Christ, offers a literal rendering of the life of Jesus that follows the Gospel of Luke (although it too fictionalises details of the Gospel narrative for the sake of "dramatic continuity").[10] It was shown on a Sunday night with a superimposed telephone number on the screen, which viewers could call to obtain counselling.

The pop style of Scorsese's *The Last Temptation of Christ* was the source of its threat, much more than was the film's controversial story-line. Scorsese had violated several genres, both artistic and social. The older Hollywood genre allowed for certain unorthodoxies, such as supplementary dramatic subplots introduced for effect (*Ben Hur*), sermonic elaborations of material, extravagant characterisations (*The Ten Commandments*), and sentimental, somewhat Gnostic portraits of Christ[11] (*The Greatest Story Ever Told* [1965]), but it did not allow for such an extreme attempt at contemporary relevance.

Before exploring the mechanisms of Scorsese's film, it is useful to note that its controversy had been foreshadowed three years earlier in Jean-Luc Godard's *Je vous salue, Marie* (*Hail, Mary*, 1984). In Godard's film, a young Swiss virgin girl, Mary, who loves basketball, becomes pregnant without intercourse. Her boyfriend, a volatile cab driver named Joseph, suffers the confusion of the ordeal with her and then marries her. A child is born who begins to display an aloofness that troubles Mary and Joseph. Mary eventually becomes an ordinary sensual woman. Godard's intentions in the film were to suggest the spiritual dimensions that characterise the lives of common people. Many of his individual compositions linger as still-life paintings on natural objects, and evoke an aura of mystery. Mary's body is displayed naked in several scenes in beautiful and graceful poses. A subordinate narrative plot has a college philosopher questioning whether the body has a soul, or the soul has a body. Godard's point is obviously the latter: the physical universe is a continuous manifestation of spiritual force taking on material substance.

Although *Hail, Mary*, because it was "foreign", never achieved among the viewing public the level of controversiality of *The Last Temptation of Christ*, it was condemned as blasphemous by Pope John Paul II and Cardinal O'Connor, and blocked from release on American cable networks. Since it originated in France, cross-references to it during the Scorsese controversy were few. Nevertheless, the film stands as a useful counterpoint in that Godard's allegorical approach serves a similar function to Scorsese's apocryphal approach: an attempt to update the Gospel by reshaping it according to modern themes.

Both *Hail, Mary* and *The Last Temptation of Christ* were called "blasphemous" for drawing portraits of Christ that appeared too human. Yet, misguided though the attempts may have been, both directors were attempting the opposite – to lift the human to an understanding and embrace of the divine. The films move towards a convergence of heaven and earth, as did the older epics.

In Scorsese's film, the influence of scriptwriter Paul Schrader is apparent in the film's structure. Schrader and Scorsese had previously collaborated on two films dealing with unusual religious pilgrimages, *Taxi Driver* (1976) and *Raging Bull* (1980). In *Taxi Driver*, Travis Bickle, a New York cabbie, becomes an agent of divine retribution as he plunges into a madness that leads him to save a young prostitute who is at the centre of a drug ring. In *Raging Bull*, Jake LaMotta, a middleweight boxer, finds his boxing persona and real character becoming confused to the point where both begin to disintegrate in a growing frustrated rage. When he is finally jailed, and rejected by family and friends, he comes to a new sense of himself and begins to rebuild his life as an entertainer, his performance recitations mocking his former sense of self-importance (the substance of his "rage") and so becoming a form of penitential confession.

In films directed by Schrader, a redemptive motif is usually driven to a single moment of resolution captured in a frozen last image, a symbolic stylistic gesture that Schrader borrowed from Robert Bresson[12] (although its usage has been wide in films – for example, *Les Quatre cents coups* [*The 400 Blows*, 1959], *Bonnie and Clyde* [1967]). The same occurs in the Schrader-Scorsese collaborative works. The last sequence of *Taxi Driver* contains a prominent shot of Travis Bickle glancing into the mirror of his cab, which the viewer sees from a position behind him, a symbolic gesture that is used throughout the film to reinforce the viewer's inability to penetrate the mind of the characters. The last sequence of *Raging Bull* closes on a view of Jake LaMotta as he begins a recitation of the "I could've been a contender" speech from *On the Waterfront*, as part of a stage performance after his release from prison. The gesture and attitude of mind contrast with the film's earlier slow-motion sequences of Jake's fury in the ring: the ritual of destruction that has grown out of Jake's indomitable pride has led to the inevitable consequence of the loss of all love in his life. In his new life, born out of the ashes of the old, Jake penitentially makes public confession of his personal tragedy as a warning and entertainment to others. In the last shot of Scorsese's *The Last Temptation of Christ*, the camera freezes on the jubilant face of Jesus after he returns from the temptation to die his appointed redemptive death on the cross. The screen then flashes brilliant colours, over which bells ring in the background before the credits are introduced.

Much of the film builds stylistically towards the religiously potent conclusion, and many of the devices of the old Biblical spectacular and the sacramental style recur: dissolves and montage, slow-motion, sudden close-ups, alterations in lighting, and musical cues. All the devices concentrate the viewer on the subject of redemption in a moment of symbolic, sacramental union.

From the earliest scenes of *The Last Temptation of Christ*, the viewer is drawn to identify with Jesus. However, the terms of the identification are compromised by the nature of Jesus's trials: he appears in Mary Magdalene's brothel and takes part in the voyeuristic spectacle of her giving herself openly to her customers; he is forced to aid the Romans in a crucifixion of a Jew; he pleads with Judas for support. In these and other unorthodox scenes, the camera concentrates on Jesus's face. He is paradoxically pained and horrified with his spiritual struggles, but then exuberant in them as he tells Mary and others of his special call by God.

This torment and alternate joy of the religious man, a staple of the older films, drives the plot of *The Last Temptation of Christ* forward as Jesus gathers his disciples and then must withdraw from them. He is never able to find social equilibrium, for his following compels him to move in the direction of opposition to Rome – Judas and other patriots continue to urge him to be a public leader – while God moves him to die at the hands of the Romans. Similarly, Jesus's miracles torment him. He raises Lazarus from the dead, but the act appears grotesque, as Lazarus remains physically corrupted and later is murdered. He heals the sick, but gatherings of sufferers and worshippers, as in a scene where he meets John the Baptist, are presented as a wailing and unappealing mass. His special audience with God similarly leads him to journey alone into the desert and suffer physical and supernatural temptations there. The conflict of soul comes to a climax as Jesus asks Judas to betray him to the Romans because he knows that he cannot be the leader against them.

Scorsese drives the narrative forward by the growing conflict of Jesus's love for God vs. his love for men in the world. In so doing, he shakes the viewer, who is more prepared for the generic standard which dismisses Jesus's own struggles against evil and typically scapegoats a handful of vile Jews and Romans. Here Jesus's torment is located internally, and his messianic mission is ambiguous and potentially ineffective. By this reversal, Scorsese foreshadows the last temptation in which Jesus will be led to consider renouncing God for a normal life in the world.

In the last temptation, Jesus is led from the cross by an angelic young girl, who dresses his wounds and encourages him to become a husband and father. Throughout the lengthy sequence, Jesus's disciples are mostly absent from the screen, and so the previous conflict appears to be resolved. Jesus is first husband to Mary Magdalene,[13] and then, after her death, he is husband to Mary of Bethany (and also, apparently, her sister Martha).[14] His life is simple and fulfilled. He works, rests, raises children, and grows old. It is not until the last sequence of the film when his disciples come to him at his death bed that the previous conflicts are reintroduced.

In this scene, Jesus is lying on a bed with the angelic girl beside him comforting him for choosing the right path. The disciples enter through a door beyond the foot of the bed. Outside the door, the world looks as if a storm has overtaken it. The sky is cast in a surrealistic red darkness unlike anything previously on screen in the temptation sequence. The disciples enter and begin to warn Jesus that the world needs him to save it and that the girl is a temptress trying to seduce him into forsaking God's purpose. The girl is then transformed into Satan, visualised, paradoxically, as a pillar of fire, and Satan begins to mock Jesus. At this, Jesus cries out and crawls from his bed to return to the cross. The journey to it is full of artificial, surreal effects. All these effects, cued by the storm outside the door and culminating in the transformation of the girl into Satan, highlight the film's climactic religious moment. The spiritual war within Jesus's own soul has physically taken shape on the screen, symbolised by these cues, and the viewer has been drawn to identify with the powers of heaven without and within Jesus. Jesus's return to the cross becomes the triumphal redemptive celebration towards which the complete film performance has moved.

What is especially noteworthy in this stylistic religiosity is that, without it, the film fails to make a coherent religious statement. Jesus's message is muddled, alternating between righteous anger, a plea to love everyone, and a stoical acceptance of whatever God should choose. He is neither fully secularized (he does perform miracles), nor spiritualized (his neurosis outweighs his courage). Similarly, as Garry Wills has observed, Scorsese's style alternates between a creative reconstruction of scenes recorded in the Gospels, such as the highly effective purging of the temple, and a stylised attempt to design sets reminiscent of classical religious painting.[15] Thus, it is difficult to know what the film is attempting, and most early critics noted the uncertainty of theatre audiences as to when to laugh and when to be sober.

The theme of *The Last Temptation of Christ* follows that of big-budget American films in the 1970s and 1980s. Firstly, the main character struggles to find an integrated and guilt-free identity in the midst of compromise and torn allegiance. Secondly, the form of the inner conflict is defined by sexual desire – it is significant that the tattoos on Mary Magdalene are serpentine, and serve to relate her physical image, which first prominently occurs as she gives sex to a customer, to the satanic manifestations that threaten Jesus's ministry. Thirdly, and this is an addition to the film's style, the intensity of the plot builds from one sensational visual image to another – the scene in Mary's brothel; the first crucifixion; the desert temptations; the meeting with John; the removal of Jesus's sacred heart; Jesus's Crucifixion; the transformations in the room and return of Jesus to the cross; the triumphal last image of Jesus on the cross.

The religious power of Scorsese's film is thus purely symbolic: it uniquely integrates the core stylistic material of the older genre with more modern themes and an up-dated visual structure. It replaces the standard Hollywood Biblical epic with a half-reverent, half-lampooning retold Gospel story that seems to be designed primarily to produce dramatic and visual effect. It does so neither to overturn the Gospel story (Scorsese's intentions were apparently sincere), nor to improve it, but to draw attention to the purpose of the story and the manner of telling, and to question the continuing validity of the generic stereotype. *The Last Temptation of Christ* illustrates the full break from the Hollywood Biblical epic in one definite direction: the outer form of the epic, the story of the Messiah or the saints, has been challenged and replaced.

Another kind of break from the Hollywood spectacular emerged in the 1970s and 1980s, and gained much wider usage than the apocryphal approach of Scorsese's film, due to its greater field for exploration. It is the secular story that is structured according to the thematic and stylistic principles of the older genre. The many fantasy and science-fiction epics of the 1970s and 1980s that follow clearly religious motifs are the obvious outgrowth of this thread of development.

The Biblical epic found an easy replacement in epic fantasy films and religiously significant science-fiction thrillers, both narrative types developing around heroic conquests and transcendent powers and experiences. Themes that had previously been played out in the Hollywood Biblical epic now emerged in tales of heroes and quests – *Lord of the Rings* (1978), *Excalibur* (1981), *The Princess Bride* (1987) and *Willow* (1988) – and in tales of interplanetary confrontation – *Star Wars* (1977), *E.T.* (1982), *The Terminator* (1984) and *Cocoon* (1985). The artificial methods of the religious style employed in the Hollywood epic likewise emerged in these films – a reverential aura; pageantry; moments of transformation conveyed through technical artifice; and intrusions of non-diegetic celebrative music (for example, the powerful theme that suggests the spiritual victory associated with the landing of the spacecraft in *Close Encounters of the Third Kind* [1977], or the triumphal choruses of the *Star Wars* series). As evangelicalism led traditional credal and historical Christianity towards a subjective and positivist experience, so the religious epic lost its traditional base, and evolved by applying its thematic and stylistic substructure to other subjects and other genres.

However, it is not only in fantasy and science-fiction that the evolution can be traced. Beyond these new variants, there have been several successful dramas that have applied the principles of the older style to historical or character narratives. Among these are *Chariots of Fire* (1981), *Tender Mercies* (1982), *Amadeus* (1984), *The Bounty* (1984), *The Trip to Bountiful* (1985) and *The Mission* (1986).

The most recognisable film to have grown out of the older genre, in terms of its integration of religious techniques with religious themes and events, is *Chariots of Fire*. Like another film of this group discussed earlier, Roland Joffé's *The Mission*, but to a greater effect,[16] it bases its narrative on an historical event (the stories of several runners in the 1924 Paris Olympics), but compels the viewer to read through its thematic arrangement to discover a religious parable or allegory (a credit for the account is given to the family of the Scottish missionary, Eric Liddell). *Chariots of Fire* is subtle in its religious intentions, although its climactic moments are brought to screen with notable technical artifice. Because of the largeness of its religious gestures and the inherent Protestantism of the film, it gained great authority among evangelicals. In fact, it is the one secular production that appears on film and video lists in fundamentalist schools, such as the Moody Bible

Institute and Wheaton College, where in earlier years the viewing of films at theatres had been discouraged among students.

Chariots of Fire received critical praise, and its success did much to bolster the rise of the new British cinema. It is a film that captures a spirit of revived British nationalism, and succeeds in doing so through the popular means of what might be called "shepherd to king" films – *Rocky* (1976), *Breaking Away* (1979), *Flashdance* (1983), *The Karate Kid* (1984), *The Color of Money* (1986), and so on. Two runners – one a Jew, Harold Abrahams, and the other the future Scottish missionary, Eric Liddell – compete in the 1924 Paris Olympics as sprinters, and both succeed in defeating talented American runners to win gold medals. Both compete for deep personal motives, and both overcome seemingly impossible odds to win. Underneath this optimistic nationalist theme, however, the film follows a curiously strong religious format.

Harold Abrahams, the arrogant and ambitious son of wealthy Lithuanian immigrant parents, comes to the University of Cambridge after the First World War with the intention of proving, by his scholarship and athletic prowess, that he can beat the Gentiles. He begins a series of competition victories that ends only when he is beaten in an Olympic preliminary race by Liddell. Abrahams then hires a professional trainer, an Arab named Sam Mussabini, and the two work to improve to the point where they can beat Liddell and capture the gold at the Olympics. Abrahams also falls in love with a beautiful English stage performer, Sybil Gordon, and makes friends of many high-born young Englishmen, all Gentiles.

Eric Liddell is the son of Scottish Presbyterian missionaries to China, who have prepared him to follow them into China to carry on their work with his devoted sister, Jennie. However, Liddell is presented as having been given the gift by God to run, and he sees the forthcoming Olympics as an opportunity to show the world that there is a dignity and strength in Christianity beyond the usual stereotype. Liddell arrives at Paris for the Olympics, only to be told that his qualifying 100-metres heat is to be run on a Sunday. He will not run on the Sabbath.

The film plot is resolved when Liddell is offered an opportunity to run the 400-metres race, which is not run on Sunday, instead of the 100 metres. Abrahams runs the 100-metres race and wins, and Liddell wins the 400-metres race. In the moments of victory, both runners are celebrated by the film, and yet it is Liddell's victory which marks the film's final climactic moment. Whereas Abrahams has run for personal and social motives, Liddell has won for the glory of God. Abrahams's victory allows him full entrance to the Gentile community – he returns to England to wed Sybil – while Liddell's victory points the Gentile community to a redemptive event. As Liddell finishes his race, the camera freezes on an astonished Abrahams watching from the crowd.

The emotional conclusion of *Chariots of Fire* is driven home by a series of slow-motion shots of Liddell crossing the finishing line and the crowd cheering him. These had been foreshadowed in several earlier scenes, where Abrahams, Liddell and other British runners were shown in slow-motion or in frozen images while competing. The conclusion is also reinforced by the entrance of the non-diegetic theme music that has followed the runners throughout the film, Vangelis's "Eric's Theme", the most powerful in terms of its integration, volume and emotion. The many highly composed shots of the crowd, cross-cut with others of the runners, effectively reinforce the viewer in the position of spectator and participant.

The final celebration of *Chariots of Fire* is even given a frame for interpretation, not unlike the liturgy of Word that precedes the Eucharistic celebration in Christian worship. This occurs as the film cross-cuts between Liddell reading Isaiah 40: 15 in church ("All nations are but a drop in the bucket") and the British team losing a steeplechase and Abrahams losing a preliminary heat on the Sunday that Liddell would not run. This device makes all the human pageants that are celebrated in the film – from the war to the university, to the stage and to the Olympic stadium – trivial when not sanctioned by God or done to His honour. Abrahams is thus placed in the position of a foil to the superior man with the better intentions, and only redeemed by virtue of participation in the redemptive celebration that concludes the film.

Chariots of Fire, like *The Last Temptation of Christ*, represented something new in the evolution of popular film in America, another step away from the genre that had dominated religious filmmaking for so long. It represented a secularization that corresponded to the larger secularization of popular religion in America, but, more than that, it demonstrated that the tools and contents of religious filmmaking can shift to other story patterns than that of the Biblical epic. *Chariots of Fire* nevertheless succeeds as a sacramental expression in its own right.

Notes

[1]   There is, of course, a long tradition of Hollywood films that appeal to Jewish-Americans, but these films treat Jews more as an ethnic group than as a religious group. In addition, despite the Jewishness of Hollywood's production moguls, there is no Jewish style or Judaic genre in film. See Lester D Friedman, *The Jewish Image in American Film* (Secaucus, NJ: Citadel Press, 1987).

[2]   Mark Winokur, "Improbable Ethnic Hero: William Powell and the Transformation of Ethnic Hollywood", *Cinema Journal* 27: 1 (1987): 5-22. See also John Higham, *Strangers in the Land: Patterns of American Nativism 1860-1925* (New York: Atheneum, 1963); Patricia Erens, *The Jew in American Cinema* (Bloomington: Indiana University Press, 1984); and the opening chapters of Bruce Babington and Peter William Evans, *Biblical Epics: Sacred narrative in the Hollywood cinema* (Manchester; New York: Manchester University Press, 1993): 1-90.

[3]   Gerald Eugene Forshey, *American Religious and Biblical Spectacular Films* (Westport, CT; London: Praeger Publishers, 1992).

[4]   The other 1960s films similarly went to the symbolic top of the genre for material – John Huston's bomb, *The Bible* (1966), and George Stevens's long cameo-pic, *The Greatest Story Ever Told* (1965).

[5]   It is the common practice in the Jesus films to shift the antagonist role from the Jews to the Romans, to avoid charges of anti-Semitism. Typically, the Pharisees and Sadducees and court of the Sanhedrin are either entirely omitted from the films or introduced in crowd scenes where Jesus's ministry is momentarily opposed.

[6]   See John D Woodridge, Mark A Noll, Nathan Hatch, *The Gospel in America* (Grand Rapids, MI: Zondervan, 1982). For a complete description of the birth and rise of evangelicalism, see George Marsden, *Reforming Fundamentalism: Fuller Seminary and the New Evangelicalism* (Grand Rapids, MI: William B Eerdmans Publishing Company, 1987).

[7]   The most notable study of this type is Eric Rohmer and Claude Chabrol, *Hitchcock: The First Forty-Four Films*, translated by Stanley Hochman (New York: Frederick Unger Publishing Co., 1979). More recently, see Leo Braudy, "The Sacraments of Genre: Coppola, DePalma, Scorsese", *Film Quarterly* 39: 3 (1986): 17-28.

[8]   Scorsese's intention was to show God's care for human suffering and temptation: "The beauty of Kazantzakis' concept is that Jesus has to put up with everything we go through, all the doubts and fears and anger. He made me *feel* like he's sinning – but he's not sinning, he's just human. As well as divine." Martin Scorsese, quoted in Richard Corliss, "Body... ...And Blood", *Film Comment* 24: 5 (September-October 1988): 36. Emphasis in original.

[9]   It is significant to note that apocryphal literature typically attempts to fill gaps in canonical history. The large gap filled in much of the Old Testament Apocrypha and the Pseudepigraphical writings is the period of Jewish oppression after the Babylonian captivity and release, 450 BC–AD 70. After the prophet Malachi, there was no consensus of authority on the interpretation of Jewish historical events. The most common story type within New Testament apocryphal literature addresses the silent years of Jesus's life; for example, what miracles did he perform as a boy? See James H Charlesworth (ed), *The Old Testament Pseudepigrapha* (New York: Doubleday, 1983); G R Beasley-Murray and F F Bruce, "The apocryphal and

apocalyptic literature", in D Guthrie and J A Motyer (eds), *The New Bible Commentary Revised* (London: Inter-Varsity Press, 1970): 52-58.

[10]   For the most part, the film is developed like a Bible story book in which secondary characters, like the paralytic or the rich young ruler, are given extra dialogue better to match Christ's responses. The inevitable problem with any adaptation of the Gospels is their loose narrative structure, which is hardly conducive to the film medium.

[11]   Gnosticism defined Christ as essentially a spiritual being, since it grew out of Hellenistic ideals which made the flesh an evil. Kazantzakis and Scorsese work to avoid this common heresy, but inadvertently fall into another. The theology of both the film and novel versions of *The Last Temptation of Christ*, in which Christ's nature suffers in a near paranoia from the dichotomy between God and man within him, strongly parallels an ancient theological position which the Church rejected. This was the theology of Theodore of Mopsuestia (died 428), which was condemned by the Fifth Ecumenical Council in 553. Theodore based his conception of Christ on the idea of the "indwelling" of the Holy Spirit. As with Old Testament prophets and holy men, the spirit of God indwelt Jesus to draw him uniquely into union with God. In Jesus, God dwelt "as in a Son", uniting himself to Him at the moment of conception and becoming mature and full as Jesus continued His struggle against evil. In the full expression of God's spirit, Jesus is raised in the Resurrection to show that the human and the "logos" are one functional identity. Thus, the union of God and man in Christ is the product of God's graciously working with His people, fully in Christ. So the union of God and man in Christ is drawn in terms of *will*, not *substance*. God is present with or absent from people by the disposition of divine will, His indwelling, and the responsive will of His people. Christ is the two substances, two concrete realities of different kinds agreeing. This split in the notion of "substance" was the cause for Theodore's censure. For a discussion of the complete evolution of Christological thought in the Church, which helps to place the ideas of both Kazantzakis and Scorsese, see Richard A Norris, Jr (ed), *The Christological Controversy* (Philadelphia: Fortress Press, 1980).
    It should be stated, in Scorsese's defence, that the theological problem of the film resulted from a devotional curiosity, rather than what the Puritans would have called a "pernicious" spirit: "Over the years I've drifted away from the Church, I'm no longer a practising Catholic, and I've questioned these things [Orthodox dogma]...I found this an interesting idea, that the human nature of Jesus was fighting Him all the way down the line, because it can't conceive of Him being God." (David Thompson and Ian Christie [eds], *Scorsese on Scorsese* [London; Boston: Faber and Faber, 1989]: 124.)

[12]   See Peter Fraser, "*American Gigolo* & Transcendental Style", *Literature/ Film Quarterly* 16: 2 (1988): 91-100.

[13]   The union of Jesus and Mary, although much criticised in the hysteria of the film's release, is, in fact, handled with discretion and a modest distance by Scorsese. Kazantzakis exercised little restraint: "Jesus seized her, threw back her head and kissed her on the mouth. They both turned deathly pale.

Their knees gave way. Unable to go further, they lay down under a flowering lemon-tree and began to roll on the ground...Purring, Mary Magdalene hugged the man, kept his body glued to hers." (Nikos Kazantzakis, *The Last Temptation*, translated by P A Bien [Oxford: Bruno Cassirer, 1961]: 459-460.)

[14] This reduction of the three women to a universal role-type is an apparent clue to the evil of the vision that tempts Jesus.

[15] Garry Wills, "Jesus in the Mean Streets", *The New York Review of Books* 35: 15 (13 October 1988): 8-10.

[16] Both films base their narratives on "realistic" drama, and yet both are presented with a thematic arrangement that compels the viewer to read them either as religious parable or as allegory. *The Mission* can be read as an allegory that speaks to the plight of South and Central American Indians, who have faced similar tragedies in the struggles for power in the 1970s and 1980s between the socialist East and the capitalist West. It earned mixed reviews due to this political intention. See, for example, David Denby, "Odor of Sanctity", *New York* 19: 44 (1986): 109-110; Judith Williamson, "Carry on up the waterfall", *New Statesman* 112: 2900 (24 October 1986): 25-26; Stanley Kauffmann, "For God's Sake", *The New Republic* 3750 (1 December 1986): 26-27.

Filmography

The following abbreviations have been used:

ad	art designer	*m*	music
aka	also known as	*p*	producer
bw	black and white	*pc*	production company
col	colour	*pd*	production designer
d	director	*ph*	cinematographer
ed	editor	*s*	story
m	minutes	*sc*	scriptwriter

Andrej Rublëv
USSR 1966 185m bw/col
pc Mosfilm *d* Andrej Tarkovskij *sc* Andrej Mikhalkov-Končalovskij,
Andrej Tarkovskij *ph* Vadim Yusov *m* Vyacheslav Ovchinnikov *ed* N
Beliaeva, L Lararev *ad* Evgeni Tcheriaiev *cast* Anatoli Solonitsyn (Andrej
Rublëv), Ivan Lapikov (Kirill), Nikolai Grinko (Daniel the Black), Nikolai
Sergeyev (Theophanes the Greek), Irma Raush (deaf and dumb girl),
Nikolai Burlyayev (Boriska).

Babette's Feast
Babettes gæstebud
Denmark 1987 103m col
p Just Betzer, Bo Christensen *pc* Panorama Film International/Nordisk
Film/Danish Film Institute *d, sc* Gabriel Axel *novel* Isak Dinesen [Karen
Blixen] *ph* Henning Kristiansen *m* Per Nørgård *ed* Finn Henriksen
pd Sven Wichmann *cast* Stéphane Audran (Babette Hersant), Jean
Philippe Lafont (Achille Papin), Gudmar Wivesson (young Lorens
Löwenhielm), Jarl Kulle (old Lorens Löwenhielm), Bibi Andersson
(Swedish lady-in-waiting), Hanne Stensgaard (young Filippa), Bodil Kjer
(old Filippa), Vibeke Hastrup (young Martine), Birgitte Federspiel (old
Martine).

Black Robe
Canada/Australia 1991 100m col
p Robert Lantos, Stephane Reichel, Sue Milliken *pc* Alliance
Communications/Samson Productions *d* Bruce Beresford *sc, novel* Brian
Moore *ph* Peter James *m* Georges Delerue *ed* Tim Wellburn *pd* Herbert
Pinter *cast* Lothaire Bluteau (Father Laforgue), Aden Young (Daniel),
Sandrine Holt (Annuka), August Schellenberg (Chomina), Tantoo
Cardinal (Chomina's wife), Billy Two Rivers (Ougebmat), Lawrence
Bayne (Neehatin), Harrison Liu (Awondoie), Wesley Cote (Oujita),
Frank Wilson (Father Jerome), François Tasse (Father Bourque), Jean
Brousseau (Champlain).

Diary of a Country Priest
Journal d'un curé de campagne
France 1950 120m bw
p Léon Carré *pc* Union Générale Cinématographique *d, sc* Robert
Bresson *novel* Georges Bernanos *ph* Léonce-Henry Burel *m* Jean-
Jacques Grünenwald *ed* Paulette Robert *pd* Pierre Charbonnier
cast Claude Laydu (priest of Ambricourt), Jean Riveyre (Count), Marie-
Monique Arkell (Countess), Nicole Ladmiral (Chantal), André Guibert
(priest of Torcy), Nicole Maurey (Louise), Serge Bento (Mitonnet), Jean
Danet (Olivier), Martine Lemaire (Séraphita).

A Farewell to Arms
USA 1932 85m bw
p Frank Borzage, Benjamin Glazer *pc* Paramount *d* Frank Borzage
sc Benjamin Glazer, Oliver H P Garrett *novel* Ernest Hemingway
ph Charles Lang *m* Ralph Rainger *ed* Otho Lovering *ad* Hans Dreier,
Roland Anderson *cast* Helen Hayes (Catherine Barclay), Gary Cooper
(Frederick Henry), Adolphe Menjou (Rinaldi), Mary Phillips (Helen
Ferguson), Jack La Rue (the Priest).

Gallipoli
Australia 1981 111m col
p Robert Stigwood, Patricia Lovell *pc* Associated R and R Films *d* Peter
Weir *sc* David Williamson *s* Peter Weir *ph* Russell Boyd *m* Albinoni,
Brian May *ed* William Anderson *ad* Herbert Pinter *cast* Mark Lee (Archy
Hamilton), Mel Gibson (Frank Dunne), Bill Hunter (Major Barton), Bill
Kerr (Uncle Jack), Robert Grubb (Billy Lewis), Tim McKenzie (Barney
Wilson), David Argue (Snowy), Ron Graham (Wallace Hamilton), John
Morris (Colonel Robinson), Graham Dow (General Gardner).

The Gospel According to St Matthew
Il Vangelo secondo Matteo
Italy/France 1964 142m bw
p Alfredo Bini *pc* Arco Film/CCF Lux *d, sc* Pier Paolo Pasolini
source Gospel According to St Matthew *ph* Tonino Delli Colli *m* Luis
Enriquez Bacalov *ed* Nino Baragli *ad* Luigi Scaccianoce *cast* Enrique
Irazoqui (Jesus Christ), Margherita Caruso (Mary as a girl), Susanna
Pasolini (Mary as a woman), Marcello Morante (Joseph), Mario Socrate
(John the Baptist), Settimio Di Porto (Peter), Otello Sestili (Judas
Iscariot), Ferruccio Nuzzo (Matthew), Giacomo Morante (John), Alfonso
Gatto (Andrew), Enzo Siciliano (Simon).

Hardcore
aka The Hardcore Life
USA 1978 108m col
p Buzz Feitshans *pc* A-Team/Columbia *d, sc* Paul Schrader *ph* Michael
Chapman *m* Jack Nitzsche *ed* Tom Rolf *ad* Ed O'Donovan *pd* Paul
Sylbert *cast* George C Scott (Jake VanDorn), Peter Boyle (Andy Mast),
Season Hubley (Niki), Dick Sargent (Wes DeJong), Leonard Gaines
(Ramada), David Nichols (Kurt), Gary Rand Graham (Tod), Larry Block
(Detective Burrows), Marc Alaimo (Ratan), Leslie Ackerman (Felice),
Charlotte McGinnis (Beatrice), Ilah Davis (Kristen VanDorn).

Jesus of Montreal
Jésus de Montréal
Canada/France 1989 119m col
p Roger Frappier, Pierre Pierre Gendron, Doris Girard, Gérard Mital,
Jacques-Eric Strauss *pc* Max Films/Gérard Mital Productions *d, sc* Denys
Arcand *ph* Guy Defaux *m* Yves Laferrière, François Dompierre, Jean-
Marie Benoît *ed* Isabelle Dedieu *ad* François Séguin *cast* Lothaire
Bluteau (Daniel Coulombe), Johanne-Marie Trembley (Constance
Lazure), Gilles Pelletier (Father Raymond Leclerc), Rémy Girard (Martin
Durocher), Robert Lepage (René Sylvestre), Catherine Wilkening
(Mireille Fontaine), Yves Jacques (Richard Cardinal), Denys Arcand
(judge), Cédric Noël (Pascal Berger), Monique Miller (Denise Quintal).

The Mission
UK 1986 125m col
p Fernando Ghia, David Puttman *pc* Goldcrest/Kingsmere Productions
d Roland Joffé *sc, s* Robert Bolt *ph* Chris Menges *m* Ennio Morricone
ed Jim Clark *ad* George Richardson, John King, Peter Melrose *pd* Stuart
Craig *cast* Robert De Niro (Captain Rodrigo Mendoza), Jeremy Irons
(Father Gabriel), Ray McAnally (Cardinal Altamirano), Chuck Low (Don

Cabeza), Ronald Pickup (Hontar), Aidan Quinn (Felipe), Cherie Lunghi (Carlotta), Liam Neeson (Fielding).

On the Waterfront
USA 1954 107m bw
p Sam Spiegel *pc* Horizon *d* Elia Kazan *sc* Budd Schulberg *ph* Boris Kaufman *m* Leonard Bernstein *ed* Arthur E Milford *ad* Richard Day *cast* Marlon Brando (Terry Malloy), Eve Marie Saint (Edie Doyle), Karl Malden (Father Barry), Lee J Cobb (Johnny Friendly), Rod Steiger (Charley Malloy), Pat Henning (Kayo Dugan), Leif Erickson (Glover), James Westerfield (Big Mac), John Heldabrand (Mutt), Rudy Bond (Moose), John Hamilton ("Pop" Doyle).

Rome, Open City
Roma, città aperta
Italy 1945 101m bw
p, d, ed Roberto Rossellini *pc* Excelsa/Mayer-Burstyn *sc* Sergio Amedei, Federico Fellini, Roberto Rossellini *ph* Ubaldo Arata *m* Renzo Rossellini *ed* Eraldo da Roma *ad* R Megna *cast* Aldo Fabrizi (Father Don Pietro), Anna Magnani (Pina), Marcello Pagliero (Manfredi), Maria Michi (Marina).

The Word
Ordet
Denmark 1955 124m bw
p Erik Nielsen *pc* Palladium Film *d, sc* Carl-Theodor Dreyer *play* Kaj Munk *ph* Henning Bendtsen *m* Poul Schierbeck *ed* Edith Schlüssel *ad* Erik Aaes *cast* Henrik Malberg (Morten Borgen), Emil Hass Christensen (Mikkel), Preben Lerdorff-Rye (Johannes), Cay Kristiansen (Anders), Birgitte Federspiel (Inger), Ejner Federspiel (Peter Petersen), Gerda Nielsen (Anne), Ove Rud (pastor), Henry Skjær (doctor), Anne Elisabeth (Maren), Hanne Aagesen (Karen).

You Only Live Once
USA 1937 87m bw
p Walter Wanger *pc* Wanger Productions *d* Fritz Lang *sc* Gene Towne, Graham Baker *ph* Leon Shamroy *m* Alfred Newman *ed* Daniel Mandell *ad* Alexander Toluboff *cast* Henry Fonda (Eddie Taylor), Sylvia Sidney (Joan Graham), Barton MacLane (Stephen Whitney), William Gargan (Father Dolan), Jean Dixon (Bonnie Graham), Jerome Cowan (Doctor Hill), Chic Sale (Ethan), Margaret Hamilton (Hester), Warren Hymer (Buggsy).

Bibliography

Andrew, Dudley. *André Bazin* (New York: Oxford University Press, 1978).

——————. *Film in the Aura of Art* (Princeton: Princeton University Press, 1984).

Auerbach, Erich. *Mimesis: The Representation of Reality in Western Literature*, translated by Willard R Trask (Princeton: Princeton University Press, 1953).

Saint Augustine. *Christian Doctrine*, volume 4 of *The Writings of St. Augustine* (Washington, DC: Catholic University of America Press, 1966).

Aulén, Gustaf. *Christus Victor: An Historical Study of the Three Main Types of the Idea of the Atonement*, translated by A G Hebert (New York: Macmillan, 1969).

Ayfre, Amédée. "Neo-Realism and Phenomenology", in Jim Hillier (ed), *Cahiers du Cinéma. Volume 1: The 1950s: Neo-Realism, Hollywood, New Wave* (Cambridge, MA: Harvard University Press, 1985): 182-191.

Bacon, Thomas I. *Martin Luther and the Drama* (Amsterdam: Editions Rodopi, 1976).

Bainton, Roland H. *Here I Stand: A Life of Martin Luther* (Nashville; New York: Abingdon Press, 1950).

Bazin, André. *What Is Cinema?*, essays selected and translated by Hugh Gray (Berkeley; Los Angeles: University of California Press, 1967).

——————. *What Is Cinema?*, volume II, essays selected and translated by Hugh Gray (Berkeley; Los Angeles; London: University of California Press, 1971).

Beasley-Murray, G R and F F Bruce. "The apocryphal and apocalyptic literature", in D Guthrie and J A Motyer (eds), *The New Bible Commentary Revised* (London: Inter-Varsity Press, 1970): 52-58.

Belton, John. *The Hollywood Professionals: Howard Hawks, Frank Borzage, Edgar G. Ulmer*, volume 3 (London: The Tantivy Press, 1974).

Biskind, Peter. "The Politics of Power in 'On the Waterfront'", *Film Quarterly* 29: 1 (1975): 25-38.

Bloom, Harold. *The Anxiety of Influence: A Theory of Poetry* (New York: Oxford University Press, 1973).

Bondy, François. "On the Death of Pasolini", *Encounter* 46: 6 (June 1976): 53-55.

Bordwell, David. *The Films of Carl-Theodor Dreyer* (Berkeley; Los Angeles; London: University of California Press, 1981).

——————. *Narration in the Fiction Film* (Madison: University of Wisconsin Press, 1985).

Bourdieu, Pierre. *Distinction: A Social Critique of the Judgement of Taste*, translated by Richard Nice (Cambridge, MA: Harvard University Press, 1984).

Bragin, John. "Pasolini – A Conversation in Rome, June 1966", *Film Culture* 42 (1966): 102-105.

Braudy, Leo. "The Sacraments of Genre: Coppola, DePalma, Scorsese", *Film Quarterly* 39: 3 (1986): 17-28.

Bresson, Robert. *Notes on Cinematography*, translated by Jonathan Griffin (New York: Urizen Books, 1977).

Bruce, F F. "The fourfold Gospel", in D Guthrie and J A Motyer (eds), *The New Bible Commentary Revised* (London: Inter-Varsity Press, 1970): 64-70.

Brunette, Peter. *Roberto Rossellini* (New York; Oxford: Oxford University Press, 1987).

Bultmann, Rudolf. "The Task and the Problems of New Testament Theology (the Relation between Theology and Proclamation)", in *Theology of the New Testament*, volume 2, translated by Kendrick Grobel (New York: Scribners, 1951): 237-251.

Cameron, Ian (ed). *The Films of Robert Bresson* (New York: Praeger Publishers, 1969).

Campbell, Richard H and Michael R Pitts (eds). *The Bible on Film: A Checklist, 1897-1980* (Metuchen, NJ; London: The Scarecrow Press, 1981).

Carroll, Noël. "The Future of Allusion: Hollywood in the Seventies (and Beyond)", *October* 20 (1982): 51-81.

Caughie, John (ed). *Theories of Authorship: A Reader* (London; Boston; Henley: Routledge & Kegan Paul, 1981).

Charlesworth, James H (ed). *The Old Testament Pseudepigrapha* (New York: Doubleday, 1983).

Collins, Jim. *Uncommon Cultures: Popular Culture and Post-Modernism* (New York; London: Routledge, 1989).

Corliss, Richard. "Body... ...And Blood", *Film Comment* 24: 5 (September-October 1988): 34, 36-39, 42-43.

Dempsey, Michael. "Light Shining in Darkness: Roland Joffe on *The Mission*", *Film Quarterly* 40: 4 (1987): 2-11.

Denby, David. "Odor of Sanctity", *New York* 19: 44 (1986): 109-110.

Dresner, Samuel. "The Vanishing Hero Christian Drama, Jewish Tragedy", *Midstream* 28: 6 (1982): 44-46.

Dunne, John Gregory. "Interview with John Gregory Dunne and Paul Schrader", *Esquire* 98 (July 1982): 85-89.

Edwall, Pehr, Eric Hayman and William D Maxwell (eds). *Ways of Worship: The Report of a Theological Commission of Faith and Order* (New York: Harper & Brothers, 1951)

Eisen, Ken. "The Young Misogynists of American Cinema", *Cineaste* 13: 1 (1983): 31-35.

Eisenstein, Sergei. *The Film Sense*, edited and translated by Jay Leyda (New York: Harcourt, Brace, Jovanovich, 1975).

Eisner, Lotte H. *Fritz Lang* (New York: Oxford University Press, 1977).

Erens, Patricia. *The Jew in American Cinema* (Bloomington: Indiana University Press, 1984).

Falkenberg, Pamela. "'The Text! The Text!': Andre Bazin's Mummy Complex, Psychoanalysis and the Cinema", *Wide Angle* 9: 4 (1987): 35-55.

Forshey, Gerald Eugene. *American Religious and Biblical Spectacular Films* (Westport, CT; London: Praeger Publishers, 1992).

Fraser, Peter. "The Musical Mode: Putting on *The Red Shoes*", *Cinema Journal* 26: 3 (1987): 44-54.

——————. "*American Gigolo* & Transcendental Style", *Literature/Film Quarterly* 16: 2 (1988): 91-100.

Friedman, Lester D. *The Jewish Image in American Film* (Secaucus, NJ: Citadel Press, 1987).

Gibson, Arthur. *The Silence of God: Creative response to the films of Ingmar Bergman* (New York; London: Harper & Row, 1969).

Green, Martin. "The Cult of Young Manhood", *Commonweal* 109 (March 1982): 181-184.

Green, Peter. "The Nostalgia of the Stalker", *Sight and Sound* 54: 1 (winter 1984-85): 50-54.

——————. "Apocalypse & Sacrifice", *Sight and Sound* 56: 2 (spring 1987): 111-118.

Greene, Marjorie. "Robert Bresson", *Film Quarterly* 13: 3 (1960): 4-10.

Hanlon, Lindley. *Fragments: Bresson's Film Style* (London: Associated University Presses, 1986).

Hentzi, Gary. "Peter Weir and the Cinema of New Age Humanism", *Film Quarterly* 44: 2 (1990): 2-12.

Hertz, Neil. *The End of the Line: Essays on Psychoanalysis and the Sublime* (New York: Columbia University Press, 1985).

Hey, Kenneth. "Ambivalence As a Theme in On the Waterfront: An Interdisciplinary Approach to Film Study", *American Quarterly* 31: 5 (winter 1979): 666-696.

Higham, John. *Strangers in the Land: Patterns of American Nativism 1860-1925* (New York: Atheneum, 1963).

Hirsch, Foster. *The Dark Side of the Screen: Film Noir* (San Diego; New York: A S Barnes & Company; London: The Tantivy Press, 1981).

Houtart, François and Emile Pin. *The Church and the Latin American Revolution*, translated by Gilbert Barth (New York: Sheed and Ward, 1965).

Hurley, Neil P. *Theology Through Film* (New York: Harper & Row, 1970).

Jaehne, Karen. "Schrader's *Mishima*: An Interview", *Film Quarterly* 39: 3 (1986): 11-17.

Jones, Cheslyn, Geoffrey Wainwright and Edward Yarnold, SJ (eds). *The Study of Liturgy* (New York: Oxford University Press, 1978).

Jowett, G S. "From Entertainment to Social Force: The Discovery of the Motion Picture, 1918-1945", *Current Research in Film* 2 (1986): 1-20.

Jungmann, Josef A, SJ. *The Early Liturgy To the Time of Gregory the Great*, translated by Francis A Brunner (South Bend, IN: University of Notre Dame Press, 1959).

Kazan, Elia. *Elia Kazan: A Life* (New York: Alfred A Knopf, 1988).

Kazantzakis, Nikos. *The Last Temptation*, translated by P A Bien (Oxford: Bruno Cassirer, 1961).

Kinnard, Roy and Tim Davis. *Divine Images: A History of Jesus on the Screen* (New York: Citadel Press, 1992).

Ladd, George Eldon. *A Theology of the New Testament* (Grand Rapids, MI: Eerdmans, 1974).

Lamster, Frederick. *Souls Made Great Through Love and Adversity: The Film Work of Frank Borzage* (Metuchen, NJ; London: The Scarecrow Press, 1981).

Lawton, Ben. "Italian Neorealism: A Mirror Construction of Reality", *Film Criticism* 3: 2 (winter 1979): 8-23.

Le Fanu, Mark. *The Cinema of Andrei Tarkovsky* (London: British Film Institute, 1987).

Lehman, Peter. "American Gigolo: The Male Body Makes an Appearance, of Sorts", in Jeanne Ruppert (ed), *Gender: Literary and*

Cinematic Representation (Tallahassee, FL: Florida State University Press, 1989).

Leith, John H (ed). *Creeds of the Churches: A Reader in Christian Doctrine from the Bible to the Present*, third edition (Atlanta: John Knox Press, 1982).

Lewis, C S. *Miracles: A Preliminary Study* (New York: Macmillan, 1947).

Lewis, G H. "Uncertain Truths: The Promotion of Popular Culture", *Journal of Popular Culture* 20: 3 (1986): 31-44.

Livingston, Arthur. "Theresa", *The Living Church* 194: 16 (1987): 12.

'Longinus'. *On the Sublime*, translated and edited by T S Dorsch (New York: Penguin, 1977).

Lourdeaux, Lee. *Italian and Irish Filmmakers in America: Ford, Capra, Coppola, and Scorsese* (Philadelphia: Temple University Press, 1990).

Loyola, Ignatius. *The Spiritual Exercises of Saint Ignatius of Loyola*, translated by Louis J Puhl (Chicago: Loyola University Press, 1951).

MacCabe, Colin. "Theory and Film: Principles of Realism and Pleasure", in Philip Rosen (ed), *Narrative, Apparatus, Ideology: A Film Theory Reader* (New York: Columbia University Press, 1986): 179-197.

Macdonald, Susan. "Pasolini: Rebellion, Art and a New Society", *Screen* 10: 3 (1969): 26-32.

Machen, J Gresham. *The Origin of Paul's Religion* (Grand Rapids, MI: Eerdmans, 1925).

Marsden, George. *Reforming Fundamentalism: Fuller Seminary and the New Evangelicalism* (Grand Rapids, MI: William B Eerdmans Publishing Company, 1987).

Martz, Louis L. *The Poetry of Meditation: A Study in English Religious Literature of the Seventeenth Century* (New Haven: Yale University Press, 1954).

May, John R and Michael Bird (eds). *Religion in Film* (Knoxville: The University of Tennessee Press, 1982).

Metz, Christian. *The Imaginary Signifier: Psychoanalysis and the Cinema*, translated by Celia Britton, Annwyl Williams, Ben Brewster and Alfred Guzzetti (Bloomington: Indiana University Press, 1982).

Milne, Tom. *The Cinema of Carl Dreyer* (New York: A S Barnes & Co; London: A Zwemmer; 1971).

Monaco, James. *American Film Now: The People, The Power, The Money, The Movies* (New York: Oxford University Press, 1979).

Montagu, Ivor. "Man and Experience: Tarkovsky's World", *Sight and Sound* 42: 2 (spring 1973): 89-94.

Moore, Brian. *Black Robe* (London: Jonathan Cape, 1985).

Murray, Edward. *Ten Film Classics: A Re-Viewing* (New York: Frederick Ungar Publishing Co., 1978).

Neale, Stephen. *Genre* (London: British Film Institute, 1980).

Nichols, Bill. "American Gigolo: Transcendental Style and Narrative Form", *Film Quarterly* 34: 4 (summer 1981): 8-13.

Norris, Richard A, Jr (ed). *The Christological Controversy* (Philadelphia: Fortress Press, 1980).

Pasolini, Pier Paolo. *A Violent Life*, translated by William Weaver (London: Jonathan Cape, 1968).

—————————. *Pasolini on Pasolini: Interviews with Oswald Stack* (London: Thames and Hudson, in association with the British Film Institute, 1969).

—————————. *Lutheran Letters*, translated by Stuart Hood (Manchester: Carcanet New Press; Dublin: Raven Arts Press; 1983).

—————————. *The ragazzi*, translated by Emile Capouya (Manchester; New York: Carcanet, 1986).

Pelikan, Jaroslav. *The Emergence of the Catholic Tradition (100-600)*, in volume 1 of *The Christian Tradition: A History of the Development of Doctrine* (Chicago; London: The University of Chicago Press, 1971).

—————————. *The Spirit of Eastern Christendom (600-1700)*, volume 2 of *The Christian Tradition: A History of the Development of Doctrine* (Chicago; London: The University of Chicago Press, 1974).

Rayns, Tony. "Truth with the Power of Fiction", *Sight and Sound* 53: 4 (autumn 1984): 256-260.

Rohmer, Eric and Claude Chabrol. *Hitchcock: The First Forty-Four Films*, translated by Stanley Hochman (New York: Frederick Unger Publishing Co., 1979).

Ryle, John Charles, D.D. *Expository Thoughts on the Gospels: For Family and Private Use*, 4 volumes (London: William Hunt and Company, 1887).

Schrader, Paul. *Transcendental Style in Film: Ozu, Bresson, Dreyer* (Berkeley: University of California Press, 1972).

Siciliano, Enzo. *Pasolini*, translated by John Shepley (New York: Random House, 1982).

Sklar, Robert. "Interview with Denys Arcand", *Cineaste* 18: 1 (1990): 14-16.

Skoller, Donald (ed). *Dreyer in Double Reflection* (New York: E P Dutton & Co, 1973).

Snyder, Stephen. *Pier Paolo Pasolini* (Boston: Twayne Publishers, 1980).

Sontag, Susan. "Spiritual style in the films of Robert Bresson", in *Against interpretation and other essays* (London: Eyre & Spottiswoode, 1967): 177-195.

Tarkovsky, Andrey. *Sculpting in Time: Reflections on the Cinema*, translated by Kitty Hunter-Blair (London: The Bodley Head, 1986).

Teresa of Avila. *The Interior Castle*, translated and edited by E Allison Peers (New York: Image Books, 1961).

Thompson, David and Ian Christie (eds). *Scorsese on Scorsese* (London; Boston: Faber and Faber, 1989).

Thurman, Judith. *Isak Dinesen: The Life Karen Blixen* (Harmondsworth: Penguin Books, 1984).

Tolstoy, Leo. *Resurrection*, translated by Louise Maude (London: Oxford University Press, 1931).

Vronskaya, Jeanne. *Young Soviet Film Makers* (New York: George Allen and Unwin, 1972).

Wainwright, Geoffrey. *Doxology: The Praise of God in Worship, Doctrine and Life* (New York: Oxford University Press, 1980).

Wall, James A. *Church and Cinema: A Way of Viewing Films* (Grand Rapids, MI: Eerdmans, 1971).

Warfield, Benjamin Breckinridge. *The Inspiration and Authority of the Bible*, edited by Samuel G Craig (London: Marshall, Morgan & Scott, 1951).

Webber, Robert E. *Common Roots: A Call to Evangelical Maturity* (Grand Rapids, MI: Zondervan Publishing House, 1978).

Wilkerson, David, with John and Elizabeth Sherrill. *The Cross and the Switchblade* (Chicago: Moody Press, 1972).

Williamson, Judith. "Carry on up the waterfall", *New Statesman* 112: 2900 (24 October 1986): 25-26.

Wills, Garry. "Jesus in the Mean Streets", *The New York Review of Books* 35: 15 (13 October 1988): 8-10.

Wilson, George. "*You Only Live Once*: the Doubled Feature", *Sight and Sound* 46: 4 (autumn 1977): 221-226.

Winokur, Mark. "Improbable Ethnic Hero: William Powell and the Transformation of Ethnic Hollywood", *Cinema Journal* 27: 1 (1987): 5-22.

Wood, Robin. "Robin Wood on Carl Dreyer", *Film Comment* 10: 2 (March-April 1974): 10-17.

——————. *Hollywood from Vietnam to Reagan* (New York: Columbia University Press, 1986).

Woodbridge, John D, Mark A Noll and Nathan Hatch (eds). *The Gospel in America* (Grand Rapids, MI: Zondervan, 1982).

Yacowar, Maurice. "Dick, Jane, Rocky and T. S. Eliot", *Journal of Popular Film* 6: 1 (1977): 2-12.

Index

200

ISBN 0-275-96464-7

90000>

EAN

9 780275 964641